PRAISE FOR GREY DIVORCE

"When Ann Evans' devoted husband left her after thirty years, she was plunged into the depth of despair. Like other women who have been suddenly abandoned, she suffered greatly as she tried to make sense of something that inherently didn't make any sense. In her book, *Grey Divorce: A Right to Mourn*, Ann not only takes the reader on her journey of recovery but more importantly, shares with us her profound thoughts about spirituality, forgiveness, friendship (her angels), the legal nightmare, and retirement. She opens her heart so that we can understand at increasingly deeper levels how to make sense, move on, and rebuild a life no matter what it brings our way. A lesson we all need to learn."

– Vikki Stark, MSW, MFT, Author of the bestselling *Runaway Husbands*, *The Abandoned Wife's Guide to Recovery and Renewal*, www.vikkistark.com

"Grief comes to all of us as we journey through life. There is a wide selection of books supporting us through grief, death, and bereavement. However, *Grey Divorce: The Right to Mourn*, fills an important gap in that literature. Ann's unique journey through abandonment by a life partner late in her life unfolds with candour and authenticity as she redefines her identities at this "grey" stage of life. Her deep spirituality and long-time experience as a psychotherapist and pastoral counsellor are reflected in the literature she deftly weaves throughout her book…What struck me deeply is Ann's tenacity to define her own journey – to not be straight-jacketed by societal norms regarding "proper grieving" timelines and expectations… Her indefatigable spirit kept me rooting for her throughout the memoir.

Her actions—both tentative and bold—provide many concrete actions for others seeking healing paths forward through their own pain. Ann's story is a testament to this profound realization."

– Carol Rolheiser, Professor Emerita, Department of Curriculum,
Teaching and Learning, University of Toronto

"This book is such a vulnerable expression of pain and loss that the reader cannot help but be gutted by it. Yet it's also a book of such hope, beauty, and the wisdom of a psychotherapist who has walked with many through their own pain. Both a guide to walking through grief and a profound personal story of courage, I will recommend this book as a source of hope to many of my clients."

– Brian Klassen M.Ed., R.C.C. Psychotherapist

"Ann Evans' memoir is an unflinching account of her devastation after she is rejected by the man she has loved and adored through thirty years of marriage. She is an inspiration as she forges her own path to healing, drawing on a deep faith, her belief in the unconscious, and the loving support of her family and friends."

– Darlene Bamford, United Church of Canada minister
and psychotherapist, retired

"Despair does not begin to capture the life that Ann Evans was shockingly catapulted into when her husband of 28 years left with no warning, taking not only their life together but their entire world. A cross-country move to facilitate his work in a congregation meant that when he left the church, she also lost her community. And she was not young – starting over at 76. This is a profound story of a woman taken to the depths. I was there and honestly was not sure she would recover any semblance of her former self, or a meaningful life. She proved me wrong and…will inspire you when you meet her in these pages."

— Rev. Dr. Anne Simmonds, Minister Emerita, Rosedale
United Church, Spiritual Mentor, Companion,
Grief Support Specialist, Institutional Ministry, CASC

"With resilience, wisdom, and hope, Ann Evans takes us on a difficult journey of loss and recovery. The narrative is inspiring, courageous, and insightful. The legal chapter reveals some of the challenges and costs when dealing with family law and mediation."

— Moyra Dhaliwal, Lawyer, British Columbia, Retired

"In *Grey Divorce*, Ann Evans shows how we never lose the yearning to be loved and desired no matter how old we are, and that betrayal and abandonment cut especially deep later in life…a brave and important book."

— Genevieve Fox, PhD; Founder-Director, Manuscripts & Mentoring:
an editing and coaching service for writers; Author, *Milkshakes and*
Morphine: A Memoir of Love and Life; www.genevievefox.com

GREY DIVORCE
Copyright ©2025 by Ann Evans
All rights reserved

Cover Design: David Drummond / Salamander Hill Design
www.salamanderhill.com

Design and Composition: Tim Ogline / Ogline Design
www.oglinedesign.com

Editor: Joy E. Stocke

ISBN: 979-8-9897464-9-1

Publisher's Cataloging-In-Publication Data
Evans, Ann
    Grey Divorce: The Right to Mourn

Categories: Memoir, Family

Tributaries Press
102 Sandy Ridge-Mt Airy Road
Stockton, NJ. 08559

A Memoir

Grey Divorce

The Right to Mourn

ANN EVANS

Tributaries
Press

Dedicated to

David and Mary

And all who choose to be present with those who mourn.

ACKNOWLEDGEMENTS

When my whole world collapsed, I fell into the arms of angels. In this way I survived and even began to thrive. This book celebrates each of these angels and the wondrous ways in which they were present with me. Whatever I am, I am because I was and am blessed with community.

In addition, I wish to thank so many others. One woman thought to send me an unsolicited cheque to recognize a gift I had given her a long time ago. With her endorsement I used it to take a course in memoir writing. There are several unnamed angels in my life who just consistently took the time to regularly ask how it was going and to encourage me to continue.

I am grateful to the hosts from all over the world who exchanged homes with me during the writing of this book. Through the Vancouver-based exchange homelink.org, I was able to connect and trade homes with people in Vienna, Scotland, Aruba and Sicily. In Australia, I exchanged homes in Byron Bay, Palm Grove and Bribie Island. In Canada I was fortunate to stay in an architectural gem of a converted church in Guelph, Ontario. The hosts were generous with their instructions and ideas of places to visit. Each home was an oasis that allowed me to take delightful walks and explore different cultures before, and after, many hours of writing.

I want to recognize Kris Rothstein, my first editor, and her patience with me through the first drafts. Genevieve Fox steadily mentored me, pushing me to write memoir with the liveliness of a novel. She demanded that my descriptions be both meticulous and captivating. And kudos to Joy Stocke and Tim Ogline of Tree of Life Publishing for their expertise bringing my book to its final engaging form. I am grateful for the production expertise of Kurt Von Hahn who created the audio book read with meaning and heart by my dear friend and angel Moyra Dhailiwal. As a visual person I delight in David Drummond's cover which states so clearly my central message. We all have a right to mourn.

The love of my children David and Mary, their spouses, Cheryl and Chris, my four intrepid grandchildren, Ben, Henry, Nora and Miranda sustain and encourage my well-being with presence and encouragement. For them, my gratitude always.

CONTENTS

Do not brace yourself against suffering.
Try to close your eyes and surrender yourself,
as if to a great loving energy.
This attitude is neither weak nor absurd.
It is the only one that cannot lead us astray.
Try to "sleep" with that active sleep of confidence
which is that seed in the fields in winter.

– Teilhard de Chardin

Never to lament casually and if one is to
express the great inevitable defeat that awaits
us all, it must be done within the strict
confines of dignity and beauty

– Leonard Cohen,
Prince of Asturias Award Acceptance Speech

PROLOGUE

"Hope you enjoy those walruses," my client, a marine biologist, chuckles as he and his partner are leaving after their final counselling session with me. "You helped me use my tusks to keep me from drowning more than once."

"We chose our parting gift for you together," his partner adds, glancing at the pair of jade green walruses with prominent white tusks just placed on my table model of Noah's Ark in my consulting room. "We want a place in your menagerie. Thank you so much, for all your help."

In the falling light of a December late afternoon, I close the door softly behind them, my last couple. Forty-five years of work as a psychotherapist is coming to an end. I turn and my eyes settle on the latest couple to board the Ark, settling among the sea animals. A little like Noah, I have worked with couples and, with their willingness, have kept them safe during terrible floods.

By now there are many animals chosen and gifted to me by clients as they finished therapy with me. Kangaroos hop and platypuses hide. Hand-carved Scottish Highland sheep stand uniquely among the farm animals and sealskin mosquitoes the size of apricots bring a giggle to those from the far north who know them so well. All bring memories of my lifetime of work as a psychotherapist.

I had prepared well for this day. The tinge of sadness quickly trans-forms to deep joy. Work well done and such a bright future lie just ahead. I leave my home office and bound—well, in my mind I bound—up the stairs, two steps at a time, to our living quarters. I burst in on my husband who, at his desk, is doing a final check through the page galleys of his latest book which expresses his thoughts on love.

"I am so happy," I exclaim.

Christmas is just ahead, the last payment on the mortgage will be made, and we are escaping to Florida for the winter. My husband's fifth book will be published, we have just purchased a pied-à-terre for ourselves in the city where our children live. It will make our visits longer and easier. Our life project, articulating evolutionary Christianity, is in full swing. People around the world are excited and supporting us. I am, as my dad, a Blake afficionado, loved to say, "kissing the joy".

My husband looks up. I see his face wrinkle. My heart goes out to him.

"Soon, soon, your last edits will be done," I whisper, my hands massag-ing his shoulders. "Today I received photos of the great beach house where we will be staying. It is fantastic. We are so blessed."

It is almost a regular morning as we stand, a few days later, in our dou-ble shower.

"Please scrub that sweet spot on my back," I say. "You know the one." He does and then I watch him dress. It is a pleasure because he chooses his clothes thoughtfully. I like that he always cares to look his best.

This morning he is going to his last therapy appointment. He has been seeing this therapist for three years to deal with what he has told me is childhood trauma. (She is a chiropractor who practices sacral cranial thera-py, a form of therapy that explores the mind/body connection.) I am proud he has been doing this work. I think about the times when he came home from therapy and took me in his arms in a very intentional, intimate hug to tell me I am special. I want to celebrate this journey he has made. I fan-tasize buying a huge bouquet of flowers and waiting outside her office and when he comes out, giving her this thank you for the careful work she had done with him. While I like this idea, I talk myself out of it.

Instead, I choose to go to her office and wait on the street for him to leave. We hug and decide to go for a walk to celebrate. We head for the sea-wall and the stunning vista of the ocean and the Vancouver city skyline. In December there are still fallen leaves to kick and the freighters are decked in Christmas lights. It is a Vancouver custom to count the freighters that are out there "on the nod on the bay" as Bruce Cockburn, our favourite art-ist sings in his iconic song, "Wondering where the lions are". I eagerly tell my husband that this song is dancing in my mind as we take in the glory of English Bay with the majesty of the Lions piercing the sky above us and the colourful freighters bobbing on the sea beside us as we walk.

"You did it!" I add. "You put your trauma to rest."

"Yes, I don't blame anyone anymore," he says. "I understand and I have been able to heal and in healing, accept."

I note a pensiveness in his tone. I know his body has psychological scars from his early years.

Then I hear him tell me, "Ann, just now at the very end of the session, she asked me to stay for an extra ten minutes. She said to me, 'If you decide to leave your wife, I want you to know that I want to be with you and I want to have a family with you.' I think," he pauses, "I want to do this and be with her."

In one, swift, shuddering instance my whole world dissolves into fragments.

Chapter 1

STARK NAKED GRIEF

The woman is perfected.
Her dead
Body wears the smile of accomplishment,
The illusion of a Greek necessity
Flows in the scrolls of her toga,
Her bare
Feet seem to be saying:
We have come so far, it is over.
– Sylvia Plath

I hung onto the words "I think I want to" for dear life. It was not a done deal. In the shock of it, the choices were flight or fight. For me it was all fight. This was crazy and I had to make him see the folly of it. We both told no one and carried on with life as normal. There was the rush of Christmas. He was the lead pastor of a large liberal church. There were gifts to get and to give, a Christmas message to compose, and the house to prepare for the renters who were moving in on January 1, as we left for three months in Florida. There were workshops there and in Arizona to prepare for and deliver. I had mostly stopped sleeping. The nights were for trying to understand what was so wrong with us. Nothing was making sense.

The big Christmas party for the congregation was just two weeks away. This year it would be held in the home of the new co-pastor and new organist. I had already purchased a glorious red dress for the event. The song "The Lady in Red" will now always turn my stomach. Being obsessed with the fact that my eyelashes were almost invisible, I made the call.

"Kinjou Eyelash Extensions, how may I help?"

I made an appointment and very soon was supine on a table in a stranger's salon.

"Is this for a Christmas party? I can help but you will have to hold still and relax, please."

Eyelash by eyelash I tried to be more beautiful. I had not known that I could not cry, or these meticulously glued lashes would wash away.

Party night arrived and with it a hundred people, more or less. We were the centre of attention. This was our tribe and we were the leaders. We circulated and performed.

"Hello Dennis, it is so good to meet you. We all look forward to your music. Is this your partner, James?"

"Yes," he said, turning to a tall guy nibbling on an hors d'oeuvre. "He just arrived from South Africa. He is a professional photographer, and he is looking for work. If you can help, please pass the word."

A photographer! I was hooked. If I can help an artist I will. He was so personable and fun to chat with and a much-needed distraction for me. Before long I had booked him to take professional photos of my husband and myself because I knew we needed them for our promotional materials for the upcoming gigs. Welcome to absolute denial!

James made the photo shoot such fun. He was excellent at his work. I flirted with the camera and he got great shots. We changed clothes many times. There were indoor and outdoor photos. He was trying to establish himself in a new country and we were the ideal couple. He drew us into a perfect couple pose, the Pacific Ocean as the backdrop and the waves crashing at our feet, a jaunty tweed cap barely constraining my curls. Little did he know.

At last, the renters arrived, we left for the airport and the Florida beach house awaited.

The condo was deeply shaded from the hot sun, the gated community had multiple pools, there was an excellent tennis academy and a water taxi to an exquisite beach. It was more than we could have hoped for. The weather was outstanding and remained so. All the warnings about Florida being cold in January were wrong.

The church community that we were welcoming as a sister church in the evolutionary project was warm and generous. They greeted us with a dinner party for fifty people. We did what we did. He worked the room and I made significant individual contacts. It was at dinner that I met Sister Carol. She was an interpreter of my husband's work for the Roman Catholic and Lutheran communities in Florida. Over food, we bonded.

This was a second marriage for my husband and me and we had been together for thirty years. It was an unusual coupling. I was seventeen years older than he was. We had to be very intentional, and we were. We committed to a strong and loyal bond. We held ourselves and others to the Jewish and Christian vision of marriage where, over a lifetime, the two become one. I never doubted this, not even once, until it was not so.

Now I was all mixed up, fighting for my marriage and performing professionally. I could not sit still or be still. I could not wait for red lights and made many right turns. I ate small amounts and slept fitfully. We walked and walked and talked and talked. "Why, why, why?" pulsated through my mind and body. Sometimes we walked and talked all night. I looked for signs of hope and clung to crumbs.

I knew we needed a therapist. I drew on my years of experience to find one and I did. We were no easy clients, and she took us on for one hour every day. Rosemary, a family and marriage therapist, tried to manage the tornado that entered her office. Within a week, my husband told me in a session that he had made up his mind and he was going to leave me. He refused to work with Rosemary any longer. He had no willingness to try to repair the marriage. I was devastated. This made no sense. We were both therapists as well as clergypersons. I had always believed if ever there was trouble, we would seek help and make an earnest attempt to repair. It is what we encouraged others to do. I could not stop fighting for us to have the chance to repair. Refusing to give up, I used my connections to find a rock star therapist who was the world's best at dealing with our situation. Esther Perel, the esteemed therapist who championed the concept of erotic intelligence in a relationship, was in Miami giving a workshop. I called her and she called me back and heard my story and offered to see us if we would come to Miami. He said no. His definitive refusal remains, for me, unforgivable.

"Hundreds of couples work on their relationships and in most cases heal," I said. "And if they don't heal, they at least understand what has happened. What have I done that you would refuse us this?"

Sometimes he would answer, "Nothing." And once I remember him saying, "If we try to repair it, we will, and I don't want to. It is too late for me."

Another time I pleaded: "So many of the couples that worked with me did repair their marriages and those that did not at least tried."

"What proof do you have of that?" he asked and then answered his own question. "None. You just want to believe it is so."

I was crushed for years by what I heard as a denigration of my lifework.

"God is calling me to be with her," I heard him telling me. "You and I have been very good together and now I have received this call from God to advance toward her."

This was the reason he managed to put forth. He appealed to my deep faith. There were times I tried so hard to believe this. I prayed for help to accept this as truth. He wanted me to tell our church community this. He believed that they would accept this. He was and wanted to remain their leader, without me by his side as I had always been. He wanted me to write a letter to our church community back home and explain this to them and to say that I was supportive and understood. I did what he asked and he edited the letter. This is an excerpt of what I wrote:

12:56 a.m. on January 23, 2013.

On Jan 10, my husband told me that he wanted to exit our marriage, be totally free and take a year to decide who, if either me, his therapist or neither of us, he would choose.

Gradually, as the shock has lifted, it has become clear to me that my husband is choosing freedom to establish patterns of his own rhythms free from the domesticity of everyday relationship with me and that also he is choosing to explore with his therapist a loving relationship. He has no assurance of outcomes.

For now, I have not been chosen. He does not want to, nor will he, explore any possible renewal with me at this time. Please know that I have attempted everything I can think of to change his mind and have him see what I think. For me, this is the crisis we have needed to awaken our relationship to its next stage. Neither he nor I can think of any relationship that we know of that was any better or deeper, more loving or more adventurous than ours. We did however both long for and envision more than we had. You will recognize that my husband is a person who is either driven at worst or allured at best to the more ideal. This is true of me as well only in a less intense manner.

I have been in daily therapy since January 2 here in Florida. I have been praying and meditating and studying the latest literature in both the marital area and the spiritual area.

My husband is giving me no option but to stand down while he explores life with his new beloved. I have only acceptance as an option. I know that my husband and his new love are also radiant souls, beloved by God. I want to accept what has been thrust upon me, to accept with the deepest integrity and love for myself that God in her abundance is surely giving me. Of course, my heart breaks and I know that God is restoring my soul and my heart hour by hour. I need and want your love. I want to live out the time I have on earth as a lovable and loving soul. Any support you can give me in this is like refreshing water and a green pasture to this emerging soul whose name is Ann.

I am deeply ashamed I even wrote this letter. After I wrote it, I became more ill and was doubling with cramps. I was physically ill. I kept seeing my daughter Mary in my mind, reading such a letter. Her disdain for me would be overwhelming. I would betray her every sense of her mother as a person of integrity. Acceptance seemed like the option my husband had designed for me. Outrage was what I truly felt.

In Florida, we worked out at the gym every day. He stunned the tennis academy with his outstanding skill as a tennis player, and we kept our obligations to the church in Florida and ran a stellar workshop. I prayed our shared interests and competence would demand he choose me and the sanctity of our marriage. We distracted ourselves with long walks and outings to the botanical gardens and the golf course. At the driving range, I gave every ball I hit his or her name. My drive improved exponentially. We managed to tell my children, his daughter, his parents and two friends each. My daughter was demanding to come to me, but I asked her to wait. I still believed he would come to his senses. He had intense dreams, and I was a therapist who had worked with dreams my whole life. I was sure they indicated what he was doing was showing him as hurting and damaging not only me but all our community. While we had always told each other our dreams and interpreted them for one another, he was no longer interested in any of my wisdom, though he continued to share his dreams with me. He appeared to listen to what I read in them and at times I saw that the truth of what I offered rattled him.

We were to go to Arizona in early February to give a workshop. It was now late January and when the time came for him to leave, he insisted that I not come. He left me for four days alone in the condo. When he was gone, I could not manage. I wanted to be dead. The physical pain in my stomach was intolerable. I had given birth to four children, but this was pain so sharp and relentless it made childbirth seem easy. There were moments when I was screaming, bent double in agony.

My husband and I had sleep medication for jet lag while traveling. I had a bottle full of sleeping pills. I decided to take them. I had never seriously considered suicide in my life. I had never suffered from even mild depression. I was a person with a level mood. All I thought about was ending the pain. I rarely drank alcohol. I never took recreational drugs of any kind. These were not escape options. I was committed to the life I had and the future I was anticipating. I had worked hard for it, and I believed in our mission for the wider world. Now I had no hope and no light. I wanted to be gone.

I fetched the pills and a glass of water and I got into bed. I kept checking the computer. I hoped for a message from my husband, a message of willingness to try to repair our marriage, a message of hope. None came. I started taking the pills. I was unable to see beyond my own misery. I knew suicide was a selfish act but I did not want to subject myself to anyone in this much agony.

None of us take our own life easily. As I lay in bed, I remembered a newspaper article I had read that reported that many of the rare survivors of Golden Gate Bridge suicide attempts recall regretting their impulsive decisions instantly—even as they were falling. Knowing this, I paused, but then reached for another pill, swallowed and once again checked my computer for messages. I was feeling some sweet cessation of the terrible cramps. Then, at that critical moment, came a message from the photographer, James. It was 2 a.m. in Florida. He was sending the file of the photos he had selected. I opened the file and what I saw took my breath away. There I was, a vibrant, fashionable, beautiful woman. I could barely recognize her. She had existed only four weeks ago. I imagined her pleading with me for her life. I expect I was losing at least a pound a day. I started weeping sobs of compassion for this woman in the picture. I realized I knew her, and I could not kill someone so compelling. I hid the remaining pills in their bottle in a small empty ice cream container at the back of the freezer but I knew where they were.

I was a long way from giving up the option of suicide, but I had come through what I knew was a very close call. It would be two days before my husband would be back to find me. No one would have known. The woman in that picture had reached out to a photographer who needed affirmation and work. She had done this over and over with other artists over the years. She had enabled the creativity of her husband at every opportunity. There was goodness in her. Somewhere on the floor of her fractured self, broken pieces began to stitch together.

Some three months later, I had the photo framed. It sits beside my bed where it is the last thing I see each evening and the first I see each morning.

I still had not sent the letter.

The suicide option remained in that hidden bottle of pink pills. I didn't know if it was a lethal dose that I had accumulated. Later I learned it was.

Chapter 2

FIGHT NIGHT

Fighting means different things for different people. You'll know for yourself what to fight.

> – Miriam Toews, *Fight Night.*

We are individuals, yes, but individuals whose live blood is connection.

> – Terry Real, *Us*

Many of us know the famous question with which Mary Oliver ends her poem "The Summer Day".

> *Tell me, what is it you plan to do*
> *with your one wild and precious life?*

I know my answer was to create a "we" out of "ones". For years my husband and I led pre-marriage workshops which we called "On Becoming One". We understood this as a vision for marriage available for every couple to choose. We taught that a thriving relationship was one where two individuals began the journey to become one. It would be a place where individuality and connection were in balance. We viewed this as a holy call available for every couple and one to which we had personally committed. We understood that this journey would have many stages and would take a lifetime to build.

We ended each of these workshops in the sanctuary with a recording of Marc Cohn singing "True Companion" as a celebration of this vision. For me Cohn's lyrics gave me a warm and evocative image of my husband and myself growing older together doing the very simple things of true intimacy. I had no illusions that this vision of marriage would be easy for us, or for any couple choosing it.

For me, this vison of holding healthy individuality and the authentic intimacy of deep connection in balance in a marriage was my answer to Mary Oliver's famous question. I knew that in our highly individualistic world, this journey would involve over and over the surrender and sacrifice of the one into a whole. It was a movement from individuality toward abiding connection. I did not see a straight trajectory but one which progressed toward the connection of deep love; that was the goal. My husband's abandonment of this commitment was devastating, first for our coupledom and then for those we had encouraged to choose as we had.

As a marital and relationship therapist, I view seeking this balance as a redemptive and much-needed direction for a thriving relationship in our present culture, where self-individualization often takes precedence over connection. American philosopher Martha Nussbaum acknowledges this in her 2018 book *Anger and Forgiveness*: "[I]t is always difficult to strike a balance between healthy self-preservation and a kind of self-withholding that is incompatible with deep love."

I thought our marriage was on the solid and well-developed foundation of this vision. I saw us as inspirational to others. Later, I would believe for many years that because my marriage had failed, I could no longer champion what I could not achieve. My marriage had been blown out of the sky by a missile and my very being shattered beyond recognition, but back then, I was convinced I simply had to fight for all we were and all we meant to others. I had to stop this desire of his. I did not want to be relegated to "gone".

I also thought that confessing that I was suicidal would change his mind, but it did not. Upon his return from Arizona in early February he was strengthened in his urgency to have me send the letter, for the next workshop to be over and for him to be closer to the end of his life with me. I saw this last workshop we were to do together as my one last hope. He would surely see how meaningful the work that we were doing was and feel at least duty-bound to continue it. I did not see that his plan was to continue without me in this endeavour. How could I be expendable both as a work partner and a life partner?

For this last workshop together I dressed well, smiled and connected with all the participants, helping them understand the difficult concepts of evolutionary spirituality. But some of them found him a confusing teacher/ guide.

"Please," they begged me, "help him speak more simply. He needs to connect with us and recognize where we are and what our difficulties are. He needs to acknowledge all that we are doing to embrace evolution into our spiritual thinking. This is Florida."

I pushed him to go slower, and to be kinder to the people in the community. As he practiced his lecture with me, I made suggestions, as I always had, to help him respond more thoughtfully to his audience. In the end, we were outstanding, and it was not enough to alter his desire to leave me. The community surrounded us with affection and God's blessing in communion, and this too was not enough.

The next workshop was scheduled for mid-February in Vancouver. It had been planned that this one he would do on his own, leaving the day after Valentine's Day and returning to Florida four days later. We were then scheduled to return to Vancouver and our home by April 1. That would give us all of March together. I wanted this time. I was fighting for us.

The days leading up to Valentine's had a surreal quality. We went shopping a lot. On a particularly breezy evening, I left a glass of water resting on a book beside my laptop on the nightstand in the bedroom. When I came back in the bedroom, the glass of water and the book had tumbled to the floor and my computer keyboard was soaked in water. I panicked. I did not know that this would be fatal to my computer, but it was. He was sure I had knocked it over. I was sure I had not. I still don't think I caused this accident. It will always be my word against his.

We had been careful with money for so long, trying to pay off the mortgage and afford this new life plan we had. Now we had to purchase a new computer. We did and he got himself one of the first iPads at the same time. In my mind there was no way that we had enough money to dissolve this marriage. I argued this fact with him, and he claimed to be ready to embrace poverty. I was born a kid on the other side of the tracks and poverty held no allure for me, spiritual or otherwise. Maybe she was rich?

We had always shopped for clothing together. I suppose we were meticulous dressers. We enjoyed clothing. In my younger years, I had thought I might be a fashion designer. I had learned to make my own clothes very early in order to dress well. It also freed me from my mother's ineptitude with a sewing machine.

I had not noticed that none of my clothing fit me. He did and took me shopping. February was early season for clothes shopping in Naples, Florida. The tourists had gone home, and the shops were just getting in their new lines. Tommy Bahama had an early shipment of their summer season wear. It was exotic to us as Canadians. I remember the spicy smell of the shop. I picked out some shorts and tops in size 6 or size 8, which I thought to be my size. In the dressing room, we both saw that they were too big. He began bringing me smaller sizes. Finally size 2 and then size 0 fit. I was happy he was choosing my clothes and fetching things for me to wear. One pair of shorts was a delicious pistachio green. My mind ignored the change in size and excused it as some strange American sizing thing. We left the store with several new outfits for me.

Sitting at a fancy outdoor patio, we ordered drinks. It was warm and sunny. We were in Florida in the Canadian winter. We had been shopping. He cared that I looked good. He was the thoughtful man I loved, and he would never leave me. Just maybe, retail therapy had opened a treasured and familiar channel between us. I hoped.

As he made the arrangements to fly back to Vancouver six days later, I saw he had not booked a return flight. He was literally not coming back. He was not only going to end our marriage; he was also going to leave me alone—well-dressed—in Florida.

Why would he not come back? My mind refused to believe that he was leaving our marriage in February. I thought if he left at all it would be after we returned to our home in Vancouver on April 1. I never thought he would abandon me in Florida. For me, this seemed like a stunning, unbelievable act of cruelty. I tried to make sense of it. Maybe he was leaving earlier because he despaired of ever getting me to send the letter to the church community claiming I understood and accepted. Maybe my pain was too much for him as it named him the cause. Maybe his dreams were shaking his resolve to leave the marriage and he thought he better go before his dreams became even more explicit in portraying the negative enormity of this plan. Maybe he was afraid that she would not wait much longer.

When I realized there was no return ticket, in a moment of reality, I agreed my daughter could come and be with me when he left. The plan was for me to drive him to an airport hotel where he would spend the night and leave the next day for Vancouver. I would pick up my daughter that same night at the airport.

At some level I knew the woman he was leaving me for would pick him up at the airport in Vancouver and they would have sex. I created the scenario where this union would collapse. He certainly encouraged me to believe that it could all come to nothing but a wild and furious infatuation.

He did not know her as anything other than his therapist. He told me she had already given up her membership in her professional college, to avoid any ethical repercussions I presumed. He did know I was toying with the idea of reporting her and was terrified I would. He told me he would be resigning from his position as head pastor of our church. I hoped that the two of them would quickly see that their infatuation came with too high a price tag.

I had a lot of professional experience with marriages that survived affairs. This helped me keep my hope alive. It also contributed to me unwisely ignoring the advice of my accountant and lawyers.

Our time together leading up to his departure was tumultuous, to say the least. There were the shopping trips, walks at the botanical gardens and beach walks. On the outside we looked like a tourist couple enjoying an escape from the Canadian winter. On the inside I was approaching insanity. Finally, while I drove us back to the condo, it all erupted in a huge fight. Eventually we were just screaming at each other.

"Yes, I am going," he yelled.

"No, no, no!" I yelled back.

I would not agree to send the letter to the church board. I would not accept that this was God's will. He could not convince me. Though I wavered, I would not agree. I remember that "no" resonating in every part of my shrinking body.

Giving up was not in my DNA. That's something I came to realize over a lifetime. I was a woman raised in a post-WWII *Leave It to Beaver* world. The feminism of my suffragette grandmother had been replaced by the happy housewife in suburbia. Prior to my first marriage I had to promise I would never work outside the home, even though I had two postgraduate degrees at that time. I had been a combination of compliant and resistant. Gradually the compliance dwindled. With my first-born son in a highchair, I read Betty Friedan, researched my grandmother, and became a committed feminist and a professional working woman. I fought for what I believed to be good and true. A righteous rage for justice flowed in my veins. I had long ago quit giving up.

As he packed, I realized he was taking his guitar, the guitar I commissioned for him by a famous Canadian luthier. I wanted to hide that guitar so that he could not take it. I knew it was his most precious possession. I did not do this. I wanted him to think of my love for him when he played the instrument I had made possible. Abalone dolphins were set in the neck of the guitar as a symbol of our playful joy with each other. Twenty-four hours later, we drove to the hotel near the airport where we would wait for my daughter's plane to arrive at ten that evening. I knew that he was leaving. Yet, I hoped.

It was like most airport hotels out in the boonies. Unremarkable. The clerk was alone on the job.

"Yes, I have you registered. One night only, is it? Please sign here. This is your key. You will find the Wi-Fi code in the room on the desk."

We went to the room. Having lost so much weight I was shivering, and I drew a hot bath for us as was our custom.

"This is a small tub. But it has never stopped us before." He even smiled. It was so normal.

"I am so cold," I said. "I am so scared." Even so, I forced myself to focus on it being a day for lovers.

After bathing, warm now and lying naked on the bed together, we reached for each other.

Perhaps I made love and he performed? Maybe I thought if my scent was on his body, she would change her mind and not welcome him.

The clock ticked.

"It is time to go to the airport," he said. "We can wait in the cell phone parking area until Mary calls on her cell to let us know that she has arrived. You can then drop me first at the arrivals before you fetch her. I will get a cab back here." His words drew me into the present. Such a civil plan for an execution.

In the cell phone parking area, I still fought.

"I can't do this," I said "Don't go. It is not right."

The night grew dark as we waited in the Florida field filled with other waiting cars. My agitation was increasing. Runway lights were flashing in the distance. I was jumping in and out of the car, contemplating running away. The cell phone waiting area was bleak, the fields dark and foreboding. I thought about the alligator warning at our condo. Nothing prepared me for this.

My cell rang and it was Mary. "Mom, I'll have my bag and be out in about fifteen minutes. Love you."

"You drive." He handed me the keys. I still hoped and believed that this nightmare would stop. He would not really leave me. I drove to the arrivals level and stopped just before the pickup zone, as agreed.

"Here is good. Let me out." I got out as well and we fell into a deep and close hug just as others do when saying good-bye at the drop-off zone.

Cheek against cheek, torn from a deep place inside me came these words: "Shame on you. Shame!" My tears burst out, manifesting my denied reality.

"Don't say that. Don't spoil this moment. Don't!" He pushed me away and began to run across the lanes of traffic and into the field beyond. Instinctively I ran after him, following him through the approaching cars.

"I am sorry, sorry, sorry I said that. I don't want to hurt you," I cried out. He stopped on the far side of the roadway, turned and hugged me again.

"Don't ever say that. Don't shame me." His last words to me as his wife. He withdrew his arms and took off at speed further into the field and the night.

Impatient horns sounded. I had left my car unattended in the line for the pickup area. I did the right thing and returned to the car and drove further down the arrivals road and there was my daughter.

However bad my daughter thought my grief might be, it was a great deal worse. Her mother was a competent psychotherapist with a long career to prove it. She was a together, strong, confident and interesting human being. Her mother was not someone who needed much care. Mary was not prepared for the half-mad suicidal disaster who picked her up.

I managed to drive her back to the rented condo where I was to suffer for the next two months in this foreign country, isolated from my community. Our house in Vancouver was still rented to tenants. He had gone to a posh hotel in Vancouver where he was to give a workshop. Following that, rather than returning to us in Florida, he would be with her, I presumed. As for myself, I was beyond making decisions.

Chapter 3

CHAOS AND COLLAPSE

One still must have chaos in oneself to give birth to a dancing star.
— Friedrich Nietzsche

Within hours of arrival, my daughter, who is also a trained psychotherapist and has worked for the Canadian government in suicide prevention with Indigenous people, began to assess the situation. I don't think I could have told her how distraught I was. I think I was long past knowing. I was continuously in various states of alert and alarm. Safety was gone. Reality had not yet made fissures in my denial.

My daughter is a mother of three and she knows what it is like to have an agitated child. She could easily see that I unconsciously held my shoulders and rocked myself when I spoke. She saw that this attempt at self-soothing was only moderately helpful. She got into bed with me that night and held me in her arms until I settled and stayed with me in this way through eight more nights. By day, she walked miles of beach with me. She helped me establish an eating pattern. We decided I would eat a breakfast of cereal, milk and fruit, and for other meals I would drink diet cola and eat bocconcini, basil, a little olive oil and cherry tomatoes. She abhorred the consumption of diet cola by herself or anyone, but she graciously purchased it and poured it over ice for me. She came with me to therapy daily and tried, with the therapist, to sort out what I could do when she left. I was certain I could not fly. I did not want to find accommodation in

Vancouver until our home became available. I had no family there. My husband's actions were disrupting all my community life there. I was so agitated and calming myself lasted only minutes.

She knew she had to leave to be with her family. I did not want to go with her. I could not bear the thought of my grandchildren seeing me. I was too ill. I knew this. I was too ill to fly, too ill to be anything but a full-time patient. I was mad with grief. I was hiding in my humiliation. When I had to connect with clerks or if strangers on the street spoke in greeting, I am sure I was rude and inconsiderate most of the time.

At the grocery store, the clerk checking the bags would say, "Have a good day now."

I would say, "Not possible."

My daughter would chide me, "Mom, it's not her fault. You must at least try to do better."

Walking on the beach, a passerby would comment, "What a beautiful day!" assuming I would nod and agree. I was absurdly angry with them for such a stupid assumption.

"It is about the worst day of my life," I would mutter under my breath.

I was unavailable. In *Levels of Life,* his memoir about his grief following the loss of his wife, Julian Barnes tells of this condition succinctly: "It is a time of complete selfishness." His wife had died, and he was as consumed by his grief as I was completely preoccupied by mine.

I wanted so badly to escape my reality. Dying seemed the best way. I did not want to go on without the future that I was anticipating. I was almost 74 years old. I once had a good life. It was enough and I wanted out. I thought about how easy it would be. Just take those pills.

My daughter knew I had tried and was frantic I would try again. In a moment of bargaining, she offered, "Mom, please. If you give me the pills, I will learn to play golf. Or I will become a Christian. You have to choose."

My anti-church, anti-golf daughter loved me this much? This touched me unexpectedly. Really? She was that desperate. Finally, I gave her the pills. She flushed them down the toilet. I am ashamed that I made this hard for her.

The desire to not live is very powerful. I could not see a future. The meaning of my life had been obliterated. Once suicide has been contemplated, with some, it has a habit of sticking around as an option. I found this to be so. Without the pills, I had to think about more messy options, and I was not good at this. I am very tidy and the bloody aftermath that shooting myself in the head would make was not attractive. If there were no pills, I mostly thought about drowning. On bad days, the possibility lurked on the edges of my mind.

For many years I frequently got emails from a friend who asked me the simple question, "Are you safe tonight, Ann?"

I caught my breath and tears welled up. I knew my friend knew that suicide was a persistent option in my mind. I did not ever think about people caring that much about me. It made me pause and realize that I care like this about them.

Eventually, several months after I returned to Vancouver, I felt obligated to go to a funeral of a person whose son I liked. It was at another church, and I hoped I could slip in and out unnoticed. It was not to be. An old and dear friend who had chosen not to remain my friend literally bumped into me.

"How are you doing?" so naturally came out of his mouth.

"I am here. I came," I said. But I was supposed to say, "Fine, thank you and how are you?"

My words and irritable tone were startling. Meanwhile, someone else had put her arm about my shoulder and whispered in my ear, "I don't know how you can be here. In your shoes, I could not have done this."

She meant being out in public at this funeral but for me it was much more. My experience has taught me that when suicide is a real option, being present in the world is an act of great courage.

Chapter 4

CHURCH:
ANOTHER BETRAYAL

"Did I not see you with him in the garden?" Again, Peter denied it, and at that moment the cock crowed.

– John 18:26–27

And Peter left the courtyard, weeping bitterly.

– Luke 22:62

The goat shall bear on itself all their iniquities to a barren region; and the goat shall be set free in the wilderness.

– Leviticus 16:22

Here's how I saw it. My husband and I had been engaged in a project that was much bigger than us. We were liberal Christian ministers who were also trained as family and marriage therapists. While he was officially the pastor of a church and I was officially in private practice as a psychotherapist, we continually supported and helped each other's work. We saw couples together from time to time and I participated in every possible way in the leadership and education of the congregation we served. I also acted as agent and marketer for the evolutionary Christian spirituality project that we were creating in order to revitalize the church. This was a gift of service I gladly donated. We worked as a team and, in my opinion, were perceived as such.

Over thirty years, through experimentation, participation in continuing education events, reading, discussion and courses created and taught, we had been attempting to turn a church on the edge of extinction into a vital thriving place not just locally but in the wider world. We were trying to build a church that was ecologically sensitive and scientifically relevant. It was a grand and perhaps grandiose mission; nevertheless, gradually, people around the world were engaging in it.

The ideas grew exponentially over the years. We were concerned that individuals could grow into ever-deeper consciousness, and we taught courses to encourage this. We wanted this growing awareness to be grounded biblically in the Judeo-Christian faith and offered in-depth courses in reading the entire Bible to allow this awareness to intensify and flower. We also gave workshops to encourage ourselves and others to act non-violently towards neighbour, self and the cosmos.

Evolutionary spirituality was a movement in the early stages of formation. Thomas Berry, Pierre Teilhard de Chardin, Brian Swimme, Ken Wilber, Rupert Sheldrake, John Haught, Ilia Delio and many of its other leaders from scientific and spiritual disciplines inspired us. In this movement spirituality, science and quantum physics were viewed as mutually enhancing. The biblical accounts of creation were treasured as attempts to make meaning suitable to their times. Darwin's theory of evolution was celebrated as the factual story of the universe as now understood. Unfortunately, this is still so disturbing for much of the world. More than a decade after Darwin's two-hundredth birthday, American citizens are still divided approximately fifty-fifty on the issue of accepting evolution as factual. A recent Gallup poll shows only sixty-one per cent of American public schools include evolution in their science curriculum.

Our congregation learned the scientific story starting with "13.8 billion years ago…" and progressed through the significant stages of development until present day. We ritualized this by walking around the sanctuary, passing through the various stages of evolution. In so doing the magnitude of the universe impacted us freshly. We celebrated this scientific understanding as a sacred revelation even as scripture itself is. They were not contradictory stories but evolving complementary stories, even as the two stories of creation in Genesis differ but enhance each other.

A simple but profound example was when our congregation adopted my husband's change to the wording of the famous Lord's Prayer. Instead of "our Father who art in Heaven", we now prayed, "Loving God in whom is heaven". Suddenly God is not smaller and less significant than the magnificent universe. Said another way, the cosmos itself is not separate from God.

In a similar fashion, Jesus is not bound to terrestrial existence. Jesus as Christ is the cosmic Christ. Teilhard de Chardin said it this way: "Christ isn't just an anthropological phenomenon with significance for humanity, but Christ is also a cosmic event with significance for the planet."

Other thinkers in the field take this further and see the cosmic Christ as having significance for the universe. Ilia Delio states it this way: "The universe belongs to the Christ. The Christ gives meaning and direction to the universe."

The theory of evolution and its scientific findings invigorated our faith rather than diminishing it. The field of biology, with its focus on the interconnection of all living things, amplified our Judeo-Christian embrace of relationship and connection. Biology gave us a physical universe which is thoroughly interrelated. Ken Wilber named it "an evolving web". The reality of God named the Holy Trinity composed of Father, Son and Holy Spirit now becomes the Holy Trinity composed of Relationship, Mystery and Evolution.

My husband wrote books to articulate and expand these ideas and we taught courses both in our home church and, increasingly, around the world. I promoted this work with enthusiasm and commitment. I was more naturally an educator and recruiter while he was a writer and speaker. Our local church committed to take this to the wider world. Could these ideas from academia be realized in the local situation of a church community? We as a church community were going to be the first laboratory where these ideas were tested. We wanted to become and were becoming the destination church for evolutionary Christianity at work amongst the people.

A Lutheran church in Florida invited us to be a mentor for them and become a sister church to increase the spread of evolutionary Christianity. They had sent their leadership team to us that summer prior to my husband's therapist expressing her desire to be with him. In January, as part of the exchange, we had made our way to them. There were similar commitments ahead in Arizona, Vancouver, Australia and the Maritime provinces, with others in the planning stages. We were to spend six months a year at the home church in Vancouver and the other six months writing, doing workshops and taking the mission outward. I was also in the early stages of a memoir project detailing the rise of feminism within the church and my role in it. Steadily we had built a loving and secure community that was excited and took risks personally and collectively to promote this grand experiment.

With my husband's announcement that he was abandoning me to be with another woman, suddenly our mission was in complete disarray. My husband believed in his view that leaving me was a sacred step in the evolutionary process. I just needed to understand and accept this. Shame washes over me when I confess how hard I tried to believe that my husband was correct and that I was flawed in not seeing it. I so seriously had tried to send that letter my husband helped me draft.

In those first eight days with my daughter, I knew I had to decide about the letter. He had gone back, and I knew he would be in conversation with the board of the church. I assumed he would be telling his version of what was happening as articulated in the letter he wanted me to send. I was struggling. I showed my daughter the letter.

"The lawyer tells me that I have to be careful to stay on his good side," I explained. "She said that he will never be more financially generous toward me than in the next few weeks. Maybe I should agree and send this letter?"

"Mom, do you believe this crap? Come on." Her disdain was just as I imagined it would be. I could not bear collapsing in her eyes.

I decided to not ever send the letter.

My husband had indicated to me that when he left on February 14 that he was going to resign from the local church. I believed him and thought it the right decision in these terrible circumstances. I expected he would hand in his resignation to the board and that I would be told this had happened.

During this time, as a minister in good standing, I expected that the higher courts of the church would reach out to me with expressions of concern and offers of support. In my denomination, there is a court rather than a bishop and an even higher court rather than an archbishop. They had a pastoral obligation to me, but I received no such official support. In the polity of my denomination, ministers are never members of local congregations, but rather members of the national denomination itself. My local congregation had made me a member as an honour, recognizing my service. This also obligated them to reach out formally to me. They did not.

However, I did choose to tell three of my closest friends in the congregation what was happening from my perspective. One of them did offer to organise support for me. She arranged for an ad hoc committee of lay leaders of the congregation to talk with me via Skype. This conversation happened on one of the eight days in February when my daughter was with me. I thought this committee wanted to hear the story from my side, what I was experiencing and what I knew about what my husband was doing and had done. While not an official act of support, I saw it as a step in that direction.

I wanted this meeting. I was a cradle-to-grave Christian. After school in my childhood, in the late 1940s, I often went with my buddy, Valarie, to our church where her grandfather was the caretaker. It was a spacious magical place to play hide and seek, tag or just spread out on a pew under the coloured twilight from the stained glass to gossip. It was a welcoming and delightful place.

My home was occupied most times of night and day with my eldest brother's RCAF buddies all returning home from war. My dad had replaced the dining room table with a pool table that, at mealtime, was transformed by a big sheet of plywood into an eating table. A lot of feasting and partying and dancing went on in my house. It was chaotic and noisy. I was often a nuisance, paid to get lost and not bother them. When as an adult I demanded to know where I slept, not one of them could remember as all the rooms were taken. At her house, Valarie slept on a mattress placed over the bathtub. I am sure that was not my fate, though I often was obliged to use the toilet at the gas station at the corner.

By the time I was a teenager, the minister, who knew all this, gave me full reign over the Sunday school blackboards. I filled them with chemistry equations and did my homework there where it was quiet. Eventually, twelve years later, this same church pushed all its boundaries, at both local and national level, and ordained me, its first woman pastor with a young family in tow. It was my homeplace and had all my loyalty.

"Mary, why hasn't the leadership been in touch with me?" I asked my daughter. "What is happening back there in Vancouver? Is he right that I am expendable? Do they think it is God's will?"

"Mom, you must settle down. Remember it is arranged that a small committee from the church is going to speak with you via Skype. Let's make a list of what you want them to hear at that meeting."

"Well, you could tell them."

"Yes, but Mom, let's see if you can tell them how it is for you and what you need. I want you to do it. I will sit with you, but I won't talk. I will be there, and they will see me."

"I have to make them see that I did not know. They have to see that I would never have deceived them so. Mary, I want them to love me and make room for me. How can his choices take my community away from me?"

The interview time arrived. My daughter helped me be together enough to pull it off.

We enabled Skype and there they were: the new co-pastor, the board chair, my friend who had pulled the meeting together and three others. It was happening in my husband's office in the church that was now being used by the co-pastor.

The setting was familiar, the desk we had chosen, the paintings on the walls and photos of the churches where we had been before this one. They were occupying what had been a safe space for me.

I began by telling them what I had experienced.

"I did not know. She was his therapist. I had trusted her. Now I wonder about her ethics as a professional. I wonder if things got romantic during a session. I have contacted her college only to discover that she resigned from her accrediting governing body three months before as this therapy was ending. At that last session he told me that she invited him, saying that should he leave me, she would like to explore marriage and a family with him. Of course, I pushed him to tell me more of what had happened."

These revelations shocked the board chair and caused her to pace about the room. She expressed incredulity. I turned to my friend who had organised this event for me and put her on the spot.

"You are a therapist. Would you do this with one of your clients?"

"No." She agreed that would any of these things would be simply wrong behaviour.

I asked, "When he left Florida, he had told me he was going to resign. Has this changed?"

The board chair responded, "We are an ad hoc committee, and it is not appropriate for us to speak to this." I was left with the impression that he had not resigned, and the board would make a ruling.

The energy in the room began to shift. I noticed the co-pastor was taking notes. Having heard what I wanted to say, she asked me, "Ann, you have helped other churches process all sorts of conflict. Tell us how we ought to proceed in this crisis?"

This angered my daughter, and she intervened with full professional formality. "I believe the purpose of this meeting is for you to hear from my mother with kindness and openness. This is not an opportunity for you to seek her expertise but an opportunity for you to express your care and love."

She named what I had not seen. I was being asked to serve at this moment of my deepest need.

"I would like to know if you will care for my mom and how you will do so. I remind you that my brother, by letter and telephone, has already made the same appeal and has had no response.

"You have written a letter that you intend to send to the congregation telling them what has happened and now I realize you are going to include what you are going to do about my stepfather's employment status. You have sent my mother a partial draft of the letter that does not include your decision."

I interrupted my daughter. "I am very upset about this draft. It does not say anything about me. It does not acknowledge all the service I have given to you and which you are now seeking, once again, by asking me how you should proceed."

Mary, emphasizing this, said, "I want you to make changes to this letter that will acknowledge my mother's role in your leadership."

I could see the co-pastor again making notes.

"And I want you to not send any such letter for at least ten days until my brother is in Florida with my mom. She needs family support before this announcement becomes public."

She was not finished. "I would like for you to assure me that you will care for my mother as she cared for you. She is bereft and suffering. I don't know a lot about churches, but I think they are supposed to care for her."

The interview then quickly came to an end. My daughter was left angry, and I was anxious, even frightened for the future. Something for me felt terribly wrong.

On February 26, 2013, with no family with me, I received this letter several hours before it was sent out to every member of the congregation. It is impossible, even now, for me to recount this letter without commenting on it. Here it is:

February 26, 2013

Dear friends,

I am writing to let you know about the change in personal circumstances of two valued leaders in our community. After 26 years, [X] has made the decision to leave his marriage to Ann Evans.

It matters to me that it was after thirty years of relationship, twenty-six of which we were married.

Both of these leaders have made immense contributions to the life of this church—separately and together as a couple.

It took a great deal of fight on my part and several drafts to have included that I had been and was recognized as an integral part of the contribution.

Although our hearts ache for each of them, this major change in life circumstances will not affect [X]'s position as a member of this church's ministerial team.

They were choosing him and this is how I was informed.

This is a personal issue for [X] and Ann; both are in pain as they make this passage. Please give them the gift of space and time to manage their lives in an atmosphere free of gossip. Keep them in your prayers. Keep your hearts open to both and assure them they can lean on our community as needed. Also know that our co-pastor is available for spiritual support during this time.

I did not want the gift of "space and time". I wanted care and inclusion now. I needed community desperately. If my husband was in pain, it was not noticeable as he returned on February 14 and left with his therapist for an extended holiday in Hawai'i two weeks later, as our joint visa card reported to me. In fact, I received a report from an ill-intentioned but knowledgeable friend telling of his absolute joy in his new decision.

I did not regard discussion about what was happening as private or gossip. This was my family. I wanted my community to know my truth and his as well. I needed the church community that had been our place and our family to know my story from my perspective. I did not want what the letter stated I wanted. I had never been consulted regarding this request.

Over time I came to know that many people in the community were enraged by this letter.

Please hold [X] and our church in your thoughts and prayers. Offer whatever support you can to each other. Know that we as the Board are endeavouring to do the same. Be assured of the Board's commitment to the work that we are called to bring to the world.

With sincerity…

This letter was signed by the board chair. I felt betrayed. This was a community that espoused transparency in its vision and mission. This seemed like a cover-up. I did not understand why this major change would not affect my husband's position in the community but would radically change mine. When he abandoned me, he was clear that he would resign from his ministry upon his return. I still believed he had at least this much integrity. I later learned that one of his conditions to the church was that, were he to resume his ministry, he would not preach (essentially perform his duties) if I came back into the community. How then was I supposed to lean on this community? In spiritual terms I was to be the scapegoat.

This betrayal was a public one. It was not uniquely mine. I had to share this betrayal with hundreds, maybe thousands. Many hated the letter, but it was powerful.

People I thought would reach out to me did not but for one startling exception: "WTF! I am not supposed to send this but I am." This was the title of an email I received shortly after the letter of February 26 had been sent to the parish. Her email went on to apologize for intruding into my space that I "wanted kept private". This came from a person informed by so much personal grief she knew the letter's request could never have come from me. My eyes tear up recalling what this lone email meant to me. One person sought to disobey the letter's requests and reached out to me personally.

So many seemed betrayed by what my husband did and how he had appeared to abandon not just me but his commitment to them. Like all churches, this community had both internal and external conflicting voices. The decision of their pastor bothered many of them but they wanted to survive. They had embarked, not without controversy, on the evolutionary Christian spirituality project as the way to thrive. The letter invited them to support each other but not me. And they did what they were told.

A parallel process was born: my grief and theirs. They spoke to each other and had many discussions. I did not want them to lose the project. Most fervently, I did not want them to lose me. Gone from my husband's life, I did not want to be gone from theirs.

I was losing my husband. I was losing my church. Nothing made sense. Once betrayed became twice betrayed. No friend and no objective person outside our church community that I spoke with, from doctors, to therapists, to lawyers and to clergy from other church denominations, could make any sense of it. They simply shuddered.

As I experienced my church family slipping away, I felt even more alone. Typical of a pastor's family, I did not have an active circle of friends outside that church community in Vancouver. My children did not live in Vancouver, and old friends lived elsewhere in the world. I truly thought that my home congregation, given the circumstances, would keep me and nurture me and extend themselves to help me heal. I thought my husband, by promising me that he would resign, was making this possible. I was not only a clergyperson but, by their choice and as an honour conferred by them, a member of this local parish. The worldwide church at its best prides itself on the preferential option for the poor and the broken, though of course, its historical record in this endeavour is abysmal.

Betrayal is as old as time itself and repair is possible, as the disciple Peter experienced. He betrayed Jesus and as soon as he realized it, the repair began; he wept bitterly. As a result, friends of Jesus, who founded a worldwide church, acclaimed Peter as the rock at its foundation.

For at least two years following the February 26 letter from the board and all the pain that ensued, I believed that, given time and facilitation, reconciliation between the local church and myself was possible. Sometimes I wonder, had my abandonment occurred in Vancouver, would church leadership support have happened more organically? I was far away, and my husband had returned and was there in their midst, telling his story in his way. It looked to me like it was simpler to judge me as a liability and betray their loyalty to me. My story was a raw, ugly story of abandonment. He cast his as a call from God to which he responded with profound courage.

My husband and I had taught several courses in the community on the work of René Girard. He was a French philosopher and social anthropologist who taught most of his adult life in the USA. He focused on the presence of violence, tried to understand it and find ways to change our proclivity for it. He taught that when communities are most distressed and afraid, they reach for ritual to help them. A most ancient and common ritual for these confrontational occasions is found in Leviticus in the Hebrew scriptures. Instead of further turning against each other, the group's collective fear and distress are poured into a single scapegoat, who is then banished to a barren wilderness. It is important that the scapegoat be viewed as evil, a monster, the one whose soul is dead, as it seemed my husband viewed mine. Then the community, having rid itself of evil, is cleansed, can breathe again and is ready for a new day. René Girard showed this reality functioning throughout literature, religion and history. I felt this violent banishment of my body and my soul to a barren wilderness.

For Girard, Christianity attempts to change this by having the victim be without fault. Jesus, innocent, hanging on a cross, redeems all victims. Victims no longer need to be scapegoated and banished. Jesus can be experienced as redeemer and reconciler. Better ways for resolving conflict are possible. My church community was schooled by us to know this but, alas, the older ritual of finding a scapegoat upon which to load and then banish existing problems was and still is faster and easier for too many.

Church had been my safe homeplace since I was a child and it had never failed me. I, like legions of others, began now to join the community of people hurt by church.

Chapter 5

ARCHANGELS/SERAPHIM:
THE FIRST RESPONDER, MARY

I am the Metatron...
I am a seraphim.
The highest choir of angels?
You do know what an angel is, don't you?
Metatron acts as the voice of God.

— Alan Rickman, *Dogma*

As a pastor and as a psychotherapist, I am required by my professional accrediting bodies to do regular continuing education. In the early 1990s, I chose to study under Professor Walter Wink, biblical scholar, theologian and activist. He introduced me to angels in a way that intrigued me. He wrote an acclaimed trilogy about "principalities and powers" that made the world think about how congregations have good and bad angels. They can be ruled by a parsimonious angel or a generous one; a closed-minded or an open-minded one; one to preserve the status quo or one to reach out to the marginalized. Saint Paul recognized these forces in the various congregations throughout the western Mediterranean region that he founded and supported with his visits and letters. Paul called these forces principalities and powers. Wink called them angels and I do as well. I think of them as forming a great corporation with many departments under the direction of the CEO, God.

Angels did appear in my life. They came from inside and outside the local and the wider church. It took me a while to discern the good ones from the fallen ones, the Lucifers. I am blessed that most have been dear guardians of my well-being.

Archangels are the angels assigned to do the really heavy lifting. They fly in, assess the situation, and remain supervisors of the project and do the best they can to accomplish transformation and healing. Alan Rickman starring as the Metatron in the film *Dogma* is an example of an archangel. John Travolta in Michael may be a more well-known example.

My first angels to fly in, literally, from Ottawa and Guelph to be with me in Florida and then stay by me with such loyalty and constancy were my children: a son and a daughter. I was amazed. I did not feel deserving. As Dr. Winnicott, famous British paediatrician and psychoanalyst, had already helped me to see, I was a good enough parent, but I never thought that I would ever be desperately needy. I had the arrogance to think that I was the parent who was entirely self-sufficient. I expected and desired to stay firmly entrenched in being the giver. Alas that identity was now dismantling.

My youngest child, Mary, was the first to arrive on the scene in Florida. She is a person of great heart, yet under pressure she can be very calm and professional. She is the one whom I picked up at the airport as he fled across the field into his new life. In those early days she was able to take charge of her distraught mother.

In those first eight days with me, her youngest daughter had her seventh birthday. Mary brought a gift for me made by her, my youngest grandchild. It was a love note.

I sat at the kitchen table to open it. The envelope was decorated with hearts and the careful script of a child learning cursive writing. Drawing the card from the envelope, a big red paper heart attached to six inches of accordion-pleated straw sprang forth into the air. As I continued to open the card, out flew seventy-four very tiny red hearts all hand-cut by her with such patience. Love spilled out all over the table. I wept.

The image and the memory of that best card ever sustain and fill me still. She was also giving me her mom who, for the first time in her life, would not be with her on her birthday.

After the attempts to connect with the church in Vancouver, two immediate problems were before us. First there was a seven-day gap in my care. My son, David, who lived in Guelph, Ontario, was scrambling to get a passport so that he could come to me in Florida. I could not imagine returning to Vancouver to find and live alone in rented accommodation. The leadership of my church was not indicating that it would support me. If anything, it was indicating that it would not.

Secondly, following my son's stay, there would still be a month before my house in Vancouver was available. I am sure that the thinking was that, given this much time, I would be more able to fly and face what awaited me in Vancouver. My family was scrambling to find solutions. I was struggling with the desire to kill myself.

While Mary was with me, her husband Chris' family stepped in and provided childcare for my grandchildren so that Chris could continue working. Cheryl, my daughter-in-law, began sending gifts, writing and calling. Eventually we began sharing photos on our cell phones. Such a practice encouraging the visual creative expression of us both became a regular habit that still connects us several times a week. We were Instagrammers before that program even existed.

Time was ticking on. Mary now needed to return to her family, but David's passport was a week away from delivery. We had to address this seven-day gap. We tried to think of who could take care of me in this time period. We explored getting a professional caregiver. We did not have the contacts to make this happen easily. My therapist was trying to help us, but her leads did not work out.

If my nature had been to seek flight and not fight, I might have been an easier patient. Not requiring so much of a caregiver, I might have gone to bed and pulled the covers over my head. Think the opposite. Day after day, I was hyperactive, wild, not eating or sleeping and unable to stay quiet. I wanted to walk constantly at all times of day and night, swim and go on outings to distract myself. When I tried to eat, I was in gut-wrenching pain that I did not understand. I was consumed with my situation. I mostly wanted to quit this life but knew I could not. I wanted the nightmare to stop.

In this anxious state I remembered the woman, Sister Carol, whom I had chatted with at the dinner given to honour my husband's and my arrival in Florida. I had felt drawn to her and that evening, had discovered that she directed a retreat centre close by. Maybe I could go there?

I was hesitant because Sister Carol was a member of a religious community of women and she was supportive of my husband's work and books. I felt protective of her. It felt risky to go to her. Her face had been kind at that dinner and throughout the workshop. I decided I had to trust it. In my distress, I now suggested to Mary that I reach out to Sister Carol. Two days later she agreed to meet with my daughter and me in confidence.

Florida is a winter escape destination for many Canadians, as it had been for me in so many previous winter vacations. Like other "snowbirds", as we are called, I headed to oceanfront spots. I favoured the eastern seaboard where the beaches are long, and one can walk for miles on firm packed sand. The rolling Atlantic Ocean surf never failed to ease work stress and invite relaxation and play. However, this time we had been invited by that Lutheran church desiring to be our sister church. It was on the west coast of Florida where it is warmer and the beaches are smaller. I was now staying with my daughter in the condo they had helped my husband and me secure as our Florida living accommodation. Tropical flowers, bougainvillea, poinsettias, and hibiscus adorned fabulous gardens. Royal palms lined the streets. Golf courses spread out, lush green and manicured. It was a paradise.

Driving from this oasis to the retreat centre, my daughter and I discovered a different Florida. This was where the citrus fruit orchards grew. We found ourselves passing through farms where horses, llamas and cows intermingled. It was hot without the ocean breeze. The land was brown and dry. The royal palms were stunted and small. It was in the interior, a part of Florida that I did not know. While it was only a forty-five-mile drive inland, it was a long forty-five miles in topography.

I was increasingly unsure that this was a good idea. I felt it was too much to ask. I wanted to disappear. This was the first time I would admit to an outsider that my husband had abandoned me. Sister Carol held a lot of power in my mind. Maybe my motives were unclean. I was turning to her to hurt him. I had so many doubts and I was so desperate.

"Mom, here is it is, I think."

The roadside sign indicating our arrival was tired and the reception centre small and unimposing. I stopped the car, parked it in what I thought was a visitor's parking lot, stepped out and looked about me. The land was cleared. I could see a struggling row of incongruous palms along a path. In the distance I could see a house and some buildings. Everything was modest. I had been at several retreat centres in my lifetime and of them all, this was the humblest by far.

I found a person in the reception centre who said she would let Sister Carol know we had arrived. Soon, we were directed to another modest building that I assumed held meeting rooms and possible housing rooms for visitors. I could see Sister Carol waiting there at the end of the palm-lined pathway.

She took us into her cozy office, and we sat down. After courteous hellos, I got straight to the purpose of our visit.

"Sister Carol, I am so hesitant to come to you. Will you, within your order, be able to keep our confidence? Are you obligated to relay to the power structure in your order what we are about to tell you?"

I could see that she was taking her time and thinking it over. I knew I was asking so much. What I would tell her would change a piece of her lifework too.

"Ann, I have only just met you at dinner and at the workshop. Still, I will assure you that whatever you have to say I can keep in confidence, and I will. I will not report anything with the staff of the Lutheran church where you gave the workshop or with my superiors in my own order anywhere in the world."

I began by telling her what had happened to me. Afterwards, I left the room so that she could speak privately with Mary. She and I had discussed the fact that Sister Carol would need to get Mary's perspective on my condition.

While they talked, I looked about. I could see I was in the main retreatant quarters. I looked in the kitchen refrigerator and there were shelves designated to the various retreatants. There were the bedrooms, all with their doors shut. I saw a few retreatants walking about or sitting and reading or meditating. Since there was no one speaking or meeting in a group, I assumed this was a silent retreat. One of them smiled at me with curiosity, the new kid on the block. There was a library, and I noted the books were up-to-date and progressive in content. Out one of the windows I noticed a screen-enclosed swimming pool in need of some repair and cleaning but a pool, nonetheless. I knew how to vacuum it.

If Sister Carol agreed, this was where I would be for one week. Mary found me and brought me back into Sister Carol's office.

"Welcome, Ann," Sister Carol said. "You can have sanctuary here."

Without hesitation, she had welcomed me. Instinctively I felt in the presence of a gracious angel. With my daughter's help, she quickly assessed the fact that I was too erratic to be in the retreat house that I had just nosily scoped out. My incessant twitching and restlessness would affect the others who were making a retreat. She lived in the director's house with her dog, Buddy. She offered me a room in her private quarters for the one week it would take for my son David to arrive in Florida. She also offered me use of her kitchen, any shelf in the fridge I wanted and a private room and bath with rural views of the land and the sky. She promised to keep a careful eye on me and in return I was to walk the dog. She agreed to spend an hour a day with me in spiritual companionship. Since this was sanctuary, it was all offered to me without cost. I knew a donation would be acceptable. The next step for me was set in place. My son and daughter were grateful and relieved. An immediate problem had been solved.

It was with relief we made the drive back to the ocean and the condo. When Mary left, I would go directly to the retreat centre and wait there until David arrived. One problem solved to make room for others. How would I see my therapist daily? She agreed to meet with me by phone.

Even more importantly, how would I sleep without Mary beside me, comforting me? I had never been so unable to manage myself. Our relationship had reversed. Nights were going to be so very difficult. Little did I know this would turn out to be a long-haul problem.

On February 22 Mary's departure day arrived and after taking her to the airport, I drove straight to the retreat centre. As my church was closing its doors, another church had opened hers, admittedly a Roman Catholic one. As a profoundly Protestant person, I had always been a tad cautious about Roman Catholics. Fortunately, I had evolved a long way in my spiritual journey and now I was going to share a home with Sister Carol. No, not just share, but be completely dependent upon her mercy.

Sister Carol was expecting me and met me at her door. Her face was round and cheerful. She was dressed casually but simply. Looking at me directly and warmly, she said, "Welcome, Ann. It must have been hard to say good-bye to Mary. She is such a beautiful and kind woman. How blessed you are with such a daughter."

I nodded, immediately tearing up.

"The house key is hanging here right beside Buddy's leash. Please put your food in the fridge. I have made lots of space for you."

She took me around her home, showing me where her quarters were and what would be our common quarters: a living room with a television, a library of CDs for me to use as I wished and a screened-in porch.

"This is so spacious and comfortable. This is all just for you?" I queried.

"No, until three months ago, another sister shared this space with me. The order is presently seeking a new person to join me. Meantime, I am here on my own and this makes having you possible." She smiled.

"This will be your room," she said, leading me into a bedroom. The freshly picked wildflowers, the fluffy towels and plenty of pillows told me I was in a place of love. I noted that she had placed an evocative tissue collage of a broken heart on the bedside table. I knew in time I would ask her about it.

"I will be working a lot and away part of every day," she said. "You can swim in the pool if you wish. There are several retreatants here and their privacy and silence must be respected. Feel free to use the grounds as you wish. There is a grove with the Stations of the Cross in it. There is where you park your car. It is a bit tight so watch the fence. Here is the Wi-Fi code. I will spend an hour a day with you as your spiritual companion at four each afternoon."

It was as I expected. The retreatants were in silence. I was glad that I did not have to engage with anyone but Sister Carol. I was also very appreciative I would not have to be in total silence myself, but could use my phone and computer and distract myself with CDs if I liked. Sister Carol would offer me her guidance. I knew how privileged I was.

"Remember Buddy is always ready for a walk," she added.

Buddy's ears immediately flared, and he was at the door at the ready. "Walk", as I would quickly discover, was his favourite word. With this, Sister Carol left me to unload the car and move in.

She was warm and matter-of-fact. Buddy was all over me and I was not ready to be so insistently drawn out of myself towards the needs of an animal. A dog? I was not prepared for a dog.

At first Buddy irritated me. I discovered that the sanctuary Sister Carol so generously gave me protected me from the other retreatants but not from him. He was overjoyed to have my company. I would no sooner sink into my despair than he would jump and lick and plead. "Love me, love me" begged his eyes and tail. He was a mix but mostly border terrier. He was rambunctious. He delighted in my frenetic energy.

When I took him for a walk, I wanted to sink into my thoughts. Having none of that, he whimpered and pulled hard on the leash, dragging me to his latest discovery. He drew the llamas over to the fences with his barking. Heeling at the end of the leash was not his idea of fun. There was no walking in a straight line. Sometimes I just sat down with him by the side of one of the deserted country roads and tried to explain my grief to him. I would hold him and cry. His patience for this was limited and he would somersault away, forcing me out of myself. Increasingly, I felt responsible for him. What if I let him off the leash, which he so desired, and I lost him? My host's dog?

It was hard to consider suicide with Buddy at my side. I suspect Sister Carol knew a thing or two and in her concern for my safety employed her dog. I think this might be called pet therapy. Untrained though he was, Buddy was certainly a recovery dog for me. He forced me to think about him and his wishes against my desire to focus on myself and my pain. For just a little bit of every day for the next eight days, he became a grief practice.

Chapter 6

A GRIEF PRACTICE: PRAYING THE STATIONS OF THE CROSS

How ironic that the place where Jesus falls for the Third time, there was once a palm tree fallen against the fence, literally broken in half, one side on our neighbour's property and the other on the House of Prayer side. This tree and this fall depict the absolute brokenness we occasionally experience in our lives – the kind of brokenness from which we absolutely cannot rise up again.

– Mother of God House of Prayer, Jesus' Way

Let the same mind be in you that was in Christ Jesus.

– Philippians 2:5

It was my hour with Sister Carol. I was eager for her wisdom. Spiritual companioning is similar to counselling. For Sister Carol, this meant setting time aside to focus on my relationship to what was spiritual for me. A force, energy, God, Jesus, Spirit. I had spent many hours with a spiritual director or companion. I fully understood the process.

Sister Carol usually did her spiritual companioning in her office in the retreat centre. With me, we met in her living room in the mother house.

She asked how my relationship with God was going. We talked. It is common for the spiritual companion to make a homework assignment at the end of the session.

She put this idea before me, a prayer exercise that I could do over the course of the next eight days. "It is Lent, Ann, and there is a most simple yet special depiction of the Stations of the Cross here on the property. We call this place the Way of the Cross. I am not sure how familiar you are with this prayer practice but let me share with you a little of how this happened here. Mother of God House of Prayer is a rustic retreat centre for sure. We also have humble origins which means we do not have a big bank account."

As this book goes to press, sadly, I have learned that the retreat centre no longer exists.

Sister Carol patiently told me the story.

"In 1982, when this place was founded, there was certainly no money for a crafted Stations of the Cross. Of course, these Stations were essential to a House of Prayer and much desired. The founders began trudging around in the woods. They started paying attention to the trees and how they grew. They began contemplating the trees, forest bathing you might say. Eventually they began to see possible symbolic representations of the last days of Jesus' life. With magic markers and signs, they chose places for the fourteen events that mark Jesus' walk on his last days. In time, someone was kind and mowed a path. This is how it all happened. We here at the centre think that this is one of the unique things that draw people to this place. Here is a booklet about it," she said, handing me *Jesus' Way*. "I invite you to consider spending time there, and then tell me about your experience with the stations, in our time together."

I felt the old familiar resistance to things Roman Catholic. My mind flew back to a time, aged just six years old, when I noted that the women on my street were abuzz with gossip. It was 1946. They were talking about my oldest brother. I was very proud that he was in the RCAF killing

Germans. I had been very careful on my way to school every day to do as I was instructed by my mother, "Step on a crack and break a German's back!"

I was all ears to hear what the street was saying now that my brother was coming home from the Front.

"Ida's son is coming home from war," I heard one woman say. "She says he has an English girl who has a French name—Blanche, I think. A bit odd, don't you think?"

My parents were glad the neighbours were thinking the way I reported it that afternoon. But at our evening meal the buzz was very different.

"How can it be? An English girl with a French name and she is Roman Catholic? Not possible." My mother was clearly distressed.

My dad responded, "Now, Ida, we must try. The neighbours don't know she is a Roman Catholic. We don't have to tell your father. Not yet. Maybe it will come to nothing."

My father was speaking very loudly and slowly. I thought the street could possibly hear him. My mother was deaf and wore big hearing aids that were not much good. He was also writing what he was saying down so that she could read it. She was so torn, wanting nothing more than to hug her son, her son who was alive. Blanche was in the way. Why did she have to be Roman Catholic?

I was absorbing the fact that Catholics were bad as girlfriends. This was Orange southwestern Ontario, but it operated like a miniature Northern Ireland. I was only six. Over my lifetime, I have been dismantling such prejudices. Neither Sister Carol nor I knew that her invitation to read *Jesus' Way* would trigger such long ago memories in me. Once acknowledged, they lost their power, and I opened the booklet.

I felt driven to this practice I had not chosen in a place I had not expected to be. My mother would just have deal with it in eternity. I had to do something with my eight days in this place and this ancient Roman Catholic practice was my best option. Over the next week, I spent many hours praying and walking the Stations of the Cross in this magnificent natural grove. I totally identified with the broken and crucified body of Jesus. Just as Paul instructed the Philippians, I found that the mind of Christ fully inhabited mine.

I discovered that the Stations of the Cross provide an opportunity to recall and meditate on the fourteen selected events of the last day that Jesus spent on earth as a human being. The easiest way to see what this looks like is to visit any Roman Catholic cathedral. You will see that there is a walkway about the cathedral with fourteen possible stops. Each stop is marked by words from the Gospels and some form of visual art. Usually it is a painting, a sculpture, or a craft in a traditional representational form. Sometimes the events are in very modern art forms. In 1947 Matisse placed all the stations in one place on the back wall of the Chapelle du Rosaire in Vence, southeast France. They look like rough charcoal sketches of a pained trip to crucifixion. Increasingly more modern interpretations have appeared. The founders of the retreat centre saw in the shapes of trees visual representations of the this walk of pain made by Jesus. I did as Sister Carol bade me do and entered this sacred grove.

I did the Stations daily, and sometimes more than once a day, for eight days. I quickly got used to seeing Jesus' journey in the subtle positions of the trees. The setting was enchanting. Northern cardinals, red-winged blackbirds, as well as house finches and palm warblers were everywhere in the trees, singing their hearts out, especially towards twilight. The shimmering sunlight on the eucalyptus trees was mirrored on the surface of the lagoon. I was always quite alone while there. It was Lent, the time in the Christian year set aside to remember Jesus' journey to his death. The timing was perfect. Sometimes I walked the Stations in order and stopped when I could go no further but at other times, I made all fourteen stops. Often later in the day I returned to the one or two that most spoke to me.

At the first station, I met Jesus being condemned to die. As a well-informed Christian, I know the story well. Jesus has been arrested for sedition. The Jewish authorities, his own leaders, want him put to death publicly which means, at that time, crucifixion. He is taken by the chief priests to Pilate, the Roman authority, for sentencing. Pilate's wife has been warned in a dream that this Jew, Jesus, is a "good" man. Pilate becomes anxious. He can find no fault in Jesus, refuses to make a judgment, and decides to turn him over to the crowd who shout for his crucifixion. Thus, Jesus begins the inescapable journey to his killing field.

At this point in my life journey, I identified with Jesus. Jesus was condemned by the very people who one week earlier had loved and celebrated him. I felt and thought I had been condemned. The person I most loved and wanted to spend my life with had abandoned me. He had judged me. He found me lacking and dispensable.

When I had asked him why, I heard him say to me, "Ann, your soul is shrivelling up. It is stagnant and nearly dead."

I was shocked. I had no thought that my soul was anything but engaged and vital. He condemned me in the place of deepest meaning for me. It is hard to explain in secular terms how excruciating this was for me. I was being told that my essence had become so contaminated that he would not engage with me in any opportunity for redemption. I had always trusted and considered his opinion. These words traumatised me. Now barely a month later, I looked at the depiction of Jesus condemned, and it resonated with what I felt in my body. My church's decision only amplified this.

I could imagine Jesus finding in Pilate a person who saw that he was a good man. And then Pilate washes his hands of the whole affair and turns Jesus over to the crowd, who condemn him. I thought my church was doing this, washing its hands of me.

I think the aim of the spiritual practice of walking the Stations of the Cross is to experience the pain of Jesus deeply enough to inspire us to never commit such violence against another. For me, at this time, rather, the practice allowed me to identify with Jesus and experience what it was to be violated by another.

At the next Station, I met Jesus carrying his cross. How does one carry the noose to the hangman, the knife to the one who beheads, the electric chair to the executioner, abandonment papers to a spouse?

The truth of my abandonment was more than I could carry. I remembered Jesus praying in the garden the evening before his betrayal by Judas and before he was handed over to the Jewish authorities: "Please, no God, take this cup from me." Luke tells us his sweat, as he prayed, was like drops of blood. This is a prayer I could and did make and, for so many days, still made in some form or another.

"Spare me, please. Bring my husband to his senses." I also was inspired by the prodigal son who at last "comes to his senses".

My husband, in a song he once wrote to express the weight of discipleship, put it this way: "Please take this robe, it is too heavy for me." Exactly.

Overwhelmed by this station, I frequently moved quickly to the third station. Jesus is falling. He is not able to carry the cross. He stumbles and collapses. I saw myself collapsed, weighted down by my burden and unable to get up. I was so helpless, and I hated this state of being. Jesus was there before me in this grove, on the ground, covered with moss and dirt, bearing it for all time.

There were times when this was as far as I got. I sought distraction, left the grove and returned to the director's house. On one such day, as I opened the door, Buddy was wild with excitement. He wanted to be outside. I grabbed him and headed for the lawn. I did not want to walk. I wanted to hold him and tell him once again what I was feeling and thinking. Buddy was not the best listener. Having none of it, he drew me away from my distress. He grabbed a branch and insisted on his favourite game of fetch. Animal lovers will recognize Buddy as an angel.

After this much-needed break from prayer, I returned to the fourth station. Here Jesus meets his mother, Mary. My daughter's name is Mary. She had just been with me, meeting me, violated and suffering. Over the many years of our marriage, she had come to trust my husband. Now aged forty-five, she had been his stepdaughter for nearly thirty years. She had given her children to be grandfathered by him. She too was betrayed. She had anger that I could see, but I could not yet acknowledge such anger in me. Somehow, she was fully there for the devastated person before her who was still her mother. As much as I needed her, I came to know that she needed me to be whole. This opened a little channel to life that I could barely see or experience. She, in her need of me, valued me, giving me purpose to live. I had given her the sleeping pills and passed them through that narrow chink. These are some of the things that were triggered in me as I gazed upon the scene shaped by the trees growing in the grove. I pondered the look exchanged between mother and son. I felt my daughter meeting me in deepest pain. And I knew my son was coming at the end of these eight days.

At the fifth station, out of the crowd steps Simon of Cyrene, moved by compassion. He picks up the heavy cross and, being a strong man, he carries it for Jesus.

In the heat of my grief, it was hard for me to discern who was stepping forward to help me and who was retreating from my hurt. Was Simon a friend of Jesus or a stranger? Sister Carol had only recently been introduced to me, and she had just taken me into her private home. My daughter had asked her, and she said yes without hesitation. She was helping me carry my pain. Meanwhile, back in Vancouver, the power structure of my church was in the process of saying no.

It made me think about the Via Dolorosa that Jesus walked that day in Jerusalem. Who was in the crowd? Were they the gang that shouted for his crucifixion? How did Simon have the courage to step forward when even Peter, one of his own disciples, had just the evening before denied he even knew Jesus?

Sister Carol supported evolutionary Christianity and during my stay with her, quite by coincidence, was preparing to give a paper on my husband's articulation of this thinking. She showed no signs of the conflict she must have felt. She saw my pain and had simply said, "Yes, I will help." I continue to be so blessed, as Simon after Simon has come into my life.

Now at the sixth station comes the moment in Jesus' walk when a woman named Veronica steps forward and wipes his face with her veil. This legend is not told in the Bible. It is told in the writings known as the apocryphal writings, which are contained in a separate section in most Roman Catholic editions of the Bible. I spent a great deal of time at this station. It is such a moment of tenderness and intimacy.

In the story, Jesus accepts the veil, wipes his brow and hands it back to Veronica. In so doing he hands back a veil on which his face had been imprinted. Veronica became Saint Veronica, and the piece of cloth became known as the Veil of Veronica.

The name Veronica is a translation of the Greek name Berenice or Berenike and she is known by this name in the Eastern Orthodox Church. This was then Latinized in the West. Vera is Latin for truth and authenticity. Icon is the name given to holy images that are vehicles to grace for those who profoundly meditate upon them. Gradually the cloth became a true image, a vera icon. Over time and by degree, said often quickly enough, these two words became one word, Veronica.

The physical intimacy of Jesus accepting a cloth given to him by a stranger to wipe his brow touched me. I often sat and rocked myself, holding and touching my arms in my grief, and I still do. I knew my skin was crying out for comfort.

Several years later, just before the pandemic, in a museum in Europe, I was overcome with jet lag and dehydration. I did not want to pass out and made my way to the museum cafeteria and sat down. I told the waiter that I needed water and that I did not feel well. Very quickly he appeared with ice water, and he also came carrying a towel in which he had wrapped ice cubes and he put it around my neck. I was so grateful. We know why the Veronica legend emerged. It just makes sense.

When my daughter crawled into my bed and massaged my back and was physically close, she also knew instinctively what was needed.

After the retreat, the times spent at that station compelled me to find a massage therapist in Florida. I found Cathy, who was a glorious reincarnation of Veronica. I wept profoundly through every session as she eased my sleep-deprived, shrinking and sore body. She gave me more time than I paid for and, as an evangelical Christian, prayed for me and spoke of Jesus being with me. I am the most liberal of Christians who at previous times would have found her literalism jarring. Now, it mattered not a wit, so very grateful was I for the tender touch of Cathy the massage therapist.

Jesus falls again in the seventh station. I hate the falling. I am also discovering my response is an enormous fear of all of us who are growing older. I had a reputation of being strong. My bones are strong. I lift weights. Jesus is clearly exhausted physically. He is a dead man not walking. It made me reflect on how much I hoped and believed that this was not happening to me. My husband just would not do this to me. I could not find anything I had done to deserve this. Surely, he would see this too. But he did not. Did Jesus fall this time because he could not believe what was happening to him? He had so much to do. His mission was really just beginning. He was facing a horrible public shaming and death. A version of this was facing me, and this was the meaning I ascribed to Jesus who was again splayed out on the ground. In my mind, his incredulity preoccupied him and caused him to stumble and fall.

At the eighth station, Jesus, struggling to stay upright, is met by the women he has helped in his ministry. They gather on the Via Dolorosa, and he sees them. In his lifetime he has shown them respect, recognized them and offered healing to them as equal members of the human race.

And he stops once again and experiences their courage to step forward out of the crowd and speak with him.

At this station my prayer and reflection became difficult and challenged. I saw these women as an affirmation of all that is good in Jesus. At a time when he is being betrayed by the Jewish leaders, even by his dearest companions, these women show up for him. I thought of them as the women he has inspired and liberated from patriarchy. Who are they? They are a woman taken in adultery; a woman spilling her precious oils to massage his feet; Mary Magdalene; Mary and Martha who are the sisters of Lazarus; Mary, his mother keeping a deathwatch as he is crucified; even Pilate's wife and more.

I was glad they are there on his way to being killed and witnessing his grace and goodness. I was having a hard time finding those people for me. My husband's condemnation just roared in my head. I was dead in my soul and my lifework as a family therapist meant nothing and even the care and love I gave him was dispensable.

At this station I began to think that Jesus had more support than I had. He got to die knowing he mattered. I did not know it would take years of therapy and the arrival of witnesses to quiet that roar in my own head.

At the ninth station Jesus falls for the third time. Here, I witnessed his vulnerability. He is not a king. This is a far cry from his rather humble but jubilant entry into Jerusalem for Passover a scant five days earlier. Echoing his birth in a stable, he is seen here as exhausted and just a few hours from declaring that he is "forsaken", abandoned and betrayed in his lifework.

I had no trouble identifying and moved on quickly to the tenth station where it gets worse. In this scene Jesus is stripped of his clothes and is now naked. I looked away. For me this is where Jesus is most shamed. How embarrassing at this point to suffer being stripped of your clothes, taunted by the crowd and to have soldiers throw dice to get your clothing.

I was not inclined towards feeling shame. It was hard for me to feel how my husband shamed and humiliated me in public. My daughter Mary had easily accessed this on my behalf. I had heard her say to her friends several times, "He shamed my mother."

He chose his therapist as his "alive" soulmate and indicated that my soul was dead. He said that he was courageous and doing the will of God in casting me aside and going where God was directing his heart. And the leadership of my church, for the most part, celebrated his great courage. It was easier for me to see that they were all shaming themselves than to investigate the heart of how I was shamed.

Gradually I was opening to my own nakedness and shame in ways that surprised me. One day, sitting in the hot tub with my daughter in Florida, I saw in my mind my husband with his therapist, naked in a hot tub. She was thirty-four years my junior. Her body was younger than that of my daughter sitting across from me. I looked at my seventy-four-year-old body and saw the wrinkles and skin folding from weight loss and knew that my hair was thinning with the onset of stress alopecia. I felt ridiculed. What was I thinking, to believe a younger man would find me attractive over time? But I truly thought he had. My dear parents had blessed me with an abiding sense that I was loveable. That belief, too, was now less secure.

Even now, I am deeply ashamed that I was abandoned. I am ashamed that I did not see it coming. I had lived with the idea that people thought me privileged to have an exciting and fulfilling marriage with a younger man. I felt I was the object of gossip and, worst of all, pity.

Of course, I don't know what Jesus felt, collapsed on the ground for the third time, but for me he was a man who saw his lifework coming to nothing. He saw the forces of violence and selfishness succeeding. He knew himself "forsaken". Thus, we know Jesus as fully human. Jesus as the "Christ" had not yet happened. He had no reason to think it would.

The end arrives. Station eleven marks Jesus reaching Golgotha, a hill just outside the city walls, where he is nailed to a cross. It is a nasty death and fortunately he succumbs earlier than most. Protestants don't spend much time with this scene. It is a rare Protestant church that shows Jesus' death and a rare Roman Catholic church that does not display it everywhere.

The clean cross reminds you that Jesus overcame death. It is a positive symbol. I remember making my first ten-day silent retreat in a convent in Rhode Island with about thirty nuns still in habit. There was a crucifix above my bed in my cell-like room. I carefully wrapped it up in a towel and put it under my cot so that I could sleep.

When you are in great pain, Jesus' dying broken body, by contrast, is an image that resonates with what is inside you. I gained a whole new respect for the crucifix. This sort of dying happens all the time. Beautiful people with dreams and plans are violently killed all over our world.

The eleventh station, where I gazed on Jesus' broken and dead body, allowed me the time and space to experience the death that was upon me. At this station Jesus was dead. Was my marriage dead? Denial of this fact was important to me, up until now. Without it I felt I had no reason to live. But at this station, I had to see the possibility that my marriage was truly over. I had to, I wanted to, and yet I was not able to dwell on this reality and fled from it. I could see the truth but only at moments could I acknowledge it.

At the twelfth station, Jesus' body has been laid in his mother's arms, as so often depicted, never more poignantly than by Michelangelo in the Pietà. For me it was my daughter and son who held my body that did not want to live and felt gone.

I returned to this station often. It drew me to it again and again. I strove to understand its power for me. The tender intimacy of the act of caring for Jesus' dead body spoke to me. In my acute level of pain and brokenness I was beginning to experience such tenderness from many angels. I felt myself wrapped in loving acts of conversation and gifts. From my granddaughter's card spilling forth hand-cut hearts, my daughter-in-law's gifts of books and earrings, little parcels in the old-fashioned mail, Sister Carol loaning me the papier-mâché image of a heart full of brokenness striated with light to have by my bed and from telephone calls and emails from around the world as people began to find out, I knew I was held.

The thirteenth station of the tomb is next, and the body of Jesus is laid there with the expectation that the next day the women will come to oil the body and wrap it one more time in a death ritual. This reflects such a physical intimacy.

In Christianity, this one full day after the Crucifixion and before the Resurrection is called Holy Saturday. It is rarely given much thought. Evangelical Christians do not acknowledge it. Only some Protestants do. Roman Catholics do hold a vigil on that day remembering Jesus' time in the tomb. I was a Protestant reclaiming its meaning. Through what was happening to me I would come to understand that Holy Saturday can be a long time, the time it takes to get from death to a different form of life.

The fourteenth and last station is Easter. Mary finds the tomb empty and fetches Peter who verifies that the tomb is empty. Jesus has risen. The station features a clean cross, standing on a pier overlooking a small lagoon ringed by palms and oaks and filled with birdsong. I avoided this place as rising from my agony made no sense to me. For now, Holy Saturday, the place of pain, was my homeplace.

As one dear friend put it, "I get it, Ann, you see no possibility of life, but you cannot take that hope away from me. I have the right to hold that wish for you."

I knew this to be true and I think I felt comforted by this in a way I could not understand.

Chapter 7

TRUSTING GRIEF:
THE RIGHT TO MOURN

Embrace your grief, for there your soul will grow.
– Carl Jung

Mourning demands our careful untying of every knot of connection to what we lost.
– Ann Belford Ulanov, *Knots and Their Untying*

When I prayed the Stations of the Cross, they helped me deepen my grief. As I have said, I compared my loss with the losses Jesus was experiencing. I did not pray them in the traditional manner, where a sense of my own sinfulness and complicity in betraying Jesus enabled me to want to live a better life. No, in praying them with Sister Carol's help, I found myself validating my grief and placing it in the context of my faith where suffering is lifted up as the journey we all must make.

I had to learn to manage grief at far too young an age. My pregnancies were mostly normal. Birthing was horrendous. I birthed four live children: David, Jonathan, Mary and Susannah in that order. David was born in heart failure, which he survived. Jonathan was born with a serious allergy to breast milk, difficulty with formula and debilitating jaundice and died at three months of age. Mary was a placenta previa birth, born with spurts of blood flying across the operating room. In today's world this would have been a caesarean section birth. Her first sound, a sneeze, brought from the obstetrical staff sounds of relief and prompted spontaneous applause. She did not drown. She lived precariously for several weeks; her vulnerability was exacerbated by the fact that we had different blood types. The medical team had to weigh up the possibilities of changing her blood. She began to thrive all on her own with her A blood type, different from my own O positive type.

After Mary's difficult birth, in 1968, I had the privilege to be a student of Dr. Elisabeth Kübler-Ross at Billings Hospital in Chicago. I was a student chaplain under her instruction when she was doing the research that would become her seminal and world-changing book *On Death and Dying*. She taught me firsthand the stages of grief. I practiced them with patients on my ward. I was learning ways to allow sorrow, practices that now are embedded in my way of being with others and with myself. I knew how to grieve, and I committed to do so yet again. If I was to live, it was all I knew to do.

Susannah was born minus a capillary system at the base of the back of her neck, a very rare defect. This meant that blood was shunted directly from vein to artery instead of being exchanged gradually though a capillary system. It was irreparable and she died blessedly at two weeks of age.

When I was praying the Stations of the Cross, as Mary holds the broken body of Jesus, I was quickly reminded of the night before my infant daughter Susannah's funeral. I had not slept, but rather embroidered a rose silk shroud with her name, Susannah Elisabeth. In the morning I wrapped it around her tiny body. Young as I was, I knew instinctively to do this.

When all this was happening, I was between twenty-five and thirty-two years of age. Nothing about this was regular in the Western world. My family had no history of birth trauma. My sister had six children all born lively and healthy.

The grief I was now undergoing was so different in my mind. Then,

I had the steady companionship and experience of shared grief with the children's father. I was not alone. My church community at that time was at our side through each birth and death.

Gordon, one of the members of that congregation, told me how one night, shortly after he had got the news that Susannah had died, had been woken up by a strong impulse.

"June," he said, waking his wife, "we just must do something. Remember how it was for us the night Julie died?" Julie was their daughter Karen's twin who died as a baby.

"Maybe we could take Ann and her husband to Puerto Rico with us?" June told him. "It would have helped us to get away. They could go to the ordination as well." A Cuban friend of ours was being ordained there as it was not possible in his own country.

A few days later, Gordon walked into our house, told me about his conversation with his wife, put an envelope on the dining room table and quickly left. It contained all the tickets and accommodation for us go to Puerto Rico with them, attend the ordination and then have a week on our own. This is how I understood the church responded to grief.

Few of us in our lifetime are spared loss. Sometimes it is expected and we can prepare. Often it just sneaks up and startles us. Just recently, as a therapist, I listened as two sisters told me how they were losing the man they thought their father was, as his secrets were revealed. Another client, a woman in her forties, told me how she longs for her fabulous younger self who turned heads. She confessed to her growing addiction to Instagram photos of stunning women. A man told me how he is beginning to understand that he lost the joy of Halloween the night he, at ten years of age, was rolled and beaten for his candy. None of us escape the opportunity grief gives us to explore its depths and seek its meaning for us that will enable us to live with more compassion.

Books are often amazing gifts that reach into our grief and give us words and pictures that validate and make meaning of our loss. While I meditated with the Stations of the Cross, my friend John Vaillant was writing a novel called *The Jaguar's Children*. A year later, I read it and thought about my time in meditation at Sister Carol's place.

John told the story of Mexican immigrants making an escape into the USA on a weekend in April. A large number of them had secured passage in a container truck. Things went terribly awry, and the heavily locked container was abandoned in a hot desert place. Those inside had very little access to air. They had a few cell phones with charged battery left. Unlike me, they wanted to live. They began to suffocate.

Probably not many people realize that John intentionally set this story on an Easter weekend. I checked this because the time in the container felt like Holy Saturday to me. Easter dates change each year, so the timing is not immediately obvious. I think for most readers it would not have mattered, but for me it did.

John gave Easter Saturday many pages in the book. It was a time when death was most real to the endangered immigrants. Many in the container were dying and it seemed inevitable that all would. The book described this process in careful detail. John told me that he did not know how it would end until the story told itself through him.

I have reflected many times on this "day" ever since my husband left me. In my opinion, it does not have to be literally a day. How long does being mostly dead last? What is the span of time for grief that is considered appropriate and not a sign of mental illness?

Since its creation in 1952, the *Diagnostic and Statistical Manual of Mental Disorders (DSM)* has been used by all the helping professions to diagnose and name the illness they are treating. It is widely used by clinicians, researchers, psychiatric drug regulations agencies, health insurance companies, pharmaceutical companies, the legal system and policy makers. Over its five editions, it has struggled to categorize grief and bereavement and to discern whether or not it is a disorder. While the *DSM* dealt with grief in cases where a loved one dies, it set the tone for all grief from other sorts of loss.

In 1917 Freud recognized a difference between mourning and melancholia. According to Freud, mourning is normal grief and melancholia is a loss of ego, the latter of which is what my profession has come to call complicated grief, too often diagnosed as major depressive disorder (MDD).

I think Freud got mourning right. Nine years after his daughter Sophie died of Spanish flu at the age of 26, he wrote to a friend: "We know the acute pain we feel after a loss will continue; it will also remain inconsolable, and we will never find a replacement. No matter what happens, no matter what we do, the pain is always there. And that's the way it should be. It's the only way to perpetuate a love we don't want to give up."

Following Freud's wisdom after his daughter died, in the *DSM-I* and *DSM-II*, the first two editions of the *DSM*, there was no mention of bereavement or grief as a diagnostic category. Grief was considered a normal process.

The *DSM-III*, published in 1980, introduced a clause that excluded the diagnosis of MDD for a person who is in grief. This exclusion was added with very little researched evidence. It did so to reduce the possibility of a bereaved person being prescribed major antidepressants for normal grief. There was also a desire to protect the public from possible pharmaceutical influence. In the *DSM-III* this exclusion applied for one year after the death of a loved one.

In the *DSM-IV*, published in 1994, the exclusion clause was continued but the period for normal grief exclusion was reduced to two months. To be clear, for fourteen years, the *DSM* gave a person permission to experience normal grief for one year, before the grief was considered a disease to be treated. This was then reduced to a two-month period.

In the 2013 edition, *DSM-5* (the *DSM* at this point shifted from

Roman numerals to Arabic numbers), the bereavement exclusion was removed entirely. This caused a firestorm of debate when the *DSM-5* was released. The bereavement exclusion was also a subject of great debate among the framers of the *DSM-5* themselves. It was feared that physicians would prescribe too many antidepressants to people in normal grief and that pharmaceutical companies would promote such activity. However, at present, the data does not confirm either of these fears.

The *DSM-5* did go to impressive lengths to help physicians be aware that normal grief may be ongoing and gave several helpful aids to distinguish this process from major depressive disorder. However, if the symptoms of MDD were present, then the attending physician could prescribe drugs with no time delay.

Bereavement in the *DSM-5* was included in what is known as the V code or appendix. This allowed physicians to prescribe grief counselling as the patient processed normal grief.

In addition, the bereavement exclusion was removed from anxiety disorders, which is where other forms of loss show up: loss of a job or divorce. Here a person may be seen to be impaired beyond what is deemed normal immediately following the loss and can therefore be prescribed with drugs if deemed appropriate.

And finally, the *DSM-5* created a "candidate disorder" for complicated grief which they named persistent complex bereavement disorder (PCBD) and which they also listed in an appendix. In doing all these things only in appendices, the *DSM-5* signalled that further research in this area is necessary.

Without careful reading of the *DSM-5*, the immediate implication seems to be that a speedy recovery from loss is deemed to be possible, even normative. I think the current news media echoes this as they barely give people twenty-four hours before talk of closure is offered and expected. Resilience is preached in the same breath as tragedy is reported. The average person knows better. Therapists know better as they listen to people in their offices talk about deaths and losses of many years ago that are still raw and unhealed. In Freud's terms, they are dealing with mourning just as he was, indicating appropriate sadness rather than melancholia, which would signify major depressive disorder.

As well as expecting people to bounce back quickly from loss, we have come to think that victimhood is a very limiting definition of self. In Uvalde, Texas in 2022, where a former high school student fatally shot nineteen students, there were multiple victims. The dead children, their parents, the school system, the police force and the city were all victims. People are uncomfortable with being defined as victims. As they say, it is a club none of us want to belong to. It implies weakness and powerlessness. Society finding its voice in the media encourages resilience; public interviews with the most bereft want to demonstrate that we all can handle things and move forward. A common expression at funerals is "How is he or she holding up?" Such an odd question, I think.

I used to be sure it was the right question. I wanted a person to move to agency as swiftly as possible. I think differently now. I am now of the thought that one needs to be a victim and be heard until that identity finds its rightful place in the narrative of self. I don't think about a timeline anymore. Indigenous people in Canada still need to talk about the damage that victimized them sixty years ago when they were children.

One morning, I heard a group of northern Indigenous teens on the radio responding to an offer that schools be erected in their communities so that they could stay home for high school rather than travel south to major cities. They did not push such an idea aside, but they had something else that was more important to them. They wanted to tell the story of racism and make clear that this is what needed to change. They wanted our country to know that they were victims of racism no matter where they went to school. Building high schools in their community was a solution that did not address the problem. Indigenous people have a lot to teach us about the fallacy inherent in such solutions. Those kids knew that there was no easy fix to a lifetime of grief caused by racism. Changing the location of the school was only a bandage and they had the courage to say so.

There is something about being abandoned in your marriage without warning that is fundamentally wrong, for which there is no easy fix. It is not "just a divorce", an expression mouthed all too easily. Yes, it is important to look at all the ways women have birthed resilience and found a way to live with the scars. But why are we so nonchalantly tolerating such wounding in the first place?

Divorce was once too difficult in even the most dangerous situations. The divorced person was stigmatized, ostracized and outrageously abandoned by church and community. Prior to 1968, the grounds for divorce were adultery and cruelty that had to be proven in court. After that, in my opinion, divorce became too easy. No-fault divorce states that the conduct of the spouses is not relevant to the divorce process and will have no effect on types of relief to which the spouse is entitled (such as property division and spousal support). The emotional fallout for children is not considered enough. In my experience, non-consensual divorce, which is by far the most frequent experience, is a trauma for at least one of the spouses and for the children of the marriage as well. This deserves recognition and fresh exploration.

Abandonment by a spouse mostly happens to women, as Vikki Stark, author of *Runaway Husbands* found out. Why is this? Mostly men do this to pursue a younger woman with whom they have a child. Have you ever noticed how many sixty- to seventy-year-old dads are toting preschoolers around parks, especially in affluent areas?

In the 1980s, Al Gore and his wife Tipper divorced after forty years of marriage. Then, it was shocking, and it initiated research that led to their divorce being identified as a "grey divorce". In May of 2004, the American

Association of Retired Persons (AARP) published research showing that while the overall rate of divorce was decreasing, the rate of grey divorces was doubling. In 2009, one in every four divorces included a partner who was fifty years old or older. Increasingly, grey divorces include couples who are boomers, born between 1946 and 1964, and who have been married twenty to thirty years. Statistically, more of these divorces are now initiated by women but the reasons are varied, from the women being bored with their emotionally dull husbands to women whose husbands are unfaithful, in part due to new male virility drugs.

And why is this happening in wealthy demographics and particularly among aging boomers? What role is patriarchy contributing? What role is the fear of death playing in this phenomenon? Is there a growing addiction to the "new"? There are many unresearched questions.

What role is my profession playing? I want to add my voice to that of American professor and family therapist William Doherty. He has come to promote what he called in 2005 "marriage-friendly therapy". He had been schooled, as I was, in the "divorce neutrality" position of the 1960s. According to this way of thinking, which is still prevalent, divorce is about the same as career decision. It is the client's decision and the therapist's role to enable the client to do whatever makes him or her happier.

Doherty now gives couples the opportunity to explore the meaning of their marriage in the broader context of their children and of their wider community commitments. I agree with Doherty and subscribe to what he called marriage-friendly therapy but I call it relationship-friendly therapy. With me, before a couple decides to divorce, they agree to spend some time sorting out what this will mean for them and what would be necessary for their positions to change. There is no promise that they will want to make these changes and find a thriving relationship. However, they slow down and let a therapist help them with the decision. They might find that they can let their present relationship go and create a new union with each other. The latest research continues to make clear that children do best in homes with reasonably low conflict and stable marriages. Australia has taken this research seriously and has added to their divorce proceedings the necessity that couples must engage in state-funded marital counselling before a divorce can be finalized.

The unanswered questions persist. Our culture's rapid embrace of closure does not allow time for discussion. I hoped that, by taking time with my own grief, I might begin a conversation about more than how to move on. At the very beginning I made a commitment to not cheat my grief. It was the reality that life had dealt me, and I wanted to take it very seriously and discern its wisdom for me.

With the *DSM-5*, my own profession was giving me no time before I could be a candidate for the possibility of major depressive disorder. The *DSM-IV* had given me two months before MDD could be considered. At the end of two months, I was neither eating nor sleeping. I was not able to meet the standards of the first level of psychological development. Therefore, I could have been diagnosed as having MDD and prescribed SSRIs (selective serotonin reuptake inhibitors), Zoloft and Prozac being well-known examples.

I did not like or trust this option for me. Having no history of clinical depression, I was sure I did not have MDD. I decided to seek other answers to the question of how long one grieves and what other options would help me and others.

In Vancouver, there is a centre where grief counselling is offered. I met with the director and told her my story, wondering if this was a place I would come for help. The director was compassionate and told me that in order to be on a solid road to recovery at a minimum I was looking at two years of therapy.

I went to my friend Anne who was a spiritual director and saw many people in grief. She already knew my story and had been a friend of both my husband and myself. She, by contrast, wondered if eight years was the timeline to consider as healthy for processing what I was experiencing.

I asked Ellen, my GP, next. An incredible doctor, she told me about one of her patients, a normal woman like me. "Ann, she just booked a visit. She wanted me to know she was, after five years, finally feeling well with a desire to live. She wanted to celebrate!"

I found this dose of reality hard to hear. Already I did not much want to live, and to live in such hurt for so long? I did not know if I could manage that. Did I have that much courage? Rationally I thought about wasting the little that was left of my life. Still, it was the wisdom given to me from my best sources that this was a long, arduous path.

On sleepless, warm January nights in Florida, before he left, my husband and I had walked and talked for hours. We went round and round on the streets in the gated community that housed the condo.

"How can you do this?" I asked him. "You know I believe in relationships. I don't want to be alone. I am too old for this. It is too late to start over."

"Ann, don't waste time," he said. "You need to move on. I've thought about this. [Y] is a good guy, and he is looking for someone. You could be that person."

I was horrified and speechless.

"There is also [Z]," he added. "You like him."

"He is married. I like his wife too. What are you talking about? I love you. I want to be with you."

His preposterous suggestions made me crazy and completely contaminated my thoughts about those two men, both of whom had been good friends. From his "enlightened" stance, my husband had answers that, in my opinion, certainly addressed his guilt.

Meanwhile, I was troubled by all the conflicting prescriptions for grief. There are those like my husband who think that spending time with grief would be a waste of time and a capitulation to negative energy. Some people think of grieving as indulgent self-absorption. I agree that resilience is a marvellous trait, but how can it be authentic the day after or two months after a community or a person has abruptly lost a person or persons that they deeply loved and trusted?

Our great Canadian poet and chanteur Leonard Cohen was awarded the Prince of Asturias Letters Award, given for work that represents a significant contribution to universal literature. In his acceptance speech he instructs me and all of us in how to lament/grieve.

As a young man, Cohen sought a voice and eventually found guidance for this quest in the works of the Spanish poet Frederico Garcia Lorca. Lorca gave him permission to find his own voice which over time he did. Cohen realized his voice came with a set of instructions which he shared with us that night in his acceptance speech.

We are *"never to lament casually and if one is to express the great inevitable defeat that awaits us all, it must be done within the strict confines of dignity and beauty."*

This makes sense to me and I knew that in claiming the right to mourn I also had to do so within the *"confines of dignity and beauty"*. Now I had the guard rails for my sorrow. Poetry gave me my treatment plan. I had seen people in my practice who had become embittered due to grief. I thought that when this happened, it often indicated that the grief was not being wisely processed. In my grief after the loss of my children, I knew I had not become embittered. I learned early to trust my grief. Sometimes, I even wished I had trusted it more. I knew I had pushed myself too hard after Jonathan died and I was kinder with my grief when Susannah died. I came to feel marked by a sadness that does not ever go away, a treasured sadness that was both a signal of my capacity to love and to be compassionate.

Just a few weeks ago, at Thanksgiving, my son and I visited the gravesite where my children are buried and where I will be buried. It is an old-fashioned cemetery full of giant elms and maples that were turning colour in the autumn air. My parents and grandparents are buried there. It is an hour-and-a-half drive from my son's home.

We pulled out of his driveway to make the trip and were a block away.

"David," I said, "oh dear, whoops, I'm sorry I forgot. Would you please go back and get a dustpan and brush and a trowel? I think we might have to clean up the gravestones."

Without hesitation, he turned the car around and parked at his home. Minutes later, he came back to the car with the tools and a vase with one of the last blooming roses from the garden. I was proud and touched by my son's prescience.

We found the site and, sure enough, lichen had encrusted the stones. One of them, his brother's, had tilted and sunk into the ground. I brushed and I swept. He troweled up some weeds.

"What do you think, Mom? Can I fix the stone?" There was no one around. Neither of us knew if this would be permissible. We had never dug up a gravestone before.

"Yes, let's do it," I agreed.

He pried the stone loose. We held it and with one free hand, he leveled the ground under it. We placed the stone marker back, adjusting it until it was now evenly placed. He put the rose on it. Jesus' image was carved on the stone with a child in his lap. A rose was carved along the other edge. My son held me in his arms, and we shed tears together for what might have been for both of us.

This is grief that has been fifty-five years honoured, and it is not closed over yet.

In Katherina Vermette's novel, *The Break*, Stella, a young Métis (people of mixed European and Indigenous heritage with a distinct Métis culture and language) mother who has just witnessed an assault, is trying to believe that her grandmother is wise and right when she states that "everything goin' to be alright".

But Stella knew the hole broken inside of her, and "she knew that it would never close again".

I was changed forever when each of my children died, and I am changed now.

Still, I knew I was old, at the end of my life. I was tempted by those who thought I could process this experience faster. Perhaps there would not be enough time for me to honour my grief.

I did try to believe that my grief might entrap me in a downward spiral and that I should bring this thing to closure quickly.

One family member put it this way: "Die your hair purple, buy a new dress, take your money from the house and see the world."

I could not imagine travelling alone. I could see myself with purple hair. I did not want a new husband. I wanted what was happening to me to not be true. The one thing that I just knew was that I needed to take my grief seriously. I had to make meaning of this terrible suffering. In spiritual terms, it was my calling. I accepted that time in the tomb on Holy Saturday cannot be measured chronologically.

I knew the final station of the cross was resurrection. I wondered if I would ever make it. I was in the container in the desert and this Holy Saturday was my place for as long as it took, and I might never get further. I began to think that all I could do is to do this with integrity. I became patient with myself.

During that week when I was given sanctuary, on one of the days after I had walked the stations, I decided to walk the labyrinth, which was nearby. Labyrinths have been created and used for thousands of years. Usually, they are sizeable and provide ample room for walking, but sometimes they are tabletop affairs with the labyrinth on a small board traced with a finger. Either way, you begin and the path will then lead you to the centre every time. Then you leave the centre knowing you will get out every time. A labyrinth is not a maze. It can have different patterns. Christians use labyrinths as prayer practice. I have walked many in the world. I usually walk slowly into the centre, repeating, "The Lord is my shepherd." While returning I pray, "I shall not want." I, like many Christians, have made a pilgrimage to Chartres Cathedral in France, to walk the indoor labyrinth there.

The outdoor labyrinth at Sister Carol's was in the pattern of the one at Chartres. It was marked simply with stones and was generous in size. The paths were wide and well-worn. When I was somewhere along the path out, I was engulfed by a flock of cardinals singing and twirling around my head, red and gold against the sky.

Fifty-five years ago, when Jonathan died, a woman in New York City sent me a special card, one of the first of its kind. Now the market is filled with them. It had an abstract version of a red bird on the cover and inside were the words: "Faith is the bird that sings when dawn is still dark." When I first created my counselling practice, I used the scarlet cardinal for my logo and put that quote underneath the wings.

The moment in the labyrinth was, for me, a signature over my decision to trust my grief with all the integrity I could muster. It was more. It made me begin to acknowledge every moment of song that burst into my grief.

As the eight-day retreat drew to a close, I knew I had walked with Jesus. I was committed to my grief. I did not know how to express my gratitude. Words would never be enough. Sister Carol and I said good-bye.

Chapter 8

MORE ARCHANGELS: THE SECOND RESPONDER, DAVID

What's called for is a little flare of anger, enough to guarantee our use of anger and not its use of us.
    – Carol Tavris, *Anger: The Misunderstood Emotion*

Sister Carol did not see me get into my rental car and reverse it into the fence she had warned me about that first day. The fence was fine, and I had a dent in the bumper and some white paint outlining it. I sat in the car, breathing deeply. I was flustered and felt barely functioning. Yet, I drove to the airport to pick up my son David. His sister had informed him well, and prepared him for how ill he would find his mother. I was not so ready for him, my next archangel.

I had wondered how it would be. My daughter had slept with me, and I had managed to sleep. I had barely slept for the ten days since she had left, having not yet figured out how to sleep alone. It felt weird to ask to sleep with my son. I thought, *I must not do that.*

He met me curbside at the airport and after hugs I said, "Dave, I have to drive as the rental is in my name."

Once he was settled in the passenger seat, I then asked somewhat normally, "How was the trip?"

"Trip was not too bad," he said, "but getting the passport…why does it have to be so complicated? I had to go to Toronto to get it. This is my busy season, so many contracts and bids out. I am going to have to work while here."

Sensing his churlish mood, I tried to change the subject. "I'm glad you are here. I'm not doing very well. I just dented the bumper. I wonder if I will have to pay more insurance?"

"Why are you driving? This whole thing is a mess."

He was irritable. He did not like to travel. He did not like his routines upset. He had finally come to trust my husband and his care for me. In the past, he had been a bit doubtful about our marriage. I expect that at his core he wished that his parents had stayed together. In recent years, he felt that my husband had come between me and his son some of the time. My husband had never been one to initiate engagement with children. If babies cried, he moved away. He had convinced me that the fact that he and I could not have children was never a problem in any way for our relationship. When we purchased the condo in Ottawa my son finally trusted that my husband meant to grandparent wholeheartedly and that I was safe. Now he was betrayed in his trust. However, I was not thinking about my son's grief.

"Why are you in Florida?" he said. "Why did he leave you here? I called the church, and she [the co-pastor] was useless. I reached out to Grandpa's friend there and she was kind but claimed there was nothing she could do."

David was very angry. I was not prepared for this at all. He was angry that he was in Florida, angry he had to leave his wife and son and angry that he was leaving so much work. It came out in a sort of fury which focussed on the fact that that my husband had left me in a foreign country.

I was overwhelmed. His grief was slightly constrained rage. There was clearly no room for my grief as his lashed out. I was not accessing much of my own anger. I was profoundly sad and afraid. Being a mother kicked in and I remembered who he was. I knew from experience that once he had his say, he would settle, and his heart would open to me.

"David, you are angry, and you have every right to be. It probably would be good if I could join you in it but right now, I am not able to. All that comes are my tears and I'm scared. My heart is so broken." As he heard and saw this, he became gentle with me.

He could soon see that I was not at all well. He saw that he was going to have to set aside his own feelings and be there for mine. Over the week we had together, he, an excellent cook, made meals for me that I scraped into the garbage. I could not get the food down. It must have been hard for him to take in his very functional mother so dysfunctional. He realized that I could not be still. My energy level was unmanageably high. He walked long distances on the beach with me, listening to my circular thoughts. One day, as we picked up shells on the beach, he thoroughly got that my life had changed forever. He put it succinctly.

"Mom, it will never be as good as it was for you."

My relief was immense. Something inside of me just let go. Finally, someone got it. I was known and my pain made sense. I could only weep.

David saw that I could not travel and that he could not simply take me to his home because it would be too much for his family. He could stay with me for a week, but like his sister he had to leave. He knew I could not be safely left alone and that he needed to find me care until I was well enough to travel and the house in Vancouver was freed of tenants. That wasn't until April 1, some five weeks away. He hoped the timing would coalesce. This hope was beginning to take fleeting shape in my mind as well.

I remembered how Emily Dickinson's poem describing *"the Bustle in a house, the Morning after Death"* had helped me do all those chores after the children died. Now, my son and I were trying to bustle about and make something work. I asked a friend to come and be with me, and I also asked a family member. For their own reasons, which I respected, they both said no. Next, I asked Anita, a friend whom I had made in the church community who I liked very much. She was a retired social worker who had, until very recently, been on the staff of the church.

"Anita, could you think about coming to Florida and staying with me when David leaves? If you would consider it, you could talk it over with Mary and with David and your family and see if it would work. They have both been with me so they can answer your questions."

She, too, was in grief, having worked with my husband managing the programming at the church. Like Sister Carol, she said yes. She spoke with David and Mary, and it was agreed that she would come and stay with me for the month if necessary. My children and I are forever grateful.

David and Mary immediately began to prepare me to accept Anita's care with grace. I had to behave better, they said, by which they meant I had to stop being so preoccupied with my state. I had to be kind to Anita. Mary would come again in the month to support Anita. They knew I was a handful.

David was relieved and relaxed as a result. He gave me great hugs that were long and warm. His anger had been heard and put on hold. He made bocconcini and tomatoes and basil every day and saw that I ate something. Eight years later, I still eat this for many lunches every week. He also distracted me with outings. One day we went to an island several hours away and had to endure bumper-to-bumper traffic. He is a good conversationalist and kept me engaged and distracted. I lived only in the moment. There was no future. Sometimes at night when I could not sleep, I crept into his room and lay on the bed beside him just for a little bit of time. I wonder if he knew.

I had discovered the Canadian television series *Republic of Doyle*. The comedy/drama series told the story of a Newfoundland private investigator and his son and their escapades in solving crimes. We both loved

Newfoundland music, the accent of the people and landscape. Much later we made two trips there visiting the pub where much of the series was set. He watched it with me, and it allowed me to escape from my unbearable reality.

That first Christmas anniversary of my abandonment I received an absolutely perfect gift from my daughter. She had written to the producer and director, telling them what a difference their show was making in my life. As a result, I received a photo of the entire cast, signed by each of them, thanking me by name for watching their show. It is framed and hangs in my bedroom where I see it daily.

In retrospect, I wonder why I could not travel. Why could I not go back to Vancouver and find another place to live? I don't have answers. Maybe I could not face the shame and humiliation that I would feel there. I could not be where I imagined he and his therapist would be prancing about "in love". I knew from our own early days together that his face would be flushed with joy. Maybe being in Florida supported my hope that they would come apart and he would return. I think I could not face living alone. Maybe it was just that it was a warm sunny winter in Florida, and I knew the sun was more healing than the rain. Vancouver was terribly unsafe in my mind.

As my dear son and current archangel was preparing to leave, his relief, archangel Anita, was preparing to arrive. Now I was safe for a whole month. Hopefully it was enough time for me to stabilise, get on a plane and return to Vancouver and what was our home.

Ever since, David and Mary and their families have remained a solid support for me. They are the archangels that have guided me in all that was to come. For at least two years, Mary talked with me on the phone every day and some of those conversations were harrowing. Now I chat with them weekly. Gradually, I began to heal. They all visited multiple times. My eldest grandson and his girlfriend spent four months of their summer in Vancouver enjoying this great city and looking out for Grandma A. My children take me on their holidays: Aruba, Curaçao, NYC, Sicily, Cornwall, Tofino, Vancouver Island, the Grand Canyon, the Laurentians, Newfoundland and Quebec City. I have stayed with them for many two-week visits in their homes. The support was and is incredible.

Chapter 9

AND MORE ARCHANGELS: THE THIRD RESPONDER, ANITA

He will put the sheep at his right hand…and say,
Come you that are blessed by my Father, inherit the
kingdom… for I was hungry and you gave me food. I was
thirsty and you gave me something to drink, I was a stranger
and you welcomed me, I was naked, and you gave me
clothing, I was sick, and you took care of me, I was in prison
and you visited me.

— The Gospel of Matthew, 25:33–36

[T]he ultimate touchstone of friendship is witness…to have
been granted the essence of another, to have walked with them,
sometimes to have accompanied them for a brief span, on a
journey impossible to accomplish alone.

— David Whyte, *Consolations*

As I drove Anita to the condo from the airport, she met an Ann who was radically different from the one she remembered from two months ago, who had ably, as if in denial, broken bread for her in Jesus' name at the Christmas evening midnight communion.

Naples has a long traffic artery with endless stoplights. There are incredibly slow traffic lights which are the subject of much complaint by snowbirds. I had begun to avoid them on all my outings. I would turn right, drive around the block and then right turn back onto the main artery over and over so I did not have to stop and wait. Anita, on her first trip to Naples while taking in the sights and the sun, became aware of my erratic driving behaviour.

I turned into the gates of the complex where the condo was. I checked in with the attendant and explained I had a guest. Anita received her own pass and after parking, we went up the stairs to the condo.

It was generous in size. Coming into the hallway, passing the kitchen and the sunny guest bedroom and bath on the right, we entered a large living room. Beyond that, on the right were the master bedroom and master bath. Further was a large outdoor patio. Anita was quick to get the layout.

"Ann, this will be my bedroom and bath. I like it that the sun comes in." She spoke with a firmness probably based on the preparation my children had delivered. I knew she meant that I would not be welcome in her space.

This was good because sleep was so evasive. I knew I must not go to her on sleepless nights. I had repetitive nightmares. My body felt his body thrusting into his therapist and I would wake screaming. Or I felt the weight of his arm over me as we slept spooning and would wake to find that he was not there. Getting into bed, once the most peaceful and welcome moments of the day, was now a minefield of cruel tricks of perception.

Anita was a single woman who had left her husband. I know this is a magnitude of difference from being left. However, she had many single woman skills which she taught me by example. I did not realize it at the time but have heard her instructions in my head many times since.

"Signal, Ann, when you are changing lanes. Come to a full stop and not a rolling stop. Mind the speed limit."

I drove very little in my marriage as my husband liked to drive. Anita gave me driving lesson after driving lesson. I am sure that this was also her way of staying safe, as I was the only one with a licence to drive the rental car.

"Ann, the clerk is trying to help. She means well."

She tried to help me be friendly. I was not at all good at this. I could not wait in lines and found small talk very upsetting. I was not having "a good day", as the clerk had just wished me. Her friendliness sank in, and the day eventually came when I remembered and tried, like her, to greet one new stranger a day in a kind way. I saw how it made her days more interesting for herself and others. She continually modeled the life that I was going to have to lead. She was a perfect companion.

She taught me to enjoy browsing in shops and to love shoes. I think she bought six pairs of shoes in a month. Retail therapy certainly has a place. On many days, we shared the pleasure of exploring Florida and did much beach walking. She had a goal of walking 10,000 steps a day and we easily fulfilled this.

"Ann, you have to call Ellen. Something physical is wrong with your stomach. You are losing weight. You are not sleeping. You are hypervigilant. You are not eating enough. Please call her."

Anita, retired social worker that she was, was never direct and now she was being forcefully so. In fact, she was getting visibly distressed at my stubborn refusal to do as she was asking. My children had impressed upon me that I had to treat Anita with care and consideration. I needed to step up.

I did not want to tell Dr. Ellen what had happened. She knew the work my husband and I were doing and, as a very liberal Christian herself, she was supportive. She had many patients who were members of our congregation. I knew she would find out and be concerned, not just for me but for herself. Reluctantly, I made the call to her office.

"Hello, you have reached the clinic of…. I regret to tell you that Dr. Ellen is away on her annual mission to Guatemala and will not be back in the office until April 1. If this is an emergency, please go to your local hospital or leave your name…."

April 1. It was now March 7. Relieved, I let Anita know she was unavailable for three weeks. A reprieve, I hoped.

"I think Ellen would want to know now. Please call and leave a voice message. Perhaps her office will see that she gets it."

This seemed like such an imposition, but I was cramping badly with stomach pain. I considered going to the ER in Naples. My therapist in Florida had frightened me about going down that route. Anita didn't seem to favour it either.

"Ann, I don't know what it is like in Canada," she said, "but if you go to the hospital, they could keep you in for observation. You could well be diagnosed with MDD. They will insist on medicating you. It will be on your record forever. Do you want that?"

She made me think about the stigma of being diagnosed with a mental health disorder which is so wrong but real. I made the call to Ellen and left the message.

Within hours, the phone rang, and it was Ellen from her field office in Guatemala. She expressed immense empathy for me and then asked doctor-type questions.

"How many hours are you sleeping, describe the cramps, what are you eating, who is with you, how much weight do you think you have lost?"

She determined that my cramps were probably due to the excess amounts of adrenalin entering my stomach and prescribed a medication. She was glad Anita was with me and knew who she was. She insisted that I get weighed and report this back to her ASAP. My relationship with Ellen underwent a seismic shift. I had been happy to have her as a GP whom

I saw once a year for minor issues. Now I had her cell number in Guatemala with instructions to use it.

Anita was relieved and insisted that I weigh myself immediately. I was still resistant. I was exercising and lifting weights every other day. I was walking miles and going to the driving range and hitting balls. I can't remember how but a few days later I knew I had to weigh myself at the gym or my angel Anita would fly away. I got on the scales and weighed 118 pounds. I last weighed that much when I was sixteen. I was shocked. I had lost twenty-seven pounds in nine weeks. I had never lost weight in my life without trying. It scared me. I knew my hair was falling out, but I was not seeing my physical self. I had always weighed right in the middle of a healthy weight. I had never been skinny and could not see myself in this way. I knew I had to stop the weight loss and stabilize my weight. It would take four years to do so.

Days with Anita found a rhythm. I went to therapy every day of the week and to the massage therapist twice a week. This gave Anita alone time. Most days we went to the beach together. The condo grounds were large and yielded to a long private jetty, beautiful for walking among the manatees. The jetty also had a slip for a small water taxi that transported beachcombers to the outer sandspits stretching into the Atlantic. It was a delightful thirty-minute voyage out to the ocean. Pelicans filled the air and swarmed the onshore trees. Once deposited by the water taxi, with our chairs, a book and swim gear, we walked to find the perfect spot. The white, hard-packed sand complemented the turquoise ocean. For me, the destination was always a shady spot under a sea grape tree. We both liked to keep our feet in the sun. We could swim or walk for miles. I tried to be curious about what Anita was reading and what she was thinking. It was a paradise, and it gave me moments when what was going on was not so debilitating. As beaches were always my happiest place, these jaunts called me out of myself to a future of blue sky and surf.

I took Anita to the botanical gardens because the tropical plants were particularly exotic for both of us, as we came from a northern climate. We shopped in stores and markets. When I could not bear the memories that came with a particular song I heard playing in a shop, I would flee and come back when I was sure the track would have changed. Later in the afternoon, she would have liked to have gone to happy hour in the gated community but she feared leaving me alone with my suicidal thoughts. The medication Dr. Ellen had prescribed mercifully stopped the cramps. I tried to eat more.

When Anita first came to stay with me, she had just received the letter of February 26 sent out by the church. Over the days that followed she was still digesting the letter. Meanwhile, emails from her friends in the congregation let her know how they were doing with the news. She was clearly troubled by that letter and its content.

I began to formulate my own letter that I would send to a few of my closest friends in the congregation. I wanted more than Anita alone to know how it was for me, and I did not want her to have to tell them.

The letter I eventually finished told my story in a few paragraphs, and then I concluded it with this reflection:

My husband tells me that he is radiant with his new love and is quite certain that he is doing what the mind of Christ in him allures him to do. I have never known the mind of Christ in someone to so annihilate the woman he has loved for thirty years because he is compelled to choose the new. He is remaining at the church with their support to continue to preach and teach from this position. His blogs are full of this message since Christmas. A letter dated February 26, 2013 was sent out to the congregation by the board chair indicating their decision to retain him. I understand that this is fast changing as folk are finding out. It is apparently all accessible on the internet. I think the future for our community is very uncertain. One very prominent layman in a conversation with me put it this way: "We are rent asunder". Certainly I am.

I am endeavouring to be entirely present to my suffering and grief and not cheat it. So far it is taking more courage than I can bring to it each day. Wise elders tell me that this is a unique grief, and I can expect it to take years from which to recover. At seventy-four, I do not have years and I do not want to come to terms with the hand I have been dealt. There has been too much grief in my life already. I know that the God I love is loving me abundantly every day in the faces of the many angels of light coming to me. I also know that this God suffers with me when I wish She could make it all go away. We all wish life were fair while knowing it is not.

I sent this letter to five people in the congregation. It gave me some satisfaction to tell my pain in my words. Certainly, my husband had the larger pulpit, and maintained a large presence on Facebook. I also sent it to my wider biological family and to selected colleagues and friends who did not live in Vancouver. I had not considered the speed at which this letter would travel, even without the benefits of social media. I had not considered its disruptive power either. I felt I had very little voice, and I was told nothing of the process going on in the church. The leadership was consulting with my husband but not with me.

I had served this church and the wider national church denomination my whole life. I had pushed open the doors of this denomination to ordain women with young children. My national church had decided by a slim majority to ordain me and thus all who followed me with similar circumstances. Later, I had championed pastoral counselling as a distinct and legitimate vocation and was the first woman teaching supervisor in the field of Canadian pastoral counselling education. I was the first woman to receive the Doctor of Ministry degree in Canada. I had given to this local church thousands of hours of service in teaching and pastoral care. Was I crazy to expect more consideration?

I was angry. I wanted my church to be better and do better. By contrast, my anger with my husband was and is very complicated. It was harder for me to be angry with his behaviour because, as a professional therapist, I knew he was the victim of a very unethical therapist. Every accrediting body of professional therapists prohibits a relationship with a client during and following the therapy experience. Some such bodies stipulate a length of time after which a non-professional relationship can be allowed. It is never less than a year. I was angry with her behaviour, which had betrayed me, him and our profession. By contrast, my anger with the church leadership was clean, accessible and direct. When my children died, the church I then served treated me with extravagant love. Now this church wanted as little contact with me as possible.

Angel Anita had been a colleague of my husband; she was a recently retired team member on the same staff. She said yes to my request for her to come to Florida as my caregiver, not at the behest of the church community or with their financial support, which would have been welcome, but from her good and generous heart. She has always been a very non-confrontational person who tries to see all sides and work toward peaceful resolution. Going against her nature, she wrote to our church and appealed to its leadership on my behalf. Her appeals came to nothing.

My birthday is March 27, and it was the therapist/other woman's birthday as well. I found this eerily disturbing. My daughter returned to Florida to be with me that day and also to give Anita support at the midpoint of her care for me. Anita loved baseball and Mary and I made it possible for her to spend a day at spring training. Mary also helped me pack up and get ready for the flight back to Vancouver. Then she left, assured that I would board the flight with Anita and return to the house in Vancouver. Anita had been cleaning the condo; I suspect it had never been so thoroughly cleaned. The oven and the stove glistened. My friend Ruth was going to spend the first week with me in the Vancouver home that I had shared with my husband. After that I was going to have to live alone in a house for the first time in seventy-four years.

I was also facing a return to Vancouver in the knowledge that I would not be welcome at worship services in my community. Because my husband had agreed to return on the condition that I not be in the congregation, I was basically, but unofficially, told to stay away. However, according to the church's constitution, they could not bar me or anyone from attending services. Later I learned that there were a few brave souls who, had I shown up, would have been proud to hold my arm and walk down the aisle with me and stand with me. Another told me that if I did return, she thought some people would express disgust for me for failing to see my husband's point of view. And could I take that? I was not that well. In retrospect I sometimes wish I had the courage to stand up for myself and my place in this community. When I first returned to Vancouver, I was only well enough to go back into our home on Easter Sunday, the anniversary of the day thirty years before that my husband had first declared his ecstatic love for me. There are always ironies.

I had already decided that when I went home, I would not go back to church. I could not risk further damage to my psyche. I was barely managing to eat and sleep, the first level of survival skills. I did, however, long to be officially welcomed back.

What I did not know was that after the congregation was informed by the letter of February 26 of my husband's decision to leave me, there were people in the congregation unhappy with the board's decision to retain my husband as senior pastor. They had simply left and taken their significant financial support with them. These people were talking with each other. Apparently, they could see no reason that they should have to leave a church that had been theirs for generations. I appreciated that, out of concern for me, I was told none of this, only learning of it later. My ignorance protected me legally from any accusation that I could have engineered what was to happen.

In the polity of my national church there is a way for local congregation members to initiate a complaint concerning their pastor. Ten people must sign the complaint, which is then considered by the higher courts of the church. If the complaint is found worthy, then the pastor is required to stay in place for two years as an investigation takes place. The investigative committee makes a ruling based on its findings and this is announced. Such rulings could remove the pastor from the local or even national church and take away all privileges, including pension and sacramental rites. However, more often, the ruling would require that the pastor continue his or her work under supervision for a set period of time. My husband got wind of the fact that this process was happening. In late March, when I was preparing to leave the Florida condo, he was told by the co-pastor that signatures to initiate such an investigation of him had been gathered in sufficient numbers. He resigned within hours of learning this. His resignation was announced at what would have been his first service back on April 1, 2013 following the end of his sabbatical. It became his last day of work not by choice but by threat of an investigation. It was the day, not knowing any of this, that I returned to our home in Vancouver.

After finding out that my husband had resigned, I had a naive hope that my church would want to make a place for me. I believed that even given what had happened, some form of reconciliation was possible, and that it always would be.

Chapter 10

DENIAL GIVING WAY TO REALITY

Trauma denial is a way to put distance between you and an overwhelming experience. It can be one of the many ways your brain tries to adapt and mitigate a reality collapse or a system overload, which can often happen after a traumatic event.

— Hilary I. Lebow, "Trauma Denial: How to Recognize It and Why It Matters"

Trauma is not what happens to you but what happens inside you.

— Gabor Maté, *The Myth of Normal*

Finally, March 31 arrived. The lease on the condo in Florida was over and the tenants in my Vancouver home had moved out. It was Easter Sunday; the rental car was packed, and I was to fly home. I went for an early walk, and hoped I was settled enough to wait patiently in lines at the airport.

I made it. After we landed in Vancouver, the taxi dropped Anita at her house and took me to what used to be "our" house. Ruth, a friend of Anita's and mine, had arrived ahead of me. I had told her where to find the key; it was in a magnetic container under the window box on the back deck. She was hoping to put food in the fridge and air the house for my arrival. When I arrived, she, unable to find the key, was waiting on the back deck and very glad to see me. She had been waiting outside for two hours.

I couldn't find the spare key either, which is when I realized I had no key. Peering through the mail slot of the front door, I could see the tenants had slipped it through the slot instead of returning it to the secret place. I knew my husband would have a key, but I was not going to ask him. I called a locksmith who was at home during the holiday and a good two hours away. For holiday prices he agreed to come. I was quite anxious and desperate. I just could not wait and decided to try to break in. I found a patio table, climbed on it and managed to force open a very small window into my office. It is exactly fourteen inches by twenty-two inches and six feet above the inside floor. Upon forcing open the window, the alarm was set off. I had not thought of that eventuality. It was loud and piercing and I knew I had to get in and shut off the alarm or the police would come. There was no way but to dive in headfirst. By now, Ruth was standing on the upper porch above my study and peering down at me on the patio. As she looked over the rail to see what was happening, she saw my feet flying in the window opening as I took a header into the house. I got to the alarm, shut it off and called the alarm company and the locksmith, who was en route, and stopped all their actions. I was back in Vancouver, indeed upside-down, and all we could do was laugh. It was the first laugh in months. It was a moment of grace.

The week rushed by, and Ruth left. I was truly on my own. Trying to get through the nights, I found myself literally crawling around on the bedroom floor looking for me. I think I developed a form of prayer that could be called a seeking and lamenting prayer for the middle of the night. I imagined myself in pieces on the carpet, my body parts strewn everywhere. I was desperate and sometimes frantic as I searched for bits of me that might fit together. Who was I now? Was I an athlete? Was I a Christian? Was I loyal? Was I a good person? Was I insane? Was I suicidal? Was

I a friend, and to whom? Was Vancouver my home? Who was I? Only one place in my mind was safe from my questioning. I was confident that I was a loved mother and a loved grandmother.

I would crawl around like this for an hour or two, often weeping. I touched my leg, my shoe, my nightshirt or my wedding ring. I crawled and searched, lamented and tried to fit the pieces of what was left of me into some semblance of a person often until, exhausted, I fell asleep on the floor.

One evening, after fifteen months of this frequent middle-of-the-night floor crawling, I was watching the news when I saw the BBC coverage of a plane crash in Ukraine.

"Malaysia Airlines flight MH17, en route from Amsterdam to Kuala Lumpur, was travelling over conflict-hit Ukraine on 17 July 2014 when it disappeared from radar. A total of 283 passengers, including 80 children, and 15 crew members were on board."

I could not stop watching the images of the bodies and debris on the field in Ukraine. Body parts were lying everywhere. Children's toys in pieces and bits of luggage and plane parts in fragments littered the landscape. This field mirrored my middle-of-the-night activity where I touched and held precious bits of a whole self no longer there. I now had words and an image to describe my fragmented self. I felt how that field in Ukraine looked.

One of my dearest friends, who was also terribly wounded by my husband's actions, wrote a song that was her way of poignantly telling my story and some of hers as well. Her lyrics named my brokenness:

Black is the road ahead I see
broken, the shape of my heart left behind,
ache the tune that sings in me
now that you've gone, gone, gone.

This mattered. My nighttime floor crawling now grew less frequent. Somehow, fifteen months later, my pain had a place in the history of human tragedy. I began to follow the story of flight MH17 and awaited the end of the trial of those responsible for the crash, promised for September 2022 at the latest.

The church was a twenty-minute walk from my home. I still had not stepped inside it. I met church members on the street and in shops. I wanted to do something to ease their pain and mine. As a marriage and family therapist, I proposed that if the current pastor and the chair of the board would sit down with me and a neutral facilitator, more understanding could be accomplished. At times, it seemed as though this would happen, though an initial response to my request took several months. What I knew was that, when the meeting did happen, I needed to be sure that the dialogue would be conducted in a safe place and that the facilitator would be acceptable to both sides. I also needed the assurance that there would be a commitment to several meetings to give the process a chance of working. In my professional opinion, this was a complex situation—a "complicated grief" for them as well as myself.

As a therapist and as a person who has negotiated difficult circumstances with other churches over my years of work, I thought a commitment of up to ten sessions was reasonable. It might be done in one but, from my experience, a guaranteed opportunity to be at the table for longer both reduced anxiety and created trust for everyone. With the support of another therapist, herself a respected layperson in the church, I found a competent, experienced facilitator who was unknown to all the parties and would therefore be neutral and objective. This person agreed to take on the task and I presented this name to the leadership of the church.

The leadership of the local church dithered and eventually refused to decide on a meeting and forwarded the request to a higher court of the church for deliberation. On May 13, 2014, one full year later, their decision was communicated to me by letter. Two hours of facilitation would be offered, and the church would choose a facilitator from within their staff without any consideration of my opinion. The letter also informed me that while I could not be barred from attending this church, I would not be allowed to hold any leadership positions, to ever speak about my husband while on or in that church property and I was not to teach there in any capacity. I was also invited to apply for $500 to pay for any counselling I might have required.

I was incensed and devastated. I discussed the letter at length with friends who were involved in the situation. I took it to my lawyer, who said it was quite unbelievable. She crafted a brilliant response. However, it felt hopeless and expensive to go further so I have never sent it. I stopped fighting and accepted being silenced by my church. I told myself that I was in good company, recalling many other incredible people over the centuries that the church had silenced. I thought about Galileo, who in 1633 was forced by the Roman Inquisition to recant that the Earth moves around the Sun. He was tried and convicted of heresy and kept under house arrest until his death. In 1988, Dominican priest Matthew Fox faced expulsion from his order if he did not recant his theological positions, such as calling God "mother" as well as "father" and embracing homosexuality as legitimate. He resigned. Thinking about them was my grandiose way of coping.

The official person tasked with writing the letter, also its signatory, emailed me a day or two later, expressing sadness. She thanked me and said that as a pastor with young children herself, she knew that I had opened the door for her to be able to practice ministry. I appreciated this.

At that moment, I knew that I had given my best and my survival needs took precedence over my strong need to fight for spiritual and psychological justice. I gave up, although some might say I let go and others still might say I delayed. It was probably a combination. For me, and I still think this way, my institutional church completely failed me. I did not lose my faith, but I lost the only home this faith of mine had ever known. I am able to consider that my church let its own survival needs take priority over its most sacred mandate: to encircle the marginalized. The conflict that was brewing within the church between those who had signed the document of complaint against retaining my husband as minister and those who wanted him to stay frightened them. They were afraid that their membership would split the church and further weaken it. In the face of the secularization of society, the church at large was already vulnerable to collapse. I can see in hindsight that holding me caringly in their midst would have been a risk. They "washed their hands" and passed on the challenge. The higher courts of the church assisted them, and they were free of me.

Fortunately, another church story began to take shape. While in Florida, I had expressed to my husband my deep pain about an upcoming event in Australia that I very much wanted to attend. He was to be a theme speaker and I was to give a workshop. My sister had died there a year before and I wanted to visit her burial place and see her remains interred. I had lobbied the Australian church very hard for us to get this opportunity. My husband insisted that I was but a token part of the event and that he would go alone. In my mind, he had been particularly brutal about this.

"You have got to get over this, Ann. I am the keynote speaker. It is very expensive to fly me there and house me. The conference does not have a huge budget. It is me they want and have hired. You are just an extra. They are not thinking about you or your sister."

He had told me that his contract would be honoured, and mine would not be. I had believed him. Then, when the publicity material came out in the summer of 2013 for the conference that September, there he was, front and centre. I could not see my name anywhere nor did I look beyond the first page. He had been right. I kept receiving these publicity announcements, which cut to the quick. Eventually I thought to email the committee, asking them to take my name from the email list as it was too painful to receive this information over and over in my inbox. Immediately, I received an email from the committee chair in Australia, saying that I was still invited. My expenses would be paid. I needed to open the email further and see the workshop literature to find my name. My joy was immediate and immense. I found myself reciting the words of e.e. cummings, which I knew by heart:

> i thank You God for most this amazing day:
> for the leaping greenly spirits of trees
> and a blue true dream of sky;

It meant this much. The church in Australia simply said, "YES! Please come and teach."

After this initial joy, I thought that I could not go as he would be there. My friends rallied around me, and one said, "How will you spend the days when he is there, and you are not?"

It helped me to see that perhaps I could go but I needed friends there with me. Two dear, generous friends stepped up, paid their way and made the trip with me. I did it and I stood tall. The committee there found me another invitation to a nearby state university where I could repeat my presentation. This allowed me to leave the conference before my husband had the floor.

While there, my two friends said I shone and was alive. As an old favourite hymn puts it, "And from the dust there blossoms red/ Life that shall endless be."

I fell more in love with Australia. When I left the conference after a group presenters' lunch, one of the committee members saw that I was tearful, came to me, put her arm around me and walked me to my residence. She told me that when it had come up for discussion at the planning meeting, as to whether to honour their invitation to me, the chairperson immediately and unequivocally said, "This is something we can do for Ann and for her well-being and we will do it."

The Uniting Church of Australia put their arms around me at great financial cost to themselves and it mattered. They said I mattered and that I could teach. Their generosity was in stark relief to that of my own church in Canada.

I continue to have friends who are in the leadership of the wider church. They kindly accept me where I am with the church. Four years later, a person who had been at that conference in Australia referred a colleague and pastor who had left Australia and taken up new duties in my home city to me for help. Each "yes", each endorsement of my worth, mattered.

Chapter 11

ANGELS DISPATCHED FROM THE SECULAR DEPARTMENT OF HEALING

What we are searching for is how to go on, how to keep going, how to recover the belief that life is worth living.
— Michael Ignatieff, *On Consolation*

Research shows that one of the most effective ways to benefit from the therapeutic benefits of touch is through massage. Massage therapy has been shown to ease depression, increase attentiveness and enhance immune function.
— Lindgren, Jacobsson & Lämås, 2014

As well as the archangels detailed to care for me from the very early days in Florida, angels have appeared and nurtured me. Some were sent from the department of psychology, psychotherapy and medicine. These ones did their time and moved on as my needs and their deployments changed. Rosemary, Ellen, Catherine, Richard and Heather all brought their skills to their assignment to assist me in the recovery of my emotional and mental health.

Angel Rosemary, Registered Marriage and Family Therapist (AAMFT)

Having turned down receiving help from world-famous Esther Perel, my husband consented to come with me to see Rosemary, a psychologist practising near our condo in Florida. We went to our first session at the end of our first week in Florida.

I often put Florida and strip malls in the same sentence. We pulled in and parked in a very classy strip mall. It resembled an oversize entrance for a posh gated community. Rosemary met us in the waiting area and invited us into a large living room of an office. Palms, hibiscus and tumbling bougainvillea in riotous colour greeted us in the garden on display through the enormous windows. The room, with its walls painted in pale yellow and green, was filled with sunlight. With a friendly, open smile, she invited us to sit.

I often think about what walked into that therapist's elegant office. Pure chaos and pain were what she received from me, and I expect she quickly saw that my husband was trying to remove himself from the situation.

He told her everything he had told me about the last session he had with his therapist and her invitation for him to partner with him and have a family. Then he went on to say that he had a pressing concern and he wanted to speak privately with Rosemary. I agreed to wait outside.

Rosemary soon invited me to rejoin them. As I listened, I came to understand that my husband wanted to know how serious his therapist was about trying to have a child with him. To find this out he wanted to write her a letter and chat with her, and he wanted me to be agreeable to these exchanges. I learned this mattered and would be helpful to him in determining whether he would try to repair with me or not. I took this to mean if she was clear she wanted a child then he was not ready for this idea and would return to entertaining life within our marriage. My sense of my husband was that he had never minded that we could not have children. He already had a daughter and I had two children. I truly thought in both his mind and mine that our three children were enough. I was desperate and I construed that this was a bit of a lifeline for us. I agreed that this communication take place.

On the flight to Florida, the psychological magazine I had brought to read on the plane contained an article on current research into aging male sperm. It was a complete coincidence. The article pointed out that not only old female eggs, but also old sperm contributed to the high degree of autism in today's children. To me, the findings were fortuitous, and both my husband and I researched the subject further on the internet, read more articles and found more data confirming this. There were more premature births requiring stays in the neonatal unit and childhood risks were increased for all sorts of severe mental disorders. These articles confirmed further what I thought I had no reason to doubt. He would be unwilling to parent another child.

As we had agreed, he reached out to his therapist by email to clarify her intent. I lived in hope that her desire for children would be stronger than her desire for him. We both were in very different states of agony awaiting her response.

It is no wonder at all that Dolly Parton's most famous song is "Jolene". Her lyrics described both my sincere petition and my worst fear. "Jolene" was my song.

For three days we walked the beach in the daytime and the condo grounds at night. We talked. I fought for us. If she said it was a package deal, him plus a child, then we would regroup and we would have a chance to try to understand what was leading him out of the marriage. We could begin to explore if repair for us was possible. I felt I had his agreement on this.

In those three days I also had a single session with Rosemary. She confirmed that this was the agreement and I was given to understand that his letter made clear that he had told her he would not consider having children.

Immediately after that session, his therapist's email response came.

She accepted my husband's terms and would welcome him to choose her. I then learned that the conditions my husband sent her were not what I thought had been sent. He had asked her to agree that having children was something they would discuss and that they would make a decision over time. He was not very open. Yet, he was not closed. Of course, she accepted this agreement, as I would have expected had I understood what his intentions really were.

In our third joint session with Rosemary in mid-January, my husband told me his decision was made. He would leave me a month later as soon as he had fulfilled his work obligations in Florida. He also stated he would do no further therapy with me. After these three joint sessions, I saw the therapist alone daily.

I saw this supposedly final month with my husband as an opportunity to change his mind. We did many familiar things. We explored the area where we were living, we walked for hours, he played tennis, we golfed, we shopped and we made love. I believe now that he used this time to try to convince me that this was an amicable God-directed separation that should lead to an agreeable divorce. He left on February 14, very quickly after the work obligation was fulfilled, knowing that he had failed to get me to agree to his understanding of this ending of our marriage.

Rosemary, in her concern for me, soon offered me daily appointments and often saw me on the weekends as well. Later, after he had left and Mary arrived, she attended a session with me, as did my son, when he arrived. I don't remember a lot about these sessions. I think I cried all the way there, all the way through the session and all the way back to the condo. I know I have never sobbed so much in my life. I was in an acute phase of grief. Presence for me in that grief was all that mattered, and Rosemary was there each and every day.

I know she was trying to help me remember who I was. She certainly thought the church would support me and that I would be welcome there.

I am sure she was stunned by the response of my church on that front. I was inconsolable. She warned me that if I screamed too loudly in the condo, the neighbours would call the police and I would be hospitalized and have both a police record and a medical record. This might hinder my capacity to acquire medical insurance and make easy travel to the USA more questionable in the future. She must have worried that I would kill myself. I saw her at least forty-four times in the same number of days and a few times by Skype after I returned to Vancouver.

I think she respected me and when I could, we talked about books I had read and thoughts I had about the field of psychotherapy. I think now about how much she gave to me. She reinforced that I was a person of worth. She helped me put together a few splintered pieces in the chaotic field of my shattered self. She let me see that I had something to give by letting me give to her.

She was by nature highly optimistic, I think. In one of the sessions, I learned that her friends called her "Rosie". Sometimes she tried to paint a picture of a worthwhile future for me. I remember this and it has stayed with me, though, at the time, I could not consider it and pushed it mightily away. The future I wanted and anticipated had been completely eradicated. Somehow, she managed to be present for me while at the same time pointing out a tiny chink in that despair.

For me and my family and Anita, she was an anchor. I had a place every day where an experienced psychotherapist was engaged in helping me make it through another day. She was essential. After my husband announced he was leaving, she did everything she could to make her office a safe place for me. I will always be grateful.

Angels Kathy and Janet,
Registered Massage Therapists

Kathy the massage therapist appeared as angels do: unexpectedly. I saw her card on the bulletin board of the tennis centre in the condo complex in Florida. I was not sleeping. I got the idea that the trauma was demolishing my body. Because my daughter slept with me and held me, which seemed to bring a little relief, I thought I needed to be touched and that massage might help. Kathy turned out to be a born-again Christian with a mission to convert and with a heart for those who hurt. Though I was very far left of a born-again Christian, I kept this to myself. I was simply not convertible. I just thought of her as an angel from a different wing of the company.

My body was so full of stress under her hands, it just poured forth its sorrow. She was very creative as a masseuse and tried everything she knew. I have a memory of her standing on my back in one of her more inventive moves. In long twice-weekly sessions, as she manipulated my body tissues, she also prayed over me. She wanted me to go and work with her guru in India. Here in Florida, she became my tourist guide and created outings for me in the Naples area that were places of solace and sanctuary. She persuaded me, with Anita, to attend an incredible music concert at her church with 5,000 others. I was still not able to manage my agitation, but I managed to sit in one place and stay at the concert until the first intermission, when I bolted.

I saw Kathy as akin to one of the women who took down Jesus' broken body and lovingly wrapped it with kindness. She was doing this for me. That we each had a different theology really did not matter. To this day, when I am impatient with the Christian Right, I remember Kathy and her beautiful gift she gave to me.

After I left Florida and returned to Vancouver I found Janet, also a registered massage therapist. In time, I told her my story while she, with a skilled touch, eased the stress in my body. During the three years I continued seeing her, I broke my shoulder playing hockey with my grandson and I also had hand surgery to relieve the arthritic pain in my fingers. Her skill and penetration of my tissues helped me keep those joints functioning at a high level. She was trained to be very cognizant of how trauma affects the fascia tissue and worked with this in my body. She also made me feel very positive about my aging body. I went for treatments once a month until Covid stopped this. My body misses her, and my mind misses our conversations. She wrote young adult fiction and we shared our writing lives as I lay on her table.

Angel Ellen, Medical General Practitioner

In 2017, Dr. Danielle Martin, a family doctor and vice president of Women's College Hospital in Toronto, Canada, published *Better Now* in which she outlines six big ideas to make medical general practice in Canada better. She claims each idea is affordable and achievable. The first big idea is about ensuring relationship-based primary health care for every Canadian.

I sought out my own GP, Dr. Ellen, when I first moved to Vancouver in 1997. At that time, as is still the case, it was almost impossible to find a GP. Because of her commitment to humanitarian causes and because she knew of my work and that of my husband, she stretched her already full practice and took me on. I was very aware of how busy she was, and I tried to be as healthy as possible. During the three months I was in Florida, that all changed. I am ever so blessed that she had been practising Dr. Martin's first big idea long before Dr. Martin articulated it. I came to be the recipient of relationship-based primary care at the highest level of competence.

When I got back to Vancouver from Florida, Ellen began seeing me weekly and then bi-monthly at the end of her day. Her office was modest yet homey. The chairs in the waiting room were vinyl and stiff. A radio on a high window shelf played too loudly and when no one was looking, I climbed onto a chair and turned down the volume. I was never reprimanded. The magazines were eclectic and often out of date. The files in the office alcove were in manila folders and the shelves were hopelessly crowded. The phone rang constantly. Sometimes I waited more than an hour. I started to feel at home there.

As I waited in her office, I surmised that the other patients waiting were all there for more than physical attention. We all seemed in need of emotional care that would require more time. I also learned that I was to be seen last, no matter what time the schedule said. I was just the last. Eventually, I realized this meant I was the sickest and the neediest. I might require more time than the others, and for that reason I had to wait.

As the time of waiting went by, fewer and fewer patients spoke English. I would find myself surrounded by Spanish-speaking families who were a mixture of shy and boisterous. They were shy in front of me and boisterous with each other. I could not understand their language, but I saw their faces shine as they forgot about me. I saw that they felt very welcome. Ellen would greet each of them as she took them into her office or to the door of the waiting room when they left the building. I, as a tall, well-dressed white woman, was clearly an outlier.

Impatient though I often am, I increasingly found it a privilege to wait. At last, she would see the final patient to the door, lock it and invite me into her office. If the waiting room was chaotic, her office was all the more so. It was maybe an eight-by-ten-foot space with an examining table, a desk, sink and computer. The walls were covered with photos: they showed babies delivered, medical sites in foreign places and trinkets, all breathing appreciation and relationship. On her desk were the day's files in an order only Ellen could understand.

After sitting down, I knew she would first address my physical health. Was I eating and sleeping? We both knew that the amount of stress I was in could develop into serious physical challenges for my body. With that checked out, we would talk.

From the moment I returned to Vancouver, Ellen made clear that I was her patient and that she was one hundred per cent on my side. This mattered because when I spoke with anyone who knew my husband and myself, I never knew whether I could trust them. Were they trying to stay neutral? Were they gathering data for him? Were they there for me, and for me only? She cleared up my safety issue immediately.

She took the interaction of my physical and emotional self seriously. From time to time, she would assure me that she had had patients that had made it through to healing and health. She knew this could take five years or more and never questioned that this was a very long journey. Also, she knew my Christian denomination and was a person I could talk with about my church. I trusted her completely.

My daughter wanted me to seriously consider taking antidepressants. What if they would help and I was refusing this possibility? It was true, I was strongly resistant to the idea, but I agreed that Mary could come with me to a session and we would get Dr. Ellen's opinion. Maybe I was just being stubborn?

"Ellen," Mary said, "Mom still thinks about suicide. She does not sleep all that well and she is so stressed. Wouldn't antidepressants help her?"

"Ann doesn't think she is depressed," Ellen said, "and I don't think so either. I know she is having a hard time, but I think the Dexilant medication [which stopped the stomach cramping and acid reflux] I am giving her is helping her eat and in time she will regain weight and eventually sleep."

"Ellen, are you the sort of doctor who is against prescribing antidepressants?" My daughter is nothing if not direct.

"When I diagnose depression," Ellen replied, "I prescribe antidepressants and I have many patients on them. I just don't think your mother fits the diagnosis. She doesn't think she does, and she has no history whatsoever of depression. She is grieving."

This is what Mary needed to hear. She was then able to relax about this subject with me. Ellen had gained her trust as well. Would that every GP in our country had her skills and her presence. I could not have been more blessed than I was in her healing hands.

Angels Catherine, Richard and Heather, Registered Psychologists

Many of the friends that I was talking with were themselves therapists. They gave freely of their time to me, and I received their care so willingly. However, I knew I needed to find a therapist in Vancouver where I now lived. Virtual therapy was not yet common practice and I had let Rosemary go. Ellen was my GP and firmly in that place in my life. Now I began the search for a therapist to complement Ellen's work, and I had several first sessions in the process. I felt I had to find the person who was right enough for me. I knew my body was very involved in what was happening to me. I sought out therapists with skill in somatic experiencing. I wanted my new therapist to be able to integrate the messages my body was sending with my emotional well-being.

After a few unsuccessful leads, I found **Catherine**, a psychologist recommended by two of my psychotherapist friends. I could walk to her office in forty-five minutes, which I liked. On the way there, I used this time to meditate and to prepare, and on the way home, I processed our conversations. She was gentle, compassionate and able to work with my body. She trained dogs to be recovery dogs, which are used to help ill or traumatised people manage life skills and recover better. They are trained to be a very calming presence. The Labrador retriever is a breed highly suited to this work. In my first sessions, a black Lab in training was in attendance. Sometimes the dog was not present and I thought it was Catherine realizing that I was, in my tearful state, a bit much for her dog. When I enquired, she assured me that the dog had a schedule of working certain days and not others. It still seems amazing to me that the dog was able to tolerate my deeply stressful state. It helped me experience and understand what a comforting, wise and regulating presence such a trained dog can be.

In my work with Catherine, I was convinced that I was suffering from a form of PTSD (post-traumatic stress disorder). Ellen thought it possible as well. In our last weeks together, I had begged my husband to tell me why he was leaving me. The most salient message that I was getting from him was that my soul had lost its loveliness. I was hearing that he would not help me with its repair. These thoughts tore me into pieces. I believed that somehow my soul was no longer interesting or lively. I felt this message must be true and had to be the reason that he was abandoning me with no effort to repair the relationship. In the year since he had told me he was leaving, his words played in my mind over and over, crushing me again and again. Inside me it got condensed into the idea that my soul was stagnant and dead. That might not bother some folk but for me it cut at the core of who I essentially am. When I heard those words, I felt crazy.

I often saw him as a holy person, a sort of guru. I was not alone in this. People often commented that they went to the church of ......, invoking his first name! Many saw him as gifted in a special way and I also believed he had spiritual wisdom. The idea that God was directing him to abandon me and be with her—that it was a holy call and I needed to see this— played over and over in my head. Was God ordaining that I be treated in this way? Was this some sort of lesson that God wanted me to learn? Was my husband right? Was God calling him to move on to another person? Was it because my soul had lost its luster?

In the summer after he left, I attended a performance of *Othello*. Near to where I live on the Vancouver waterfront there is an enormous festive white tent where Shakespeare's plays are mounted each summer. The venue is called Bard on the Beach. The backdrop for the stage is a view of the mountains and ocean inlet, where Vancouver is situated, seen through an opening in the tent. In that theatre, I watched Iago make

Othello mad with terrible untruths. I wept for Othello who, believing the lies, strangled his wife. I thought I knew the play well, but I now clearly saw myself in Othello's agony. I felt I was being strangled with lies.

The power of the message that "my soul is dead" distorted my concept of my reality. I began to believe it was true. Yet as I watched Othello being tricked by his trusted friend Iago, I was aghast. I wanted Othello to have the strength and wisdom to call out the trickery and not succumb to it. Alas, like me, Othello fell for it.

My therapist friends knew I was succumbing to the thought that I had a stagnant soul. One of them was trained in and practiced EMDR (eye movement desensitization reprocessing). She wanted me to see if it would help. This therapy was invented in 1987 by American psychologist Francine Shapiro. Walking in the woods one day, she noted that as she moved her eyes from side to side, the negative emotion she was experiencing diminished. She began experimenting with this eye movement with her clients who were suffering from PTSD. EMDR was born. It does not rely on talk therapy or medications. Instead, it uses a client's own rapid, rhythmic eye movements. These eye movements dampen the power of the emotionally charged memories of past traumatic events. I knew this therapy was experimental and why it works was still much debated. It is thought but not proven that an area of the brain where the trauma is residing is blocking the left side of the brain from accessing the self-soothing right side of the brain. The bilateral stimulation bypasses this block, allowing self-soothing to take place.

In my consideration of this form of treatment for myself, I was encouraged that the American Psychiatric Association had noted its effectiveness in treating PTSD and the American Department of Defense and the Department of Veterans Affairs had jointly issued practical clinical guidelines for its use in the military. I decided I was open to exploring it and discussed the possibility with Catherine. She encouraged me and helped me find Richard, a man who was Vancouver's leading EMDR therapist. In 2014, Catherine and I agreed to pause our work and I went to see **Richard**. I could only afford one therapist at a time.

The journey to and from the therapist's office was always important to me as a time for preparing, meditating and integrating my therapeutic experience. From my house, Richard's office was across the Burrard Street Bridge, the main artery to downtown Vancouver. Crossing that bridge, I was always aware that this was a favoured destination for people contemplating suicide. It guaranteed a successful end of life for those who jumped. At the same time, tourists walked this bridge to view Vancouver's expansive harbour. On a clear day, the mountains of Vancouver Island could be seen outlined on the horizon. To the north, the snow-capped Coast Mountains dropped to the sea, the lower levels filled with expensive housing. I could see the cyclists biking back and forth on their side of the seawall path, speeding past the walkers. In the inlet, tankers were carrying orange, red and turquoise containers and enormous cruise ships plied their way in and out of dock as rowers, paddle boarders, kayakers and canoers manoeuvred among them. The views had the capacity to lift me beyond myself to all that is compelling, vibrant and commanding of joy. Going and coming across the bridge, I understood both the push to jump and the pull towards life's magnificence.

I arrived at Richard's office and after a warm welcome and preliminary conversation, he took my history. He was compassionate. He wanted me, if I could, to put my trauma into one sentence. This was easy for me. I already had my belief down to one sentence.

"My soul is stagnant, and dead."

Then I added, "When my husband refused to repair out marriage, this is one of the messages I heard as a reason. I won't stop believing this is true."

"You make it easy for me," Richard said. "That is a perfect sentence for us to use for your treatment. Do you agree that we can use it? You understand EMDR, right?"

"Yes." I nodded to both questions. "But I have never experienced it firsthand. You will have to direct me step by step."

"You have some choices. Eye movement is the most traditional form of treatment. I can use a light bar and you can follow the lights with your eyes as they move back and forth from left to right, or you can put your ear buds in your ears and you will hear an alternating sound in one ear and then the other. I also can offer you sanitized headphones. Or you can sit directly in front of me, and I can tap one of your knees and then the other back and forth. This works the same way as tracking eye movement as it stimulates each side of your brain in succession."

"Let's do the knee tapping. I would like to try that." I knew that I responded better to touch than to sound due to my deaf mother.

He moved our chairs so that they were close enough for him to easily touch my knees. He checked out that I would be comfortable with this.

"You must focus on the sentence that you have just given me. It sums up everything that disables you, right?"

I nodded in the affirmative.

"If it helps, you can say it out loud, and when you do, I am going to tap one knee and then the other at one second intervals over and over for thirty to sixty seconds, and then I will stop."

I repeated in my head, "My soul is stagnant and dead." He began tapping. After the first set of taps, he asked me how powerful the sentence was in my belief on a scale of one to ten. Then, the procedure would repeat. After each set of taps, he asked me to let him know the degree of power the sentence held. He would ask me questions like "What comes to mind?" and "What are you noticing?" He repeated the process over and over for the rest of the session. Occasionally he did reflect that it was irrational of me to give such power to another person's negative words. I appreciated those moments. My mind was quicker to respond but my body needed most to be healed. There is no doubt that the repetition had a hypnotic effect on me. When this happened, my mind was stilled.

If this seems a bit like hocus-pocus to you, it did to me, too. But I was willing to try and to be truthful in my responses. In fact, the power of the sentence did vary. As I repeated it over and over, trying to believe such nonsense got harder. It was beginning to register in me the lie that it was. I wish I knew more about how the tapping assisted me and research in this matter is ongoing. In my next lifetime, I am going to be a neurologist. There is so much about how the brain works that is yet to be discovered.

"Ann, our session has about five minutes left," Richard said. "How much is this belief affecting you now?"

"It is less powerful. It started at ten plus and it is a maybe a five now."

Then, before the session ended, he chatted with me about last evening's hockey game. He was checking to make sure I was disengaging from the trancelike state the process had induced. He made sure that I left his office with my feet on the ground, ready to cross the bridge, go home and a week later come back to the next session. It was a little like hypnosis and he wanted us both to be sure I was fully awake, aware and functional before I set off for home.

I noticed after the first four weeks of treatment that my mind was becoming comfortable with the sentence when it crossed my mind. It no longer carried the same power to make me think my soul was deeply flawed. However, my body still shuddered as if a ghost were walking across my psyche when I thought about this judgment of me.

After three months of weekly sessions, I now noticed that my body had now eased. It no longer made sense to my mind or my body that the state of my soul was the cause of the marriage's dissolution. The shuddering ghost was decapitated. I am incredulous that it took eighteen repetitious sessions. My soul was recovering and even had some shine. I left Richard's brilliant if unorthodox care and rested from all psychological therapy in order to integrate my learnings.

After a few months of this therapy sabbatical, I returned to **Catherine**. I think, for her, I was an interesting client, but I was not easy.

I was not ready for a therapist to say to me that I was a beautiful woman and that I would find a new partner and live happily ever after, or anything hinting at such or any future. I was still grieving, plain and simple, and I needed a therapist to be with me for the long haul. Yes, I needed to be told if I was wallowing or if I was becoming bitter. Yet I wanted to grieve as cleanly as I could. Catherine agreed that I had a right to mourn and a right to be accompanied in that process for as long as it took.

Catherine had learned that there was some sort of "sweet spot" as she called it. She told me it was the place where she was able to both help me recognize my resilience at the same time as honouring my pain. Bless her for holding this "spot" as she conducted her sessions with me. I remember that as with Rosemary, I wept though many sessions. With Catherine I made progress. I was now able to listen and think about a future I would forge.

I spent three years with Catherine in weekly sessions and then, in 2017, she retired. She was going to move to the country and focus full-time on raising therapy dogs and assisting in their placement with the right client. I was pleased for her, the timing felt right for me and I did not feel abandoned. In our last session we talked a little about my time with her. She wanted me to know that early on she had understood that it was very important for me that my pain be seen and validated. She told me that she found my commitment unique and important. She encouraged me to sort through all my journal notes and begin to write a book. It was a future for me that I was ready to consider.

A year after Catherine's retirement I knew that I still desired psychological support. I wanted to find a very wise person who was a dream analyst. I have always valued my dreams.

In a time before television, I was brought up to be a genius at Bible trivia. As a youngster I was told and had loved Bible stories, particularly those in the Jewish text or Old Testament as it was called then. Those stories were more exciting, had more crimes and were filled with battles and sex. In the town where I grew up, Bible Baseball was popular. In this game, the pitcher threw you a difficult factual question and if you answered it correctly you moved on a base. The questions would get more difficult. "Who is the oldest man in the Bible?" Answer: Methuselah. Advance to first base. At second base, you might be asked "How long did he live?" Answer: 969 years. I got so good at this game that by the age of ten, I was on radio shows with competing kids. While engaging in this game, I learned that the scripture was full of dreams. Once, I was standing at bat with the bases loaded and the pitcher asked me not one but three questions.

"Whose dreams are recorded in the Gospel stories of Jesus' birth? How many dreams? What was the substance of the dreams?"

"Joseph, Mary's partner, had four dreams. One, marry her; two, flee to Egypt; three, Herod is dead, go back to Judea; four, no, not safe, go to Galilee."

Whew, I answered correctly. I brought in four runs!

My legacy from Bible Baseball was created. Dreams have fascinated me ever since. They have been recorded since ancient times by all major religious cultures. I knew them as complex stories with hidden meanings. They were my first taste of mystery stories, and I was hooked for life. I have recorded mine throughout my entire life since the age of eleven; I had two nightmares under anesthetic with ether when I had my tonsils out and another time for draining an abscess. Dreams gave me stories that I learned to treat as metaphors. These metaphors guided me in my thinking about my life. Freud called them "the royal road to the unconscious". In Emily Bronte's Wuthering Heights, Catherine says, "I have dreamt in my life, dreams that have stayed with me ever after, and changed my ideas: they've gone through and through me, like wine through water, and altered the colour of my mind."

I have had a handful of dreams that fit this description.

I think dreams give one clarity, and my husband and I paid close attention to our dreams throughout our long marriage. We relied on them for perspective. We interpreted them for one another. We thought of them as God's language and God's way of messaging us.

Dreams often are dismissed by people as not making much sense. They often, at first recall, do seem to be nonsensical stories. Usually, they come in separate scenes, becoming more dramatic until we wake up. Everyone has three to five dreams a night in REM (rapid eye movement) sleep. Some people have easy recall and others say they never remember a dream. Even those people can usually recall a nightmare or two.

It is possible to learn to catch dreams. Indigenous people made dream catchers out of branches and twine shaped to resemble a snowshoe and hung them near their beds to aid in the catching of good dreams and the dismissing of bad dreams. Dreams are more easily recalled if we wake up slowly and hold the space between sleep and wakefulness for a few minutes. However, a dream not immediately recorded is frequently forgotten when our feet hit the floor and we move into the day.

Sometimes, I brought dreams to Catherine. It was not her forte, and I missed my husband who had been my personal dream interpreter (and I his). I became my own interpreter, but I knew I needed more objective input. I kept an ear to the ground hoping to find such an interpreter in Vancouver. Eventually, I found **Heather.**

I worked with her for two years, 2018 and 2019, five years after my husband had abandoned me.

Her office was ten minutes from my house. I discovered she was a writer and we shared writer's angst with each other from time to time. She was near retirement. She was a swimmer and we often saw each other in the pool. She seemed a kindred spirit.

In our first session I told her how it was that my husband had left me and how I had been endeavouring to grieve fully. I described the extensive work I had done with Catherine and then with Richard. I told her my history with dream interpretation and asked if she would work with me to understand my dreams. She said yes and we agreed I would bring her my dreams twice a month.

My dreams confirmed and amplified the work I had already done in therapy. Near the end of the second year, I brought her a dream where I recalled only fragments as I had not written it down. Nevertheless, they were vibrant fragments demanding attention. I knew that it was a special dream and one I would never forget.

I dreamt that my salary was being paid to me in huge globes the size of exercise balls. First there were gold ones and I thought they were going to be hard to turn into cash because they were worth too much. There were filigreed silver ones. I thought they would be too hard to clean. There were copper ones and finally black ones. I was pleased with the black ones and thought, *Black is beautiful.* I woke up.

This was a pleasant dream. As I began my own interpretation I wondered if each ball was a phase of my life. I also noticed that I was struggling trying to keep all the balls together, but in the dream, they arrived and left me one by one.

The very first level of dream interpretation is to think about anything you might have done or heard in the last few days that might have a bearing on the dream. Often the plot of the dream can start in these events. When I woke up, I remembered that recently that my daughter-in-law told me that her friends thought I should have been the prime minister of Canada. Immediately I cautioned myself to beware of my grandiosity as I approached this dream.

At our session, Heather had me associate and reflect as deeply as I could on each ball.

I found myself saying, "Gold is heavy and desired. It is a precious metal used to back the economy of great nations. Gold matters and I, like others, own a gold piece or two."

In dream interpretation it is helpful to become every object in the dream. Sue instructed me to be the various balls in the dream.

"I am a gold ball and very valuable. Not too many people can afford very much of me. I am around at celebrations. People all over the world spend a lot of time trying to find me. I make people happy when they find me. I help people fulfil their dreams. I am found in nuggets. A little of me is important and prized."

Heather then had me turn to the silver ball.

I told her that I was immediately reminded of my almost white silvery hair. I told how people stopped on the street and complimented me on the way my curls framed my face. When I coloured my hair, I did not receive so many compliments. I told her how silver was more accessible, and many people had some silver jewelry.

Then as the silver ball I said, "I am very fine and elegant. I am like lace and I create patterns when the light shines through me. I am special since I am filigreed. I am a bit old fashioned. However, I do take a lot of care to keep clean. But when I am cared for, I shine."

I was smiling as I imagined myself at a spa, luxuriating in the care and absolutely glowing as a result.

And then, becoming the copper ball, I said, "I am burnished, and as I age, I turn a beautiful turquoise like a tropical sea. I adorn cathedrals and parliament buildings. I turn up in the most important places. I am chosen for effect when the best is desired. I do not wear out but get more stunning with time."

Now as the black ball, Heather encouraged me to keep embodying the ball as fully as I could.

"I am black marble, and on closer inspection I am striated with specks of gold, silver and copper. I am polished to a high degree. I reflect light more subtly than silver. I am used to creating both beautiful and practical objects. I could be a statue or a kitchen counter. People want to touch me. I am beautiful as Black Americans are announcing they are. It is a grave mistake not to see all my beauty inside and out. I am an original. I cannot be bent out of shape. I love that I change colour. I am not rigid. I look differently from every angle. I have a fluidity within me."

Heather called this dream a "big up". She invited me to see that I am called to reclaim my beauty and validity. It is good that I understand that dreams have a tendency to exaggerate in case we miss their invitation. This dream I took her was a "big up" and announced all my potential for my life ahead. In each dream I brought to her, I was invited to see myself differently. I was in the process of steadily reclaiming my vibrant soul. This dream I brought to Heather directly reinforced my previous work in therapy. I was beginning, after six years of therapy, to accept that I was beautiful inside and out.

Chapter 12

ANGELS DISPATCHED FROM THE DEPARTMENT OF SPIRITUALITY

Care of the soul speaks to the longings we feel and the symptoms that drive us crazy, but it is not a pathway away from shadow or death. A soulful personality is complicated, multifaceted, and shaped by both pain and pleasure, success and failure.
— Thomas Moore, *Care of the Soul*

Consolation is the process by which we escape our solitude and begin to re-establish our bonds with others.
— Michael Ignatieff, *On Consolation*

I was born into a thoroughly Christian home. In my early years, Sunday was a very special day. It was patterned on the Jewish Sabbath; food was mostly prepared the day before, shoes were cleaned the night before and a fresh and clean frock would be laid out for me. Late Saturday afternoon the ritual of turning me into Shirley Temple began in earnest.

"Fred, please bring in a bucket of water from the rain barrel," my mother would instruct my father. He did as he was told and the water would be put in a large canning pot on the stove to be heated. Only rainwater would produce the required shine.

When the water was warm, my agony began. My four-year-old head would be wrenched back over the regular sink and the washing and rinsing started.

"Stop," I choked. "In my eyes!" I squinted, cried and resisted with four-year-old gusto.

My Aunt Eualie, my mother's childhood friend, had arrived to help and began to distract me.

"You will be so beautiful. Ann, you will have curls just like your doll has." She crooned, initiating me into the cost of being female. At the same time, she was pulling out the hated bag of rags from the cupboard.

My hair towelled and the fear of drowning over, the two women, my aunt and mother, began to roll up bits of my hair in rags, which they then tied in knots. Eventually my hair was fully tied up. Only a few stray strands of hair would be escaping here and there, all over my head. My aunt and mother were indeed pleased.

"Eualie, it is done for another week," my mother said. "Try to get back at ten tomorrow morning. I will need help with the rest of it. I so wish Ann did not make such a fuss."

"No problem, Ida," said my aunt reassuringly. "It's so worth it in the end."

At the supper table, my hair in rags, I was a sight. My grandfather usually found his little way to make it all worse from my perspective.

There was a little girl who had a little curl
right in the middle of her forehead
and when she was good, she was very, very good
and when she was bad, she was horrid.

He would say this in a joking, rhythmic way and draw laughs from all but me. I knew that little curl would be escaping the rag as it dried. Now, at the age of 85, that little curl still is there facing me every day in the mirror. I finally find it more or less amusing.

Then followed a bumpy night of sleep. I can't believe I endured this once a week for three years. Finally, either Shirley Temple fell out of fashion, I grew too old or my aunt and mother moved on to a new beauty project for me, but the rag version did stop.

Sunday morning at ten sharp, my aunt arrived. By then I was in my clean frock, usually a smocked dress, and my clean shoes. Now I had to sit still while each rag was carefully removed, and each ringlet was carefully put into place. Quite a wonder they did all this without mousse or hair spray. They had bobby pins which got miraculously inserted into each ringlet to hold them in place.

"Ida, her hair is perfect," exclaimed my aunt, holding up a magazine with Shirley Temple on the cover. "We did it!"

"Eualie, let's go before it is a mess again." My mother insisted on moving quickly on the walk to church. They were both so proud that I looked as they thought I should. It was my introduction to *The Beauty Myth* long before Naomi Wolf exposed and analyzed it in her book. Parts of all this are with me still. I always dressed for church and never embraced the casual look for Sundays.

My parents took me to church every Sunday morning, my father took me to Sunday school in the afternoon and in the evening, and we often went back for the twilight service. I was not allowed to roller skate or bike on Sunday. Cards were not played; only religious books were read. When I was old enough and able to read by myself, I found in our attic a carton of books my mother had read as a child. Apparently, they were deemed suitable for Sunday reading. I was tired of children's Bible stories and *The Pilgrim's Progress*. In a single summer, I devoured a very emotional, romantic series of children's books about Elsie Dinsmore. Written by Martha Finley and originally published between 1867 and 1905, they told the stories of a very good, motherless Christian girl who lived in the days of the Civil War. The books birthed in me a love of the great plantation houses owned by slave owners and gave me a totally unrealistic and racist picture of that war.

My father and I were a bit naughty. On the way home from Sunday school, he took me to a Jewish deli which, unlike Christian-owned stores, was allowed to open on Sundays.

"Ann, Jews have their Sunday on Saturday," my father explained. "I think it is alright to buy ice cream here, but your mother might not agree."

He bought me a chocolate (my favourite) ice cream cone and we ate it before we got home.

We reported this "crime" to no one. Just before we reached our house, my father took one of his pressed white handkerchiefs from his pocket and wiped my face clean. It was our secret for always.

Following the Shirley Temple phase, a few years later, I demonstrated a rebellious spirit of my own. One of my elder brothers decided not to go to church and stayed home. To establish this rebellion, he wore his pyjamas all day. It was excused because he was brilliant and supposedly studying. Obviously, I was not yet smart enough for this privilege. It was winter and I, in the chaos of our family preparing for church, managed to get my snowsuit on over my pyjamas. I stood smiling at the door ready to go. Off we went and, of course, the church was warm, and my mother insisted I take off my snowsuit only to be appalled at having a daughter at church in her pyjamas. When they were young my grandchildren loved this story about their grandma. I was not to be outshone by all those brains of my brother. In my mind, I could wear pyjamas on Sunday too.

I digress. I was raised a Christian with a feisty edge. I was part of a liberal Protestant denomination that was deeply embedded in social activism. My grandmother, born in 1874, was one of the founding members of my local church. She was also a suffragette. My denomination was the first in Canada to ordain single women or women with grown children, and then to ordain married women of childbearing age (me), to perform the marriages of the LGTBQ community and to apologize to our First Nations people. It was a community of left-leaning liberals.

I embraced it. As a young woman, I experienced a call to study theology and became a minister. I continued to evolve as a Christian and focused my ministry on pastoral care. Ultimately, I created a private practice as a marriage and family therapist who was thoroughly informed by my practice as a Christian. If my clients wanted to bring issues of their spirituality to their therapy work, I was equipped to be with them there.

In seminary I was trying to find a way to combine psychotherapy with my call as a minister. At that time—my early twenties—I got introduced to spiritual direction, now called spiritual companioning. I went to a workshop given by Matthew Fox, an American theologian and at the time still a Dominican priest. He was the founder of the Institute in Culture and Creation Spirituality. When that workshop came to an end, I naively asked Matthew Fox to be my spiritual director. Busy man that he was, he gently refused.

"Ann," he said, "Meister Eckhart, who lived in the Middle Ages, is my spiritual director. The richness of his thinking guides me every day. What you have told me of you and your quest, I think you might explore the work of Otto Rank and he could be your spiritual companion."

I gave it a try. Otto Rank was a close colleague of Freud, a psychoanalyst and prolific writer, authoring chapters in Freud's famous works. He was a man who needed his profile lifted from under the shadow of Freud just as Matthew Fox had raised the wisdom of Meister Eckhart out of the Middle Ages, making him a wise voice in the twentieth century. I put effort into reading his work but the fit did not happen. I knew I wanted my spiritual director to be alive.

A spiritual director/companion is a person who sits with you in your spiritual dilemmas. Sister Carol is an excellent example. In hourly daily meetings, he or she offers scripture and other writings as a source of reflection for you. This often happens in a retreat setting where you may be making an eight-day silent retreat or a thirty-day silent retreat in the manner of St. Ignatius. Generally, these retreats are conducted in Roman Catholic retreat centres. In these centres usually there are creative rooms with a good supply of art materials. Often there is a chapel where daily mass is offered as part of the experience. When not on retreat, spiritual companioning occurs at once-a-month hourly meetings. Sometimes your spiritual director is deceased as was Matthew Fox's, and then you are guided by their writings and beliefs.

I decided to pursue spiritual direction/companioning for myself. Over the years I made time for many silent retreats of eight to ten days, making many of them in Narragansett, Rhode Island at Our Lady of Peace Spiritual Center. I also made a thirty-day silent retreat.

For twenty years I taught pastoral counselling at the Toronto School of Theology seminary. During this time, I met Sister Mary Ellen who was a colleague and a professor. I asked her to take me into her practice as a spiritual companion and she said yes. I saw her monthly for ten years. Both with her and at the various retreats I attended I was introduced to the work of Thomas Merton, American Trappist monk and mystic; Thomas Berry, a Catholic priest who brought the world's attention to the necessity of an evolutionary understanding of creation that was compatible with Darwin's theory; and Brian Swimme, professor at the California Institute of Integral Studies where he taught evolutionary cosmology and the work of so many more luminaries in the field.

While I was processing my devastation with secular therapists, I knew I needed to balance this work with complementary discussions with both theologians and more people like Sister Carol, specialists in the field of evolutionary theology and in the practice spiritual companioning. Church had always nurtured me in my faith and now it was gone.

I read the works of Teilhard de Chardin, Ilia Delio and John Haught, all evolutionary theologians. I figured out that I needed a very respected evolutionary theologian to assess this and tell me if this could truly be God's evolutionary thrust for me and my marriage. I knew who the luminaries were in the field as I had read a good deal of their works. Eight months after my husband left me in that Florida airport, I reached out to the one I considered the most brilliant and the truest leader in the field. Franciscan Sister and American evolutionary theologian Ilia Delio responded immediately and offered this advice:

I am deeply sorry to hear of your situation. In no way can an evolutionary paradigm justify your husband's outrageous behaviour. (By the way, I do know of your husband's work from the literature and website.) And by no means can his actions/decision be considered holy. Evolution does not invite infidelity but fidelity; deep relatedness builds on authenticity of personhood not duplicity.

I needed just such an external witness to put to rest my understanding that he saw his action as God's call. I printed Ilia Delio's response, posted it on my fridge and read it over and over as my deepest self struggled to reclaim what I knew to be true. His action was not a response to a holy call. From this moment on, this the damaging claim of his began to lose its spiritual power over me.

I missed my church life. Various online churches spoke to me, Riverside Church in New York being one. A friend and I made a pilgrimage there and I experienced nurture and followed the thinking of the pastor until he left that pulpit. Finally, I began to focus sufficiently to be able to read. Authors became friends to my journey and podcasts even more so. I find being read to or spoken to on spiritual matters a way to learn and nurture my faith. In time, I opened to finding a version of church in a group of two or three friends.

I also sought a new spiritual companion to replace Sister Carol. I was intent on keeping my psychological and spiritual healing in balance.

The Mariandale Angel

Two years after my husband abandoned me, I went with a friend, who is herself a spiritual companion, to the Mariandale Retreat Centre just outside NYC. There I was assigned to a spiritual companion to be my guide for the week. I continued to work with her online on a monthly basis for over a year. I called her my Mariandale angel. She was a very liberal Roman Catholic, and I grew to trust her wisdom. I felt so violated at the level of my soul that I doubted my every spiritual thought and feeling. When I was on that retreat, I had to fight the urge to kill myself every day.

I found the perfect place, a bridge over a deep gorge. I painted this scene in the arts room. In the scene, it is raining, and I somehow gave the person who was me a brightly coloured umbrella. Laughter lightened the painting and shifted the dark mood. My psyche (soul) spoke wisdom to me.

At my spiritual companion's suggestion, I made a huge collage of all the messages I had received from well-meaning friends and family. Some of these I judged as too positive and some as just right. I put all of them in the collage as directed. Things such as: buy a new dress that you would never have worn; dye your hair green and get outrageous shoes; turn the key on your house, leave it and never look back; outsmart the scam artists; pace yourself; stitch a serene nature scene; garden; talk with strangers; explore the world; bungee jump; remember the more of us who walk, the more of us survive; get in a canoe; make a solid match with a new person; and we are there for you when you can't be.

When I returned to Vancouver, I hung this collage where I could see it every day. I peppered my entire house with signs, sticking them to mirrors and walls with green masking tape. They were sentences that spoke to me and reminded me that I had a soul that was luminous. It was a bit overwhelming for my cleaning person, but she tidied around them. I made the walk about my house to read them on many an evening. Many came from

John O'Donohue, the Irish poet and former Catholic priest who is best known for popularizing Celtic spirituality.

Here are some lines from him that I printed and kept on the inside of my front door for at least a year:

Blessed be the mind that dreamed the day
The blueprint of your life
Would begin to glow on earth,
Illuminating all the faces and voices
That would arrive to invite
Your soul to growth...
When desolation surrounded you,
blessed be those who looked for you
and found you, their kind hands
urgent to open a blue window
in the gray wall formed around you.

Spiritual Guidance from Within

Some of my spiritual practices came at the direction of my formal spiritual companions. Others just presented themselves to me guided by my imagination.

In the first few weeks following the trauma, I spontaneously rewrote Psalm 23 from the Bible in a way that spoke to me. This is a psalm often read at Christian funerals to comfort the bereaved:

My Paraphrase of the Lord is My Shepherd, January 2013

God, you are the Protective Presence in my life and with you,
I know all my wants are respected.

You make me to lie down in green pastures where I can rest.

You lead me beside still waters that are deep and pure and

altogether refreshing.

You are awakening my soul and restoring it to life

You guide me in the path of Wisdom which is where I belong.

Yes, even when I walk into the deep shadows of my psyche, you are there before me and alongside.

With your rod, you summon my ego to account and with your staff you draw me from the precipice in order to comfort me.

You are preparing for me an abundant feast in the presence of all my enemies, both those within and without.

You anoint my head with oil and my cup is spilling out and running over like an endless waterfall.

Surely your mercy, kindness, truth, beauty, compassion and freshness shall attend and follow me all the days of my life

And I will dwell in your heart for all eternity.

Whenever I read this, I am touched. I wonder about where in me it originated. So much of that time I was barely coherent. Perhaps all the memorization of famous writings that I had to do as a child got inside for times such as the one I was in. It was an old-fashioned educational model reaping dividends.

Throughout this experience and still today I keep reaching out to the Holy One. I swim twice a week and when the lengths are done, I do a water meditation. I lie on my back on the water and recite the words of Denise Levertov from the poem "The Avowal":

As swimmers dare
to lie face to the sky
and water bears them,
as hawks rest upon air
and air sustains them,

so would I learn to attain
free fall, and float
into Creator Spirit's deep embrace,
knowing no effort earns
that all-surrounding grace.

In the summer when I swim outside with the mountains clear in the northern sky, I paraphrase Psalm 121, which I learned as a young child listening to my mother recite it as she baked. I pause and kneel in the water facing the mountains and pray as the psalmist did centuries ago:

I will lift up mine eyes unto the mountains, from whence cometh my help.

My help cometh from the Creator God who all this cosmos hath made.

It further seals my swim and begins my day.

Angel Peter

When my time with the Mariandale angel was coming to an end, I was graced to meet Peter. He was at one time the head of my denomination: our "pope". He is a pastor to pastors, and I was drawn to him. He was doing a stint as the preacher in a Vancouver congregation while they searched for a new pastor. I went to this church throughout this time. I liked the way he was with the people and with the troubled situation at that church. I asked him to be my spiritual companion. He agreed but had two conditions. He would not be of help to me in my journey with the institutional church and the way I had been treated there. He was also clear that he needed to see me in person as he was not interested in using Skype. He set very clear boundaries. When he left Vancouver, he relented on the second one and agreed that we could talk on the telephone from time to time, and we did. It helped me trust him.

We have had many conversations about forgiveness and its role in my process. He was the spiritual advisor for one of the commissioners on the Truth and Reconciliation Commission of Canada (2008–2015) and brought wisdom from there to me. He shared how his thinking was attracted to freedom as central to faith. He reminded me of the work of Ivan Illich, and I remembered how I had been consumed by Illich many years before. Illich was born in Austria in 1926. He was a thinker far ahead of his times. He was a polyglot, speaking at least ten languages. He became a priest who was appointed to teach in Puerto Rico. Ultimately, he was summoned by the Vatican who questioned his orthodoxy, and later he withdrew from the priesthood. He went on to establish a school in Cuernavaca, Mexico. It became a language school and free university for leftist-leaning intellectuals from all over North America. He had given me courage to seek ordination as a married woman with young children within my denomination, something that had never been done before. It was good to remember my audacious soul and the freedom I had exercised in following its direction.

I talked with Peter about complicity and ethical dilemmas. We shared book titles. He gave me a book titled *The Faraway Nearby* by Rebecca Solnit. On the back jacket of the book, she is described in these words:

"What Solnit offers us, I think, is the future of memoir. Not the story of the self...but the ways in which one's story opens into other stories...literary nonfiction doesn't get more beautiful and compelling."

– The American Scholar

Peter was encouraging me to write my memoir, setting the standard very high. Solnit is the author of twenty books with a huge feminist fan club. Peter pushed me into new territory over and over. Because Solnit devotes a whole chapter, "Ice", in her book to the gothic novel *Frankenstein* by Mary

Shelley, I spent a summer reading this classic. Like myself, Mary Shelley lost her first child and went on to lose two more. I felt a kinship with her in this suffering. I opened the book in anticipation, trusting I would be seen.

In it, Walton, a polar explorer, rescues a dying stranger and the story the stranger tells him turns his life around. It is the story of a scientist, Frankenstein, creating a living monster whom he calls the "creature". It is a tale of becoming steeped in complexity. It helps Walton choose to turn from polar death to connection and community. From my earliest days after my husband left, her story wrapped me round and pulled me toward life. Mary Shelley, at just eighteen years of age and wracked by grief, created *Frankenstein*, a novel that has drawn readers toward hope for centuries.

I peppered Peter with questions about forgiveness. He helped me to know that I brought gifts to him as well, and this touch of mutuality helped my soul feel alive. He shared with me one of his dreams and I was able to help him understand it. Once he made a direct suggestion that I go to a retreat given by his wife, and while there, my homework was to make a friend. I just managed to squeak this in in the last thirty minutes of the retreat, and what a great friend I have made in Lynda.

Peter is a leader in my church and it meant so much to me that he was willing to sit with me, be present for me and with these acts affirm that I was an interesting human being. Through this relationship, hope was ignited in me that one day I might be at home again in my church.

Chapter 13

FORGIVENESS: VIEWED THROUGH THE LENS OF RELIGION/SPIRITUALITY

Think of pulling a weed in a garden, a thorny weed of resentment. We can dig it up but that does not mean it won't sprout back again. We must refine the garden's soil over and over by planting other things like truth and justice, compassion and mercy that can crowd out the weeds of un-forgiveness and bitterness, creating a more beautiful garden.

— Charlotte vanOyen-Witvliet

Someone I loved once gave me a box full of darkness. It took me years to understand that this, too, was a gift.

— Mary Oliver

Until I was eight, my father always put me to bed. My mother was profoundly deaf, and her sight was poor. For years I slept beside her with her hand on my back in case I stirred and called for comfort. My father did the talking things and my mother did the touching things, and by so doing they kept me safe and loved.

From the time of my earliest memories, at bedtime, my father would tell me a story he made up and then we would pray. When I was so small that my praying hands did not reach to the top of the mattress, he fixed the problem. He knelt, placing his buttocks on his heels. Then he would gather me up, first placing my feet on his knees and then encircling my arms with his. Taking my hands between his, we then rested them in prayer position, on the pink and yellow Dutch girl patterned quilt my grandma had made for me. Together we prayed "Now I lay me down to sleep". Before long I knew the words by heart.

When I went to kindergarten at five years old, I discovered that I could retell my dad's story of the night before to the other kids at story time. The kids thought I made the story up and I did not think to tell them otherwise. I loved being the best storyteller in the class. I don't remember ever thinking I was doing anything wrong, or what I might have all too soon understood as plagiarizing.

One night when I was in grade three, my dad just stopped telling me the stories for no reason that I ever knew, and I was bereft. I tried to make up one of my own the next day, but I was nowhere near as entertaining as my father. My classmates became impatient and story time was never the same. I lost my star status. Happily, the praying practice continued.

When, at age eight, my hands finally reached the top of the mattress without any help, I graduated to learning the much more difficult Lord's Prayer. Over a winter season, I was finally able to say it all from memory. I was so proud, and he was too.

One spring morning, soon after, we were all seated in church together. We sat in the pew with the aids for the hard of hearing. My mother entered so she could sit where the gadgets were, then me and then my dad. Dad and I would leave in the middle of the service before the sermon with the other kids for a period of story time. There was always a long prayer before that moment. That prayer went on and on but always ended with a communal recitation of the Lord's Prayer.

Somehow, that morning, I got the idea that when the minister said,

"Now, let us all pray in unison," I had an opportunity to make my dad prouder yet.

At just the right moment, and maybe even a moment too soon, I stood up on the pew bench and in my loudest voice so that my mother might hear me, I said, "Our Father." Continuing slowly and carefully, apparently rising to a crescendo, I bellowed, "Forgive us this day our trespasses as we forgive those who trespass against us," before my father managed to pull me down to sitting and had me be quiet and respectful. I was just eight when I decided to lead our congregation in the Lord's Prayer. It was the last prayer my father taught me. I don't remember when he stopped kneeling with me as I prayed my bedtime prayers. As a university student, I remember occasionally catching my parents kneeling at bedtime prayer as I passed by their bedroom door, left open to "catch the breeze" as my mother would say. We were a family that slept with the windows open and to this day I still do.

Christians the world over know the Lord's Prayer by heart. I have always pondered that line about forgiveness. In fact, concern for what forgiveness is and is not has plagued me throughout my life.

I think Bruce Cockburn award winning Canadian songwriter and pioneering guitarist describes my feeling perfectly in his song, "Pacing the Cage" which appears on his album *The Charity of Night*. As I try to sort out what forgiveness is and is not, here are my thoughts as I struggle to understand the kaleidoscopic nature of forgiveness.

I do know that immediately after my husband left me, I stopped being able to truthfully pray the line of forgiveness in the Lord's Prayer. I knew I had not forgiven my husband or his therapist. Must I do this to be well? This question haunted me as I tried to make meaning of my new circumstances.

Forgiveness is a very "in" topic. It has deep roots in Judaism, Islam and Christianity. It also shows up in the political arena when an apology is offered for wrongs committed. The apology is analysed and if deemed sincere, forgiveness is extended. It shows up in the public arena in all the discussions about truth and reconciliation, which have become so important in Canada as we embark on the twenty-first century. Forgiveness also appears as central in the field of psychology where people who are hurting address and heal from the wrongs they have suffered. In the field of philosophy, it is addressed by none other than the famous living American philosopher Martha Nussbaum, the Ernst Freud Distinguished Service Professor of Law and Ethics appointed by the Law School and the Philosophy Department of the University of Chicago. In her book *Anger and Forgiveness*, she sums up its importance, stating "the familiar contention is that forgiveness is a central political and personal virtue."

Given my Christian faith and my lifework as a psychotherapist, to have integrity, I had to explore how forgiveness was impacting my road to recovery. I began by trying to define its meaning. This is as nuanced a task as describing the colour of snow.

As a boy, my son David delighted in forts. Forgiveness he was not so keen on. It was a work in progress as it is for all kids and still is for me. I made his first fort for him when he was three. I had enclosed the space under a raised sandbox in his bedroom with striped red and white cotton inserted in the proper places with screened windows and a door. We called it a circus fort. At six, he built himself a fort in a tree. He was developing the skill of hitting a nail on the head with a hammer. Building a tree fort was the perfect venue for this new passion that combined expulsion of energy, climbing a tree, a satisfying noise and the pleasure of repetition. By the end of the summer, the fort was a bed of nails and he was a master at hammering.

Long ago, during one particularly cold winter, he and three buddies created a fort under the stairwell in our basement. He was ten and Mary, his sister, was six. Always tagging after her big brother, she wanted in the fort. Of course, those lads would not let her in. She begged, and then she negotiated.

"How much does it cost to get in?" she asked.

"Ask her for twenty-five cents to get in," one lad offered.

Mary knew that was her entire allowance.

"No, ten cents," she proffered.

Her brother agreed to the price of entry and took the money and the boys all let her in. Once in, she discovered there was nothing that looked like a fort in there. There were no cushions or books or food. It was not a clubhouse. It was just five kids stuffed in a tiny space. She had been tricked out of a good cut of her allowance. She howled loudly and repetitively.

"Unfair! This is not a fort." Her escalating pain and anger demanded I show up and try to sort it out.

"The boys tricked me, Mom. They took my money and there is nothing in there. It is not a real fort at all." She was full-on sobbing.

I tried speaking with the boys. "Mary is hurt and she is mad, and if you boys did what she says you did, you have to do something about it."

David knew he had been caught and squeaked out, "I'm sorry, Mary." It wasn't the first time he had set her up and it was not his first apology to her, nor his last.

"Good," I said, nodding in approval. I went on to instruct: "More is required, David. Make her believe you mean it."

"Okay," he said, "here is the dime back." I was still holding his attention. "Okay guys, we all give her five cents from each of us."

The boys hooted their dismay, not quite realising their friend David's generosity. But they had all been caught. Mary received her ten cents plus twenty cents as payback.

"Alright," said Mary, smiling, "let's play."

I translated this as "I forgive you and I accept your apology now." Like any younger sister who wanted in on her brother's life, she hoped for a better future for their relationship.

Back then, this was how I understood forgiveness. It was transactional forgiveness. I hurt you and make you angry. Then I say I am sorry, and I make amends to show my sincerity. If I am the victim, I get an apology and some sort of payback just as Mary had.

Transactional forgiveness, as it is most commonly understood by Jewish, Islamic and Christian culture, is a practice that goes like this:

1. Admit you have done something you understand as wrong. David and his buddies tricked his sister.

2. Admit you did this "crime". David does not deny Mary's version of the experience.

3. Express regret. David tells Mary he is sorry.

4. Do something about it. David and the boys agree to give her back her money.

5. Show that you understand how it was for the victim. Did David really get how it was for Mary? Here the goal is attaining empathy for the one who is hurt.

6. Demonstrate that you, the perpetrator, know how it happened. David got caught up with his friends and they made a play for easy money.

7. Demonstrate that in the future you are capable of and want to behave better. This is repentance, literally a turning from a bad behaviour to a more noble one. David offers a solution. Each lad would contribute to her receiving more money back than she gave in the first place. An even better solution involves earning the trust of the person betrayed.

Viewing the David and Mary episode through Nussbaum's critical lens,

I could see that Mary expected that by howling that I would come to her rescue. She announced her victimhood. Her brother and his friends were unfair. They were the villains. David feels caught and admitted he did trick his sister. I didn't take time to find out and assess why he did this and how sick he and his buddies were of the bad weather that had driven them inside to make a pretend fort. He did not tell me that they made this fort to get away from her. They thought that she was too young to be one of them and they needed privacy. David saw that it was easier to just be suitably penitent and apologize. Mary received a generous payback. Thinking in this way, I could see the tinge of Mary's moral superiority in that long ago encounter with her brother. In this scenario there was a winner and a loser. It also set a pattern that Mary and David did repeat over and over. I know this form of forgiveness is acceptable to many, but unfortunately, in the longer term, I agree with Nussbaum when she says this:

> The forgiveness process is itself a harsh inquisitorial process. It demands confession, weeping and wailing, a sense of one's lowness and essential worthlessness. The penitent is tormented by the penitence. The person who administers the process is controlling and relentless toward the penitent....even if in the end, the forgiveness is given.

Still, I was very familiar with this transactional take on forgiveness. It was largely what I learned from my parents and what I was taught in church. Applying it to myself when my husband announced he was leaving, he had apologized just once. Then, in my mind, there was no attempt at repair, only an attempt to get me to sanction his decision which he seemed to think God had directed. When, after trying and failing to be persuaded by this, I would not agree, I felt called out for being spiritually impaired. I was now the villain. More howls ripped from my soul. He showed no earnest interest in amends or reconciliation.

Transactional forgiveness was clearly not working in my case, and it has no chance at all when one side of the rupture is unwilling to repair. As Ray Penning, vice president of Cardus, a nonpartisan think tank named for the ancient north–south road that connected the people of Roman cities to their major public spaces, put it in *The Hub* newsletter in April 2022, "[I]n Christian theology, the power of repentance sought, and forgiveness granted, is that a relationship is restored." My husband was not interested.

When I applied transactional forgiveness to my situation with the church, I did hope that it would offer a model for reconciliation. However, my church community did not see that it had committed any wrong towards me, but instead saw that I was wronging them by not quietly getting out of the way and making it easier for them to get on with their lives. They wanted to keep my husband as their pastor until, when challenged by some of their members, his resignation became inevitable. This did not yield any opening towards me. Rather they silenced me and stopped any sincere and acceptable form of reconciliation. Again, transactional forgiveness was not effective in repairing the rift between my church and me.

Is there any sort of alternative definition of forgiveness other than transactional forgiveness? While all three monotheistic religions defend transactional forgiveness rigorously and lay out steps for the penitent to be absolved, they also all contain another way to define forgiveness. They all offer a model of unconditional forgiveness.

The most familiar example of this is the account of Jesus dying on the cross where he is purported to have asked God to forgive those who were putting him to death: "Father, forgive them, for they know not what they do." Forgiveness before any penitence. No amends required.

This sort of forgiveness spoke to me. I often thought my husband had no idea of what he was doing. His dreams that he shared with me at the time reinforced my thinking this. Through my interpretative lens, they were dreams of grandiosity and impossibility, dreams of warning and destruction. I often did pray that God would forgive him for not being able to grasp the magnitude of what he was doing. Somehow it helped me to think that this was between God and him. Then my having to forgive was not the issue. God could do the forgiving. Sometimes this helped me but not always.

Applying the idea of unconditional forgiveness to the church situation, perhaps they did offer this to my husband in being willing to keep him as their pastor. However, this meant excluding me.

Aware of such difficulties with even unconditional forgiveness, Nussbaum suggests that unconditional forgiveness might be better replaced with unconditional love.

Still "pacing the cage", I considered this idea.

The quintessential parable that Jesus told about unconditional forgiveness is the Parable of the Prodigal Son. Nussbaum would have us rethink this and see it as a story demonstrating the power of unconditional love. Here is the story in my retelling.

A father has a large estate which he and his two sons run as a business. The younger son is restless and wants to see the world. He asks for his inheritance so he can go off and do this. The father says yes, gives him money and off goes the younger son. The elder son stays home and works.

The younger son has an uproarious and indulgent time. He spends all the money he has. Then there is a famine in the land. His new so-called friends desert him, and the work he can find is less and less seemly for the son of a wealthy landowner. He sinks so low that he is tending pigs on a farm. Before long he finds himself eating the corn husks that he is feeding the pigs. There is no lower position for anyone and particularly for a Jew, forbidden by Jewish law to raise pigs.

We are told that he comes to his senses, determines to go home and confess his errant ways and hopes that he can at least work at some lowly position in his father's business. He knows how transactional forgiveness works and begins the steps to achieve it.

Before his father knows anything of what has happened to his son, he sees him in the distance, turned toward home. Immediately he runs out to meet him, arms outstretched. Before his youngest son can speak a word of confession or otherwise, the father throws his arms around him in love. This father busies himself putting new clothes on his son and ordering the staff to prepare a feast to welcome him home.

When his elder brother hears this news, he is angry. He tells his father that this situation is completely unfair. It is not right to welcome his brother who has behaved so badly. He has not made amends. Such a brother has no place in the family business and family heart. His father is not following the rules of transactional forgiveness. His father tells his eldest son that he too is cherished and then chastises him and exhorts him to be more generous. "Your brother who was dead, is alive again." The elder brother leaves the feast and sulks.

What a story!

Rembrandt, famous Dutch painter of the 1600s, envisioned this story and painted it. His creation, *The Return of the Prodigal Son*, hangs in the Hermitage Museum in St. Petersburg, Russia. It is a canvas eight feet tall by six feet wide, painted in browns, reds and yellows. I came to understand this masterpiece through the eyes of Henri Nouwen, a Dutch Catholic priest who, after an illustrious career teaching at Ivy League universities, worked at L'Arche, a home for the mentally disabled in Richmond Hill, Canada where he was buried in 1996.

On July 26, 1986 at 2:30 p.m. Henri Nouwen was allowed, free of guards, to sit for as long as he wanted before the original painting as it was being restored in a back room at the Hermitage. In 1992, following his reflection on each of the figures in the painting, he published a record of his experience in his book *The Return of the Prodigal Son*.

This book sits on my "pride of place" library shelf reserved for the great books that have changed my life. For decades, it was my desire to go and see the original painting. My trip was booked, the tickets purchased, and I was going there for the fourteen white nights of a never-setting sun during the summer solstice of 2020. The COVID-19 pandemic made this impossible. Now President Putin's behaviour in the world makes St. Petersburg off limits for me. To my immeasurable sorrow, I will surely never see this painting in person.

Nouwen describes "being stunned by its majestic beauty. Its grandeur and beauty made everything recede into background." The reunion of father and son is radiant with light on the left side of the canvas. On the right is the tall elder brother looking on. In the distance are three shadowy figures, two women and one man. They are bystanders, maybe staff in the family business. Rembrandt has given the father his own left hand and a woman's right hand. He wanted us to know the love expressed had both a masculine and a feminine dimension.

In his book, Nouwen reflects on each of the figures, imagining their situation and how they would have felt and thought. On the back cover of the book jacket these words of Nouwen appear:

> I came to see Rembrandt's Prodigal Son as somehow my personal painting...All the Gospel is there. All my life is there. All the lives of my friends is there.

In dream interpretation I often play the role of each of the figures and objects in my dream to decipher the dream's meaning for me. Putting my stamp on Nouwen's idea, I decided to identify with the figures in the painting by inhabiting each of them in my imagination. I pretended to be the father and began to speak words I thought he might be saying as he saw his son far away in the distance.

"I love both my sons. I want my family to be together. I see him coming into view on the horizon. I don't know what is in his heart. I do know he turned towards his home. I see him. I know I must rush to welcome him. It is all I know to do. I am not thinking. I am just compelled to run with open arms towards him. I have to touch him. I grab fresh clothes. I shout orders to find a fat animal and kill it and prepare it for a feast this very night. I am trembling with hope, relief and glee. I run as fast as I have ever run!"

All the light in the painting focused on this embrace, which came before confession and penitence. It came before amends and absolution. It came before knowing what was in the heart of the youngest son who might just be a manipulative fellow who had figured out that food at home was better than in a pig pen. The father's heart vibrated with love. It is possible to hear this story and see this interpretation of Rembrandt's as having little to do with forgiveness and everything to do with generous and unconditional love for a wayward son who, never mind any reasons, has turned towards his father.

When my son David was in his early twenties, he and I had a severe falling out. He did not speak with me for two years. I was devastated. I tried in every way I could to open any doors of reconciliation. My pain was deep and my petitioning prayers endless. Friends counselled me to give up, to let go and move on. Maybe if two of your children have died this is a harder thing to do. I don't know, but I did not do it. I held my heart open, I hoped and I prayed as close to unceasingly as I could manage.

One day I was in the old neighbourhood where we had lived, where he had grown up. I stepped out of a bakery and caught sight of him. Our eyes locked. He walked on. I had not seen him for two years. On automatic pilot I turned in the direction he was walking. My head and heart were racing. When he was half a block further on, he turned and ran towards me and then I towards him. We embraced and I wept. It was just love on a busy thoroughfare in a major city. Whatever was difficult between us evaporated. We have never thoroughly processed what had caused the rift. Perhaps we have allowed each other our different understandings of what happened. Most importantly, while we have agreed and disagreed on other matters, we have never parted in anger since.

When I think about the deep pain when my husband abandoned me, I see that parental love and spousal love are two different things. Unconditional love seems more plausible, possible and redemptive in the parent-child attachment. The parental relationship is, in the best cases, temporary. We always expect and encourage our children to leave home. The very opposite is true of the spousal bond where the hope is that the terminus of the relationship will be death, even though divorce statistics tell a different story. Spousal love determines basics, from financial security to where we live, and it supports our lifework. Spouses are not engaged in the work of leaving each other but in the work of walking with each other as a couple in all the projects of life. The longer the relationship, the more the truth of this increases. It is possible to preserve a sense of self, but as time goes on, withholding a healthy self-preservation is increasingly problematic as being compatible with a deepening love. In the best-case scenario, the spiritual reality of two becoming one does blossom in the relationship.

I don't find the ideas of transactional forgiveness, unconditional forgiveness and unconditional love helpful when I consider my spousal situation of being betrayed and abandoned. This is why I am regularly attracted to the particular blog posts of sometimesmagical who identifies herself as a "bifeminist" woman who draws her inspiration from Paganism, Buddhism and Jesus. Quite frankly, I like her courage and apostasy. When she rants that "the very idea of forgiveness…is basically bullshit" I find I resonate and giggle a little with relief. Harriet Lerner, a most respected voice in the psychology of women, says it more respectably: "I told Katrina that she didn't need to forgive the unconscionable actions of her ex in order to free herself from the suffering he'd caused her."

For me the response to deep betrayal of the spousal covenant is not forgiveness in any of its definitions but rather loss and grief. The right to mourn, I believe, must be cherished as the way to a wholesome future. It is the way I chose.

Chapter 14

FORGIVENESS:
VIEWED THROUGH THE LENS
OF PSYCHOTHERAPY

Maybe the word forgive points in the wrong direction, since it's something you mostly give yourself, not anyone else: you put down the ugly weight of old suffering, untie yourself from the awful, and walk away from it.

— Rebecca Solnit, *The Faraway Nearby*

Forgiveness is a choice, and you are worthy no matter which choice you make.

— Harriet Lerner

Having considered the meanings of forgiveness as espoused by the monotheistic religions, I want to consider how my chosen field of psychotherapy views forgiveness. Certainly, it must address forgiveness as viewed by its clientele, which is often steeped in religious understandings. As a therapist who largely saw clients where infidelity was the presenting issue, the matter of forgiveness was ever present. I have seen client couples who wish to repair after betrayal be overcommitted to transactional forgiveness. In these cases, it is common that the betrayed person wants to have apologies repeated more frequently than their partners want to give them. Repetition of the apology is required and necessary for the repair, but I have seen the drive for amends last years too long. The drive for moral superiority that Nussbaum identifies shows up and the desire for there to be a winner and loser is strong. American family therapist Terry Real, founder of Relational Life Therapy (RLT), famously reminds us, "You can be right or you can be married."

I have also seen unconditional forgiveness, perhaps driven by a person's theology, offered far too soon. Without the anger and pain addressed and underlying reasons recovered, the betrayal festers underground, issuing in angry outbursts that arrest healing.

My field of psychotherapy defines forgiveness in multiple ways unique to each leader in the field. In addition, famous figures with a psychological interest jump in with their definitions. The number of definitions is exhausting.

Oprah offers this take: "True forgiveness is when you can say, 'Thank you for that experience.'"

In the film *A Beautiful Day in the Neighborhood*, Tom Hanks, playing Mister Rogers, host of the 1968–2001 children's TV series *Mister Rogers' Neighborhood*, offers this: "Do you know what it means, to forgive? It is a decision we make to release a person from the feelings of anger we have at them."

Brené Brown, previously a social worker and research professor at the University of Houston, Texas, and now famous podcaster and beloved author, puts it this way:

> Forgiveness says you are given another chance to make a new beginning. There is no love without forgiveness, and there is no forgiveness without love. Forgiveness is the fragrance that the violet sheds on the heel that has crushed it. To forgive is to set a prisoner free and discover that the prisoner was you.

Dr. Terry Hargrave, well known as the founder of Restoration Therapy, which combines attachment theory, emotional regulation and mindfulness to promote significant change and healing, states:

Forgiveness is accomplished when the victimized person no longer has to hold the wrongdoer responsible for the injustice; the wrongdoer holds himself or herself responsible.

In cases where restoration is possible, Hargrave outlines the steps that may be taken to facilitate a shift from victim to victor in the relationship.

However, he directly speaks to my situation when he says:

Whether or not a relationship cannot be reclaimed, there are pieces that can be salvaged from it and used…to protect, to prevent, to forewarn, to move on.

I do have ears for this idea. In my case of abandonment by my husband it makes sense to me. I know I need to be protecting and preventing and forewarning myself in order to move on. I think Hargrave is also implying in his definition of forgiveness that there are situations like mine where forgiveness is not what is required of me. Rather, forgiveness of self is the task for the perpetrator who must hold themselves accountable for the injustice they have inflicted.

Myisha Cherry, in her 2023 book *Failures of Forgiveness: What We Get Wrong and How to Do Better*, defends my withholding of forgiveness as an act of moral courage.

More often when forgiveness is raised in the psychotherapeutic field, the emphasis shifts to the relationship of the person with themselves, not with God or with the other person, but with themselves. The theory is that the anger and resentment a person may have toward the offender(s) is having no effect save to further embitter the offended party. Forgiving the self becomes defined as letting this anger go, resisting the desire to dwell on it and in so doing, to feel better. It is thought to help the person focus on the future with positive energy. I have read it plainly put this way: "[F]orgiveness is my safety valve against the kind of toxic anger that could kill me."

I have certainly seen single clients who came to me embittered by their betrayal. However, I do think their appropriate anger needs to be witnessed and understood. As Swiss-American psychiatrist Elisabeth Kübler-Ross defines it, anger is a legitimate step in the grieving process. Women often need encouragement to feel anger of any kind. My angel Anne, the spiritual director who reckoned eight years was how long it took to recover from grief, was my mentor in this endeavour.

At the same time, it is important to not become arrested and stuck in those feelings of anger. The future must become appealing enough to help a person, if only tentatively, explore it and hopefully ultimately embrace it. In this process, surely love and generosity towards the self is a more useful concept than forgiveness in any of its meanings.

Loving myself with exuberance means for me, as Hargraves suggests, protecting myself and keeping myself safe. I was careful not to expose myself to news about my husband and came to see him only when necessary, accompanied by my lawyer and in a safe space. I cleared what was now my home of reminders of his presence as best I could. I shut down films about betrayal for many years. I was relieved and felt safer when he and his new partner moved far away and no longer lived but a kilometre away from me, our former home, and now my neighbourhood.

Quite recently I was introduced to a new definition of evil by Philip Clayton, an American philosopher of religion and science and professor at the Claremont School of Theology. I was listening to a lecture he was giving on a course I was taking online. He offered that "evil is the choice we make when we disconnect."

I find this a fascinating idea in a world where loneliness is increasing. As 2023 came to an end, Senator Chris Murphy championed the cause of what he called an "epidemic of loneliness". In an interview on CNN he said, "Twenty years ago, 3% of Americans reported having no friends. Now 12% of Americans say they have not a single friend."

I find myself thinking about choosing to connect with people and with causes, and how often I fail to do so. I want to forgive myself for this. Forgiving myself for this makes sense to me. I also hope that my Creator will forgive me as well and be patient with me as I try to do better.

When I consider love and generosity as a deconstruction of the meaning of forgiveness and turn my thoughts to the church and its betrayal of me, I am counselled by this recent experience.

In my twenties, I had made a significant contribution to the church by being ordained during a firestorm of opposition. Much of the church did not want women of childbearing age, married and therefore not celibate, to be in the pulpit. In the final hours of debate, the courts of the church that decided matters of ordination voted in my favour, and I was ordained a few hours later. My ordination set a precedent and as a result the archives wanted my history. Their request came some eight years after my husband had ended our marriage, and my church had silenced me. I agreed to being interviewed and to having the story of my ordination recorded for historical purposes.

Two years after the initial recording, the archivist emailed me. He is someone I like and respect. He asked to send me the transcript, wanting my approval because he wanted to publish it as part of a celebration of International Women's Day 2022. I received the transcript and found a whole section redacted. It was the section that documented the church's decision to silence me. I was angry and while I understood the legal reasons for the redactions, they did not sit well with me. I think my anger was a good thing and that it was important for me to cherish what I would call a holy rage. I reported my dismay to the archivist. It felt right, if hopeless, to do so.

After he had heard my anger, the church archivist removed his redactions to my story. I thanked him for his graciousness, and he replied in writing:

> If anyone is gracious, it's you…bearing with my over-concern for legal requirements and avoiding consequences to myself. I regret that I caused any distress or further harm to you. You've already been through a ridiculous amount of that. Thank you for your honest expression of anger.
>
> The most important thing is for your voice to be heard. It's the reason for this oral history program in the first place! And, of all people, I will not be the next person who stifles your voice and your truth.

Amazing love and generosity flowed over me from an official in the national leadership in my church. My pain was eased. A door opened a crack. Many Christians from across the country took a moment to send an email of thanksgiving for what I had done. I was surprised by grace. My protective care of myself in church matters softened just a little. I was trusting the archives of my institutional church to hold one of my stories. The whole issue of forgiveness and what it means for my personal relationship to my denomination was, for just a moment, replaced by the concept of unconditional love and generosity.

Chapter 15

FORGIVENESS: VIEWED THROUGH THE LENS OF SOCIOLOGY

Forgiveness is less about absolving those who have harmed us, and more about drawing their poison from our own souls. It is an act of radical defiance of the hatred proffered by injustice. Like mercy, forgiveness is the prerogative of the strong.

— Akaash Maharaj

In a world marked by colonial and racialized violence, just as with the practise of evangelism, we simply can no longer take the meaning and expression of forgiveness for granted. An uncritical account of forgiveness is no longer morally responsible.

— William T. Barnett,
The Christian Century, March 2024

Beyond my enquiry into the meaning of forgiveness for my personal betrayals, I was curious about the role that forgiveness plays in the public arena. Is it possible that love and generosity may also be more effective than forgiveness on the national stage where my country seeks reconciliation with Indigenous peoples?

As mentioned, in 2008, Canada adopted a plan for a Truth and Reconciliation Commission based on the work of South Africans Nelson Mandela and Archbishop Desmond Tutu. Our government set up our own Truth and Reconciliation Commission (TRC) to inform all Canadians about what happened in our residential schools from the 1870s to 1996 and to report on its findings to the Canadian federal government. This report was issued in 2015. Peter, my spiritual companion, was also an advisor to a commissioner, and he opened my eyes to the work of reconciliation that was and still is facing our country.

As Canadians, we were encouraged to attend one of the seven hearings created by our TRC and held across the country. We non-Indigenous people, the colonisers, were invited to attend as the perpetrators. Indigenous people came as the victims of crimes committed in the residential school system, run by the churches on behalf of the federal government, that was set up to assimilate Indigenous children into white Canada. Children were taken from their homes at the age of six and sent to schools far away from their parents where they were routinely robbed of their culture and their language, sexually abused, malnourished, beaten and in some cases driven to suicide. Only in 2021 did we begin to discover how many died and were buried on the premises of these schools. Their bodies were never returned to their parents. This abhorrent system shames all white Canadians. We are trying to find ways to heal.

I felt compelled to attend one of these hearings which Indigenous peoples quickly renamed healing circles. In 2008, five years before I was abandoned, I attended the first circle in Winnipeg, Canada, on the traditional and unceded territory of the Ojibway, Cree, Dene and Dakota peoples. It was also the birthplace of the Métis Nation.

It was a brilliant, sunny prairie day. I went alone. It was the first healing circle and I could not find friends who felt as compelled as I did to attend. In Canada, there is a long history of prejudice. Indigenous people have been labeled a dirty drunken nuisance for too long. As a white person, I would be rightly seen as a perpetrator of such labels and I was nervous to attend. Since this was the first circle, not so many whites, except for the white dignitaries, showed up.

I walked into a sea of festive Indigenous culture celebrating in every possible way. Our Governor General was attending, and it was amazingly appropriate because she, Michaëlle Jean, was a Black woman and Haitian Canadian. The Indigenous chiefs and their families were in full regalia. Men in white buckskin jackets, delicately embroidered with beaded roses and appliqued with birds, women in fringed leather skirts and fur-trimmed beaded moccasins, elaborate headdresses, eagle feathers and ermine tails, braids intertwined with ribbons and beads, the smell of sage and burning sweetgrass, teepees, drumming circles, fresh bannock and smoked salmon, faces shining, children playing, regular Indigenous families in smart casual clothing all celebrating with each other. I was overwhelmed, hardly know-ing where to look next. On the vast green lawns running down to the fork of the Red and Assiniboine Rivers where Winnipeg now sits was a people coming together on what was once their land with pride.

Around the edges of the property were many tents. I called them the tents of the perpetrators. My church denomination had a tent as it had run ten per cent of these schools. I was comforted a little by the knowledge that my church had been one of the first to officially apologize. Other church denominations had their tents. Each tent was filled with archival material, including never-before-seen photos and objects ranging from desks and slates to pieces of clothing.

"That is your grandfather," one young man pointed out to his children in a photo. "This is why we are here, to show our respect."

I heard variations of this declaration many times.

"There I am and there is my sister, right there beside me," someone would say, and the person would get so very close, nose to nose with the protected photo. Tears were flowing in the tents. There were counsellors everywhere to help with the pain that was in direct contrast to the joy outside. The flow of people was circular: in to pain and out to joy, back and forth all day.

Some of the tents were home to healing circles. Inside, victims were telling their stories while the listeners sat encircling the speaker. I knew, as a coloniser, the TRC wanted me to go into one of these tents and sit there and listen. I wished I had a friend with me. I hung tentatively around the edges. The speeches were long and the moments to enter between stories seemed brief. I had to slip in and how long would I have to stay? I summoned the courage and found a seat in a circle.

I don't remember exact words. I remember an old man, his body no longer straight, talking very slowly. There was an empathic hum in the circle that rose and fell with his words. Hands and arms reached out to touch him, encouraging him to keep sharing. His eyes got wet in the corners, the people beside me wept. I felt like an intruder. Should I be there? What would I have done if my children had been taken from me when they were six years old and sent far away? He had been such a child, crying himself to sleep night after night and then, in the morning, he was strapped for the tears. I know the story did not stop there. It is convenient for me not to remember all of it. He was so vulnerable and brave, sitting there telling his story of abuse.

I made myself stay for another person who was speaking as a child of residential school parents. She spoke of the poverty and alcohol abuse as her parents tried to forget all the damage done to them. I rose to slip away and was touched just as the victims had been: kindly. Indigenous folk whispered softly in my ears their thanks that I had come. It was humbling.

I wanted to hear what our Governor General was saying. I remember her words: "What we are doing here today is about a refoundation of this country. And it comes from confronting history together. It's not about victims and oppressors. It's about what we can achieve together."

It pointed me toward the future, just like Nussbaum's clear point in her discussion of anger and forgiveness. She states, "[T]ransactional forgiveness gives us no reason to pave the way toward a constructive future." After the governor general's speech, I followed a young family off the grounds as I made my way to my car. I overheard the conversation.

The dad had an idea. "Let's take the kids to the hotel for a late lunch." His family pulled back.

His wife reminded him, "We are not really welcome in so fancy a place. I think it is too much."

"No," he said, "today it is right, and we are going to try."

I changed course and followed them to the very posh hotel Inn at the Forks. I watched until I saw through the windows that they had found a table. Then I noticed that they were not alone, and the restaurant was full of Indigenous families. I wondered if this was the first time in history that this was so. The management of that hotel was acting generously and lovingly. New ways of being were established right then and there.

The TRC ended in 2015 with a report naming ninety-four actions to be taken by the federal government in the direction of healing. The actions are grouped in two categories. The first category has to do with legacy: we must educate all Canadians about the history of Indigenous peoples. This is happening in many ways. The National Centre for Truth and Reconciliation opened its doors in 2015 in Winnipeg and holds all relevant archives. A national inquiry into the many murdered and missing Métis, First Nations and Inuit girls and women has been conducted and its final report, Reclaiming Power and Place, was released in 2021. Federal acknowledgement of Indigenous language rights has been achieved. The University of British Columbia, situated in my home city of Vancouver, has a programme, CEDAR, which stands for Cross-cultural Education through Demonstration, Activity and Recreation. The aim of CEDAR has been to provide fun learning opportunities in a culturally relevant context that help Indigenous youth to develop a comfortable relationship with the UBC campus, faculty and the UBC Indigenous community. CEDAR has just opened a laboratory for the preservation of thirty languages and sixty dialects.

The second category in the TRC report focuses on activities that are future-oriented with a theme of reconciliation. My denomination rejected the Doctrine of Discovery in 2012 before the report was released. This is a principle in public international law under which, when a nation "discovers" land, it directly acquires rights on that land. In 2022, other church denominations had not rejected this doctrine nor had the federal government of Canada. It was hoped that Pope Francis would do this in his 2022 visit to Canada, but while he apologized, he did not reject this Doctrine of Discovery.

As with the TRC in South Africa, these acts of legacy and reconciliation remain a work in progress in Canada. Fourteen of the ninety-four actions have been completed and many of them are in process. In 2023, we still cannot provide clean drinking water to thirty-two Indigenous communities in a land overflowing with water. It is long slow work requiring the enormous financial support of the federal government and much love and generosity from Indigenous, Métis, Inuit and white people for one another.

As I walked to my car that day, I thought that although Archbishop Desmond Tutu used traditional meanings of forgiveness, Mandela had made a different choice. He focused on love and generosity and the future. Yet, they had worked together.

Did I experience forgiveness for my participation in colonising history that day? The Dalai Lama and Tutu, in their conversation about forgiveness with each other, came to agree on this: "Forgiveness for all its difficulty and hard work, is just the right thing to do to live a joyful life."

They underline that forgiveness is a choice. I do acknowledge that on that day, I truly felt more joyful. Now, years later, my husband and church gone, what do I do? If I had a TRC to go to that would address my hurt and the hurt of others like me, I would attend. Vikki Stark, author of *Runaway Husbands* and coiner of the term "wife abandonment syndrome", offers a variation of this in her Jump Up retreats for abandoned women. It was in conversation with her that I met Els, an abandoned woman like myself, and our friendship has often lifted both of us into joyful spaces.

Forgiveness is not the word I choose in relation to my own circumstances, but I will always remember the soft touch of the Indigenous hands on my shoulder recognizing that I had come and that I had listened. I will remember the hotel restaurant tables full of Indigenous people taking their place with pride and joy. I will remember and give thanks for the unconditional love and generosity I witnessed everywhere that day. I know that Vikki Stark enables abandoned women to tell their stories and be kindly touched by each other so that healing and joy are released.

I don't do well when I push myself to find a definitive meaning for forgiveness and then comply with it. I acknowledge that, for many people, the definition they choose works and heals. I am coming to accept that, for me, forgiveness must be understood differently or even superseded by the generous and unconditional love of the father for his prodigal son, Mandela for his beloved South Africa and myself for myself and others. I have come to see that I do best when I fully enter and grieve my hurt. Pain over the loss rises and grabs my attention as it will forever. I say hello and goodbye to this pain, knowing it will come round again and again. Mourning is a way of life for me. So is Blake's invitation that "He who kisses the joy as it flies, Lives in eternity's sunrise".

As I sat in the red leather chair by the television in my house and watched the 2022 Australian Open, just as my husband and I would have done together, I wanted to chat with him about Djokovic and get his thoughts on the uproar over vaccines. I remembered the intimacy of those moments. Then loss flooded me. I paused and acknowledged this even as I remembered the depth of our friendship. Then I called a good trustworthy friend who was as interested in the game of tennis as I was. I acknowledge and I move on, over and over.

As I do this sober work, giving myself the right to mourn, I am deeply surprised by both the love and generosity arising within me for who I am as well as the love coming towards me in abundance from magnanimous and unexpected sources. Joy erupts. Then I am strengthened to take on tomorrow and welcome the grace that it will surely bring. This is what I can authentically offer myself, my friends, my church and my clients.

I think that Amanda Gorman, the vibrant young American poet, caught it in her poem "New Day's Lyric", a take on Auld Lang Syne, as she called us into the new year, 2022.

> Come, look up with kindness yet,
> For even solace can be sourced from sorrow.
> We remember, not just for the sake of yesterday,
> But to take on tomorrow.

Chapter 16

THE MULTITUDE OF THE HEAVENLY HOST: ANGELS COMMISSIONED TO BE FRIENDS

I swiftly realised how grief sorts out and realigns those around the griefstruck; how friends are tested; how some pass, some fail. Old friendships may deepen through shared sorrow, or suddenly appear lightweight.

— Julian Barnes, *Levels of Life*

[T]hree of the most common and dramatic friendship disruptors: moving, divorce, and death. Though only the last is irremediable.

— Jennifer Senior,
"It's Your Friends Who Break Your Heart"

A faithful friend is a sure shelter,
Whoever finds one has found a rare treasure.
A faithful friend is beyond price,
And there is no measuring her worth
A faithful friend is the elixir of life.

Ecclesiastes 6:14–16

Parish ministers make transitory friends. Up until the 1990s in my country and my denomination, a parish received a new minister every seven years to give the congregation the benefit of a new face. People stayed put over generations, and in the rural areas, many still do. There is a mantra in my field repeated over and over: "Ministers come, ministers go."

As adjunct faculty at a Canadian university in the 1980s, I was assigned a graduate student to supervise. He was writing his thesis on loneliness in the pastorate.

"Look, Ann," he said, "it is damned lonely in the parish. Yes, people are friendly, and my family is friendly back, but we all know there is an expiry date. We won't raise our kids together, take trips together, or grow old together. They will join with me and my family and then when we leave, they will join with the new minister. If they attach too much to me, they will not make the join with my replacement."

He had a point. In his thesis he explored this phenomenon both analytically and experientially. These conditions for loneliness start at the beginning of ministry and continue until retirement.

Until 2010, graduating ministers in my denomination, also called ordinands, were sent out to far-flung ministries to experience rural service and to serve hard-to-fill parishes. Few stayed more than the required three years. If you went on these assignments as a single person, it was extremely isolating. This was a powerful incentive to get married before being posted.

Back in the 1960s, when I was training to be a minister, my seminary was next door to a training centre for deaconesses. Those women received lots of proposals in the spring each year. When women entered ministry as I had done, there was no road map. If eligible men went to their placements, they were presented with every marriageable woman in the area. Women ordinands, by contrast, were a new thing and perplexing for the communities. Who would want to be the minister's husband? Isn't it easier to be the first lady than the first gentleman?

No pastor wants to be in a parish as single person. Making lasting friends in the parish is extremely difficult, even for couples. Children of clergy have the same problem. Loneliness is built in. I spent most of my adult life married to a minister. I made friends in congregations, knowing full well I would one day be the friend to leave. Then, when my husband and church abandoned me, I discovered that I was almost friendless in the city where I lived. Anita was the most glowing exception and, in the early days of my abandonment, she was more caregiver than friend. I did have one old friend from my college days, a niece close to me in age and three other friends that I had kept in my orbit. None lived in my city. Mine was a circle of five long-distance friends.

My husband was my BFF (best friend forever) until he abdicated. With him, I had experienced a third dimension in our connection. Together we were more than two and I miss those many moments where we created something beyond us. Once, on a road trip, while driving to our next golf destination, we reflected on the game we had played the day before and how no pesticides were used on the course. Spontaneously we began to riff on a possible book we could create. It was a long drive, and the energy flew between us. We came up with chapters headings such as "Golf and Climate Change?" and "Playing Golf as a 'We'". Before long we had a whole book in our heads and a title, *The Spirituality of Golf*. Creating together is a precious quality of friendship. I was bereft without it.

I loved to travel and over the years of our marriage I had taught my husband the joys of all sorts of travel. The trips we made multiplied, and I anticipated and enjoyed them all. I particularly hold close the experiences they brought: dinner in Egypt by the Red Sea, walking Juno Beach in Normandy, washing our feet on a boat on the Sea of Galilee, playing golf at Kauri Cliffs in New Zealand, a barbeque at New Year's under the Southern Cross on a New Zealand beach and, on many trips, just reading and walking on the world's most fabulous beaches. Travel encouraged and developed our friendship. It gave us time out to just be with each other.

I was introduced to the travel option very early in my childhood. Dad was home from work for lunch as always.

"Ann, it is the 12:09 p.m. arriving from Detroit. It is loaded with new cars. Come see!" my dad called from the porch. "It is off to the East and will leave a load here before it goes. Come, watch."

I learned the places the trains were going. Some would go to New York City! Many days, taking my hand in his, he would walk me through our back garden gate and into the rail yards to say hello to the engine firemen. I remember the feel of the steam and the sound of the whistle. My dad was teaching me the excitement of taking a journey.

Only one of my siblings stayed in our hometown. The other three of us have lived and travelled the world. Travel was central in the rhythm of the friendship I shared with my husband. I never imagined travelling alone. I never imagined making friendships as a single person, either.

After he left me, I had to begin the process of learning how to be a friend as a single person. As a couple, I could lean on the popularity and entertainment value of my husband. He was a good cook. He had been a waiter in his youth and could serve food ever so calmly. He played guitar and sang and loved to play to an audience at the end of an evening. He easily held his own in a conversation. I enjoyed lifting him up and celebrating his talents. Even in this, I thought I held my own. I thought we were a coveted couple that others enjoyed. Now I was on my own. What did I bring to a friend but my own griefstruck state? Who would want to be there for me? Would anyone ever be my travelling companion? Would our friends not rather be with him in his lovestruck state? Would some of our friends try to find a way to be there for each of us? Could I accept this? After thirty years, we held the friends we had in common and all of them were members of our church community.

I made a lot of mistakes. For a while, I thought I could be friends with those who chose to also be his friend. Shortly after I returned alone to our home in Vancouver and he was with her, I was with a mutual friend. As we walked, she told me, "It is hard for me to find a way to be with you both. He is so blissful and full of love. His face is flushed with joy and yours is red and blotchy with tears. I love you both. I am so caught between you."

As I heard those words, all I saw was his face in my mind. I saw this same face that always flushed when we made love. I simply wanted to throw up. I could barely breathe. Without thinking I reacted, "You know he never liked your husband. He thought you could have done better."

I struck out in anger. I would take it back if I could. I liked this woman and her husband very much. I was not fit for interacting with our old close friends. They triggered me and I could not yet control myself.

In her desperation to help me, another friend said, "You know him and you know he never changes his mind. You have to move on. He won't ever try to repair this."

I reacted with defensiveness and began to accumulate examples of all the times he had changed his mind. But I somehow knew that he had told her that this was the case and suggested she say it to me.

I was not able to bear that they now knew him better than I did. For a few brief months, while on sabbatical but connected to our church, he was still their pastor. He met with most of them as they were members of the board of our church. He told his version of what happened. This is what they knew. I had had only one opportunity to tell my story at the very beginning to a very small group.

It was my physician who gave me permission to no longer expect myself to stay friends with those who wanted to be with us both. I could not keep myself safe when I tried to keep up my friendship with them, nor could I keep them safe. Good people that I treasured were lost to me. There was so much cost.

Even the person in my city with whom I felt most bonded could not handle the depth of my grief. She and her husband were members of our church and great supporters. She let me go. I miss her still and expect I always will. For years, at the crack of dawn, we swam and then showered together three times a week, which is an intimacy known only to swimmers. I loved the way our energies sparked life between us, which radiated out for others to see. We travelled as couples and shared gourmet meals. I thought ours would be a friendship that survived the boundaries set by having first met in the pastorate.

Social media made the friend-making process difficult. When I went on Facebook, I was met, as we all are, with invitations to be friends with a person. These might be invites from people I knew or people who were just trolling to be on someone's friend list. Facebook itself also recommends people that you know as possible friends for you to confirm. I hated the constant Facebook messages that asked me if I wanted to be "her" friend or "his". As a result, I rarely visited Facebook and to this day I keep it only as a business tool. Social media never forgets and nine years later I still get these invitations. It also tells me who among my friends continue to be his Facebook friends, knowledge that still troubles me.

I had to dig deep. What did I know about friendships that were not with my husband or with members of the parish that would come to an end? Very little. My mom had three close friends. They had been to kindergarten together and lived their whole lives in the same city. I called them all aunties. They helped each other blow out the candles on their eighty-fifth birthday cakes. I learned from my mother that if you had friends, you made them young and you were loyal. I suspect that era has passed. After high school, in an emerging 1960s era of radical absolute freedoms, I went adventuring. Over time, my friends from that time drifted away just as I did. Some went into nursing, some to university and some to marriage. Some stayed and most left. Occasionally we saw each other at a high school reunion, if we attended. Yet my mother's lifelong commitment to her friends remains in my heart. I think it helped me know the importance of friends and to nurture the five long-distance friends I had.

My dad was a runner in Vimy Ridge during the First World War in France, and his closest friend was gassed in the Second Battle of Ypres. They both survived and it bonded them for life. When these two men came home, my dad married my mom and his friend married one of her kindergarten friends. The two families lived their lives ten doors apart. Friendship is rarely like that anymore. I had certainly disconnected from the city where I was born, the people of my childhood and also the families where together we had raised our children. I learned from my father that it is good to make friends in adversity. It was my best hope for my bereft self.

Spiritually, I grew up in a home where I learned that Jesus was my friend. The old hymns are still there: "What a friend we have in Jesus, ...what a privilege to carry everything to God in Prayer."

Another was "I come to the garden alone... And He walks with me, and He talks with me and He tells me I am His own."

Later when I grew more theologically sophisticated, I thought a great deal about the reading in John's Gospel where Jesus was doing a lot of teaching as he and disciples shared their last meal together on Maundy Thursday of the week preceding his death. He said to them, "I no longer call you servants, but I call you friends. I tell you everything. I don't keep any secrets from you."

With these words he lifted us, his followers, to the status of friend. We are raised into mutuality with the divine. I am drawn to this understanding of Christianity. Thus, my faith underlined the importance of friends. My practice in marriage and family therapy also elevated the place of friendship in emotional well-being for me. As a parent, it was easy to identify the developmental stage that is marked by the absolute glee of a three-year-old finding a first friend.

"Mommy, Ginny is my friend. Can I have her for lunch? We love each other," a glowing Mary told me one Saturday morning.

She went on to become the street friendship queen. From sand play to sleepovers to college chums, to this day she has kept her friends close, though they live all over the world. I expect this has generational roots that go back to her maternal grandmother.

Among my female clients I saw the strong bonds they had with their women friends. They talked out their joys and pains. In the 1960s, it was in such conversations that feminism took root and flourished. I learned that men, by contrast, had male mates with whom they did things: played sports, shared hobbies and built dens, boats and cottages. Or they had the memory of mates that they had done such things with in the past. If they ever needed them, they held the belief that they would show up for one another. John Gray articulated the problems this created in heterosexual relationships in his popular 1992 book *Men Are from Mars, Women Are from Venus*.

I learned that single women had a circle of friends that were like family to them. New research is telling us we need to take these bonds as seriously as we take romantic commitments. As Jennifer Senior, senior staff writer at the Atlantic, suggests in an article entitled "It's Your Friends Who Break Your Heart": "[W]e may find ourselves rethinking whether our spouses and children are the only ones who deserve our binding commitments."

I have experienced just this as two friends reached out to me for counselling to heal the threatening break in their relationship. I have also noticed that the number of single men in my practice is growing as they are struggling to find male friends and long for emotional connection.

This business of making and sustaining friends is a lifelong task begun when we are young. It is not surprising that children often lead their families to grow strong bonds with other families.

Recently, a client told me of an Easter weekend experience.

"We went to an event that the school parents just organised. It was at a farm not far from the city where we live. One outgoing parent thought it would be good for us to go away together to try to mend the arguments we were having about how to support the Ukrainian people during this terrible war."

Apparently one of the children's parents of Ukrainian descent wanted to organise a bake sale to gather money for Ukraine. However, several other students were from refugee families from Syria and Yemen. "Why Ukraine and not us?" was fiercely debated.

The children drew these families from such diverse backgrounds together. My client, a Peruvian father, was amazed to find himself in a strong hug with a Chinese man as this event came to an end. Easter indeed.

But as an older person, what was I to do? When families fall apart for whatever reason, friendship is challenged, as I was now experiencing for myself. I think my pain and my need for relationships forced me to stand before my oldest and long-distance friends in all my vulnerability. I am sure I was grief personified. I don't understand exactly how but I felt driven to reach out. Sometimes I would pull the covers over my head and weep, only to be kicked out of bed by some force I think of as "holy". I simply knew I was not safe alone. I needed friends. I reached out to the original five, hoping that our friendship would deepen in my sorrow.

The Group of Five: Long-Distance and Long-Serving Angels

Gail and I met in graduate school. She was in social work, and I was in theology. She was rich and privileged, and I was poor and into survival. She lived on a golf course with her parents and her father drove her to university every day on his way to his office. I lived across the street in a house where I took care of the cats to pay for a roof over my head while the family who owned the house and the cats were abroad. I was not a cat person, but I was desperate.

One day early in the fall semester, Gail and her dad saw me waiting for the bus, picked me up and Gail and I became unlikely friends. Sixty years ago.

During one of my graduate years, I studied abroad at the University of St Andrews and Gail came to join me in the summer semester. We were going to do the obligatory tour of Europe on $5 a day. I convinced her to do it on my budget, which entailed buying a much-used Lambretta scooter, staying in hostels and four changes of clothing fitting in a single panier, one each, hanging over the back tire. I taped "YUKON" in large letters on the back fender lest anyone mistake us for Americans.

We started with Ireland, green glossy and wet.

"Ann, it has rained all day for six days. I can't drive the scooter because I am too short to manage it. I can't see a thing riding behind you. I don't want to kiss the Blarney Stone. I want to go home."

I don't quit easily and we had just started out. I thought the sun would shine tomorrow and she knew it would rain. We are still like this.

"Let's head to Oxford. We have a friend there who has warm digs. He will help us sort this out," I said, hoping to give her time to reconsider.

Warm and dry was the right note to sound and she agreed. Dry socks and the chance to go home and give up on the trip was just a day or two away. She was now game.

Six days later, having kissed the Blarney Stone and now sitting in a cozy student pub in Oxford drinking beer with our friend, we got to the task of sorting out if we could really travel and how. I had to yield on the budget and spend more money and she had to relax with the days when we travelled under $5 a day. Her dad helped. He arranged for us to have a few days in Paris, his style. We both had to be flexible. We agreed and got on with it.

The apartment in Paris was across the street from where former French president Charles de Gaulle still lived. The digs and the location were swanky even for Gail. We parked the scooter and received a chauffeur to show us Paris, compliments of her father. We each had one dress; mine was a Black Watch tartan dimity cotton frock that I handcrafted and designed. I wore it to my first and only Michelin-starred restaurant for dinner. Suitable dates had been found for us: two delightful, kind Frenchmen.

"Les escargots, Mademoiselle?"

"Oui," I said enthusiastically to the waiter, not knowing I was about to eat snails for the first time.

The sommelier offered wines and Gail made the choices. Drinking was a very new thing for me. Fine wine was way out of my league but not hers.

Chef George came to our table and had his picture taken with us. We drank too much. Gail's father was more important than even she knew. It remains one of my top ten best dining experiences in my lifetime.

In Italy, her blond curls flying out from her helmet and both of us in skimpy shorts, we attracted our own paparazzi. She was horrified and I was thrilled. I drove too fast over a railway track, the wheels slid, and I went head over the windshield, and she got thrown. We were both fine. She said "enough", and I agreed. We were as opposite as could be, but we were friends and it mattered.

I wanted to go to Yugoslavia and Berlin in August of 1961, and she wanted to go to Salzburg and home. We agreed to part, friends forever. I asked her to take risks and she asked me to settle. We are a good complement.

Now she lives on an island a ferry ride away. Both of us lost our husbands, she many years before I did. I helped her then and when my husband left me, we committed to see each other quarterly for week-long outings. We still abide by that agreement carefully honed in that Oxford pub, in the summer of 1961: one week her style, one mine.

We love watching tennis. She cheers for Federer and I can't take my eyes off Nadal. We talk politics, where strangely she leans further left than I do. We play golf where she hits the ball short distances very straight and putts with razor-sharp accuracy. I want to belt the ball 175 yards off the tee and my short game is a disaster. As a result, we have the same handicap.

Our friendship continues to deepen as we live into in our ninth decade. Our friends debate choosing MAiD (medical assistance in dying) and some have. More of her friends have died than mine. We chat weekly and during tennis slams, daily. We truly stand up for each other. Sixty years and counting.

Anne walks with my soul. I met her in 1980 when she was becoming a chaplain and I was the director of training at an institute that trains pastoral counsellors and psychotherapists. She came to do a unit of training with me, and I was her supervisor. As women struggling to be taken seriously by our denomination, we experienced a natural attraction and after my supervisory role in her life was over, we eventually became friends. She married a man with the same name as my husband. We were a duplicate couple, as it were. We always knew which one of us was the Ann with and without the "e". The four of us were friends for years. Though in time we lived in different cities, we visited each other and stayed in touch long before cell phones and email were a reality. We shared and still share many similar theological interests.

Eventually Anne focused her ministry on being a spiritual companion. When my husband left me, she brought all this energy and insight to my most distressed self. Most weeks we had long telephone conversations during which I wept a great deal. She was the one who encouraged me to take my time and grieve for as long as it took.

"I am just furious with your husband. If my husband were to do this, either I or my daughter would murder him," she exclaimed.

I remember her stunning me with this unabashed rage. It was so immediate and forced me to acknowledge that my own rage must be blocked. To help me, Anne sent me the following poem "You Who Wronged" by the Polish writer Czesław Miłosz. So strongly did this poem resonate with me that I knew my friend had found a way to make me acknowledge my rage. She was pushing me, as good friends do, to see myself at a deeper level. When she sent the poem she changed the word from man to woman in the first line.

"You who wronged a simple man
Bursting into laughter at the crime,
And kept a pack of fools around you
To mix good and evil, to blur the line,

Though everyone bowed down before you,
Saying virtue and wisdom lit your way,
Striking gold medals in your honor,
Glad to have survived another day,

Do not feel safe. The poet remembers.
You can kill one, but another is born.
The words are written down, the deed, the date.

And you'd have done better with a winter dawn,
A rope, and a branch bowed beneath your weight."

I knew I had this feeling inside me. I thought about how much easier my life would be if my husband had killed himself. More often, unfortunately, I wished he had killed me. But this poem did help me turn my anger outward. It fueled my enthusiasm for retributive justice. I had this person inside me, the person that hoped my husband and his therapist could not walk off into their future as though they had not ripped the heart out of me. I wanted my pain to matter. The darkness of revenge found expression in me. I confess I imagined sticking needles into her womb so that it would be forever barren.

When I heard my husband was applying to be the pastor of the church in our happy holiday place that I had taken him to early in our relationship, I was outraged at his insensitivity. When this church refused to hire him, I began to sit on the lawn of the church when I visited the seaside town where it was located. I sat there and prayed my heartfelt thanksgiving for the wisdom of the good folk that had rejected his application. I still do this one. I will always be grateful I did not have to reclaim this blessed place of long beaches and crashing surf from the toxicity of his influential presence.

Anne helped me engage my rage, a feeling still triggered from time to time. Nine years after he left, I listen to the Ukrainian people shouting, "We will not forget and we will not forgive!" I like and identify with their outrage. I get it.

It was Anne who, the second summer after he had left me, took me to the Center at Mariandale, a retreat centre in upstate New York. She found a spiritual companion for me there. It is Anne with whom I went to Riverside Church in NYC. It is Anne that I still speak with regularly and we visit each other a couple of times a year in person. She regularly tells me of books to read and I return the favour. We support each other in the journey of being liberal Christians in a world where church is so riddled with hypocrisy. We stay in touch. Our friendship is steady and enduring.

Anne is thriving. Before Covid and once again now, she and her husband are travelling regularly to European capitals for short stays. They are biking in the Alps and beaching in Belize. Late in life, she is pursuing a career as an artist. Her paintings are improving course by course. She is having gallery openings of her work.

In this way she inspires my own creativity. I have always been interested in how books look: their feel and texture. I wanted to learn the craft of making one. I signed up for a course in book binding held in the city where she lives. She quickly gave me space in her house to stay while I did this course. Alas, I had no idea the skill level required to bind books. I was in way over my head. I learned. I made and bound several blank books and needed every bit of instruction offered to do the tasks. I learned that should I ever want to get serious about this craft, I would need years of training. I decided to focus on writing the words that would be on the pages of a book. I signed up for courses. I tried poetry and blogs and now a memoir.

After my husband left, Anne gave me space to find my own creativity and modelled with her own work that it was possible, no matter my age. Her paintings hang on my walls, and she is reading what I write and making many wise comments in the margins.

Envy is never absent in discussions of friendship. Socrates called envy "the ulcer of the soul". In my past friendships, such as they were, I think I was the one envied. I did not wear this on my sleeve. But I did know it and I tried to be humble when people's envy came my way. Now I was the one to be pitied. I wanted to hide in social situations. I made excuses not to go out. I discovered what it was like to envy a friend. Anne was living the life I had just lost.

Jean Garnett in the Spring 2021 *Yale Review* wrote that "it is the almostness of envy that kills, the fact that it could have been or should have been us". I am not sure if Anne thinks about how envy might affect our relationship, but I do from time to time. When it comes up, I recognize it and remember what it felt like to be the one envied. Then I am filled with a joy that her life is flourishing and must be "kissed as it flies". I manage my envy.

———— * ————

Darlene knew my husband before I did. She witnessed the chemistry growing between us and called it before we did. The age gap was big but for me, it was compelling to be attractive to someone so much younger. He was brilliant and handsome. Darlene encouraged us to go for it. She liked us both and came to love us both. At our wedding she led the community in prayer.

God of Faith, hope and love, we give you thanks and praise that you gather us under your wings, protecting and sheltering us.

Thank you for the love and joy of Ann and [X] and all of us for one another on this day when we are brought face to face with your greatest hope: that we might love each other with the passion and fidelity with which we are loved and sought by you.

Darlene was a minister and a psychotherapist like myself. We grew closer as I encouraged her development for several years. She married a scientist and the four of us were friends. Darlene was open to theological issues concerning the bridge between science and theology and also paid attention to places where theology and climate concerns met. When my husband and I were in Florida and he was in the process of leaving me, she and her husband were in Florida as well. We spent a day visiting them. We did not tell them.

Sitting in the sun at a restaurant bar, I noticed my husband's hair. "Wow, your hair is getting grey just like Darlene's," I remarked.

"No, you're seeing things," came his sharp reply. Darlene noticed what she understood to be defensiveness.

While walking on the beach that day, I walked with her husband and she walked with mine. When, six weeks later, I told them what had happened, they shuddered for themselves and with me. It is very hard for a professional therapist or caregiver of any sort to hear the story of what happened to me. It was blatantly unethical. He was allured by his psychotherapist who collapsed boundaries instead of setting them. Darlene also told me that she had found his thinking that day they walked on the beach very strange and more undisciplined than his usual conversation.

I did not know what would happen to the three of us. I knew Darlene loved us both. She totally supported our work in the church and the vision we held for it.

In our marriage ceremony there had been the moment when those attending were asked, "Will you, friends of Ann and [X], open yourselves to them and their love, giving them separately, and together, your support and blessing?"

Darlene had said with the others, "I will."

I know that for a very long time Darlene thought about reaching out to my husband with a letter. Maybe she remembered that she had promised to care about us as a couple. She had every right to think her perspective would matter. It may be that she composed a letter a few times but did not send it. I knew of others that had reached out to my husband to ask him to ponder his actions and he brushed them away. He had locked his heart away from our marriage. Darlene had also held him tenderly as a friend and her loss was significant. Much later she assured me that choosing between us was never once a question in her mind. She chose me. I think friends do that. They make a clear, unambiguous choice to be there for one another.

I expect that Darlene has an image of a God who holds out a warm embrace for all of us. We are the ones who must choose to either nail those arms to a cross or to be gathered into them. My husband never turned towards her. I think she, like me, hoped that he would come to his senses and return to me, working with me to repair whatever it was that he found objectionable.

Darlene, like my daughter and son, was afraid for me and my safety. She knew that I could not find reasons for living. She understood the depth of despair and has consistently been able to express it in her words and song. Three years after he left, she wrote this poem attempting to express what she knew I was experiencing:

Heartbreak

You
broke this heart
in ways I didn't know a heart could break.

A numbness runs not down the left arm
but circles the heart, dawning a new ice age.

The dread isn't of dying
but living without you.

The breath isn't laboured
but heaves with small cries and sobs.

The pain isn't a crushing slam on the chest
but a hand gripping the intestines and squeezing.

The heart isn't racing.
It barely moves
lying like a kicked animal
shamed by the hand that once tended it
and nowhere to go but back to the door of the shelter it knew.

I believed you were safe
Good at heart
One of life's blessings

But we can be mistaken
Terribly wrong.

Darlene is a tender and fearless angel and my very own poetess. I think one of the most important needs we have as human beings is to be heard. Darlene heard me in my darkest and most vulnerable place. She does not forget the raw pain of my first call to her after I was left. More importantly, she was not afraid to stay with me there. She never tried to fix me, knowing that her calling was to bear witness to my grief. In Julian Barnes' words, she was no "lightweight". One of the Jewish words for God, and my most favourite, is Shekinah, meaning "Presence", and she was and is exactly that for me.

She told me that even while I could not see any light or hope, she could and would hold that vision for me. I was so very grateful for this and no words of mine can express how much it has meant. I know she felt anxious for me and I deeply regret that she bore this pain.

Angel Darlene lives in the same city as my daughter. We visit and have long walks when I am there. We eat gourmet burgers at the same classy restaurant where heads of state have lunch. We buy each other little gifts: a tumbler, a face cream or a Christmas ornament with bling. We have little mementoes of each other in our houses. I wake every morning to a moon-shaped prism in my window that sheds rainbows across the floor. I wiggle my toes in those colours each sunny morning when I rise from my bed. I know that Darlene wears an apron I made for her when she bakes. We share a commitment to dreams and their meanings. We discuss ours with each other. She is writing a novel. She reads her work to me and I read my memoir to her. Slowly the relationship returns to mutuality. Perhaps I am becoming an old and present angel in her life too.

In 1989, my husband became the pastor of a church in a suburb of Toronto. We had moved into the community. On a third of an acre, with a saltwater swimming pool in a garden surrounded with high hedges, this first house of ours was love at first sight for me. I could swim nude in good weather whenever I pleased. Gradually we brought the landscape up to garden tour standards. When I swam, I could look up into the peach-tinged yellow petals of glorious David Austin roses and even catch their musky scent. The house, garden and church were our projects.

Joan bounced into service one Sunday morning and decided to stay. She was light on her feet and swift in her humour. Professionally she was the chief librarian at Toronto's largest technical high school. I organised groups for women in our church and she joined one of them. We became friends that survived the rupture that happened when my husband and I moved seven years later to a new church community, 3,400 kilometres away on the west coast of Canada.

Since the 1980s evangelical churches have been growing and mainline churches have been shrinking. The theory was that people could come to Sunday worship, feel spiritually enriched, but if after three or four Sundays they were not befriended, no matter how good the worship experience was, they would not stay. To solve this problem, evangelical churches had developed what they called small group ministries. I researched this model and incorporated it into our mainline church. These groups are led by parishioners. They consist of ten to twelve people, and they meet usually in the homes of the members. In these groups, people get to know each other, often studied the scripture for the week and prayed for each other. They became friends who cared for one another. After six months they would divide and become a new group with new members. In this way the growth of the church was assured.

Sally told her group that her teenage son had not kept his curfew on yet another weekend night and she was worried.

With her permission, her small group laid their hands on her shoulders and back and one member prayed these words, "Holy God of love, be with Sally today and guide her to act with wisdom. Hold her son in your heart and be with all the young men in the community as they grow to maturity. In your name, Amen."

"Thank you," Sally said gently. "I have never been prayed for like this, thank you."

George texted his group late one Friday night that he had to cancel this group's Saturday morning meeting at his house. Their family's garage had caught fire and burned down that very day.

In the morning when he went out to the garage to begin the sorting and cleanup, his group of new friends began showing up with breakfast and boxes and garbage bags.

Small group ministry worked, and our community grew. Joan joined such a group twenty-seven years ago. I was part of that group to help them get fully functioning. This group rebelled and at six months would not divide. They named themselves "the goddesses". As the overall director of small group ministry in our community, I knew I had to leave in order to uphold the principle of dividing and forming a new group in order to grow the congregation. They have continued to meet and are ongoing to this day. They have travelled to Europe together, continued to spend a summertime weekend yearly at a member's cottage, witnessed their children marry, became grandmothers together and have begun to bury each other. They pray for each other and hold each other in God's light.

I will always regret I had to move on. I discovered that the small group ministry mandate was not perfect. Some groups just did not feel called to divide. Joan tells me the news of the goddesses and they hold a special place for me in their hearts.

Joan and I developed our friendship that had started so long ago in that group. Friday afternoons at 4:30 was our time. Her working week was done, and I was transitioning from work as a therapist to work in the church community. She came to our house to begin our walk.

Our beautiful home was just where people came. We hosted so many events for the church community in that space in all the seasons and especially in summer. Our home was a cottage in the city. Our land was part of a narrow strip on top of the bluffs that rose from the edge of Lake Ontario, one of the Great Lakes. I likened those bluffs to the cliffs of Dover, the ones my dad described when he spoke of the Great War.

"Let's go down to the lake. I want to see if the trilliums are up," Joan said one springtime Friday afternoon.

Joan and I went off on one of our walks. As usual, we checked in on each other regarding our work, the meaning of life, her horse Licorice and the tennis both our husbands played. She made me laugh and more; she thought I was genuinely funny. I knew I was earnest, but she saw something in me that I could not see in myself. Isn't this what good friends do for one another?

When my husband and I left that community, she also moved on and joined with the new minister, but we did manage not to lose each other. When I returned east to visit my family, we met up and walked. In her training to be a minister she spent six months serving on the West Coast. When my husband left me, she knew what this was like from deep inside as her husband had left her just as harshly. She knew how to be with me. She was also losing the friendship of my husband who had inspired and mentored her new vocation. We shuddered together. Still, she gave me my first smiles after the horror that consumed me.

In the first months after my husband abandoned me, and I learned that Australia did want me to come, I struggled over whether to go. I was talking it over with Joan in one of our regular phone conversations.

"My colleagues think I need to go to Australia and do the workshop. But he will be there. He is the main speaker. He is the big deal. It seems impossible to go."

She listened patiently and was present for my pain. Then she offered, "Ann, I will go. I will take my holidays and go. I have always wanted to go to Australia. If I go, will you be able to go? Would it help to be there with a friend?"

I wept. Her "yes" to me was astonishing. I began to think about making it work. She helped my despair move towards a future. After the conference we could explore Australia together. I began to plan to do something I loved: travel.

My husband and I had been members of HomeLink, a Canadian service that facilitated home exchanges. I put the membership in my name. I found families in Sydney, Byron Bay and Palm Grove, Australia who wanted to exchange with me in the right time frames. Our accommodation in Canberra was provided by the conference itself.

I have always been an anticipator. While I was terrified about the conference and the pain of being there at the same time as my husband and not being with him, I was going with a friend who would be by my side. I held in my mind getting to see Joan galloping along the beach and into the magnificent surf at Byron Bay. It could just all work out. Joan was helping me create possibility.

With her support, five months later, we went to Australia. I survived the conference and we got on with being tourists. I was the designated driver with my supposed skills of being able to drive on what for us was the wrong side of the road.

"I think I have this," I bravely stated as I pulled into the large roundabout at Canberra Airport in the wrong direction.

Quite suddenly cars began to stop and pull over. Horns honked and windows rolled down.

"U-turn when possible" the GPS ever so politely kept suggesting.

"Hang on Joan, we are going for it." I continued driving the wrong way round, weaving among the amused Aussie drivers who had stopped their cars and were waiting for me to get to the rental exit ramp. I definitely was their morning laugh.

"Whew, I guess we are in for some moments on the road. Good these Aussies are so tolerant," Joan acceded.

A few days later, settled in Queensland, we went on a whale-watching vessel.

"See them! There are two pods of humpbacks, starboard and port, and coming right for us." The captain's enthusiasm was mounting.

The boat was swerving from side to side to help us get the best view. There they were, breaching and playing. There was nowhere to look where the humpbacks were not immediately before us. I was trying to get photos, but I could not steady myself. *What the hell*, I thought to myself, and gave myself permission to be fully in the moment. Together we were like whales mixing in the play, immersed in their journey racing with the currents. For forty minutes we kept abreast of their world. It is all recorded in the memory shared by us two friends.

"Best ever. Amazing. Fantastic!" The superlatives leapt from her very soul.

Joan was ecstatic. Her joy amplified my joy. Joan is a whale lover and a veteran of many whale-seeking excursions. She and my daughter-in-law had once spent a day together learning to care for and feed the belugas at the Vancouver Aquarium. She knew a thing or two about whales.

Together Joan and I were becoming travel buddies, and this would continue until the pandemic hit and we had to cancel a trip to see the highlights of China.

Joan, to her profound regret, was never blessed with children. During Christmas of 2017, I asked her to join my son and family for the festivities. My son's stone cottage was built in 1851 to house the sexton of the new cathedral on the Speed River in Guelph, Ontario. Think of a Currier and Ives wintry image on a Christmas card, or the 2006 romantic film *The Holiday* watched so often at Christmas, and you will glimpse the charm that this house exudes, from the soaring cathedral across the street to the giant homemade ice rink in the yard. On a winter's eve, I can skate alone in softly falling snow with the bells of the carillon filling the air.

That Christmas day, once the meal was over, we were ensconced in the living room. The blue spruce Christmas tree grown from a seedling by my son was now seven feet high and filled the room with its scent. Hundreds of decorations gathered over the years had been meticulously hung by my daughter-in-law and grandson. It had taken them two weeks to place them, smallest at the top and largest at the bottom. On this Christmas night, the candleholders were filled with the beeswax candles made by my daughter-in-law. My grandson fetched the water bucket and scoop just to keep us safe should a fire that has never happened, happen. He took out his recorder and played while we sang carols.

"Good King Wenceslas looked out on the Feast of Stephen," Joan, who loves to sing, belted out.

She later said, "Ann, this is so amazing. I can't believe I am here and that this is happening. It is magic!"

Her joy made us all feel warm. My daughter-in-law knew at that moment that all the work had been worth it. Now, during subsequent Christmases, Joan is invited to join, and in a small yet meaningful way I share my children with her.

Joan sings my song in the heavenly host. Unfortunately, we got assigned the same gig when we lost our husbands. We live far away but we visit in person regularly. We are a church of two doing studies during Advent and Lent and supporting each other's faith. We wonder together what the future will bring as we grow older.

Kathy (Kathleen) is family. I was seventeen when she was born my sister's third child. Those who know us say we are alike in many ways. We love literature, and she is writing a novel that features the house where I grew up and she played as a grandchild. We adore clothes: creating them, buying them and wearing them. We have a passion for cars. We lean politically left. We both play golf and travel well.

In our sixty-six years of relationship there have been many ups and downs: times when we were close and times of distance. She babysat for my children when they were young during summers at the family cottage. The men we married gradually pulled us apart. Her husband died young, mine abandoned me and we have grown slowly and thoughtfully closer and closer.

My family and I knew we went a long way back on my mother's side. In fact, the family home, Walmer, still stands in Portloe, a fishing village on the sea in Cornwall, England. It was listed in the Domesday Book, which records the "Great Survey" conducted in 1086 of parts of England and Wales. The home and land have been held and continue to be held by members of the Trounce family.

My maternal great grandmother, Elizabeth Ann Trounce, was born on that land in 1843 into a large family of siblings. The youngest, Peter, was born in 1847. There were so many Trounces on the land that Elizabeth and Peter felt compelled to seek new fortune in the colonies. In 1870 Elizabeth came to Canada and Peter went to Australia. Their offspring have kept in touch over the centuries.

How did she, Elizabeth, make such a long journey as a single woman "without prospects", as they would have said? There was no husband waiting for her in Canada. She surely was brave and adventurous. I like to think these genes run in me. I am named for her, Ann Elizabeth. She settled and married in London, Ontario and gave birth to my grandmother.

One day in my youth, a letter arrived at Christmas. It was blue and decorated with a large red kangaroo stamp. My mother, wiping her hands on her apron, took the precious missive from the mailman's hands. In those days of World War II, the arrival of the post was a sacred moment. A letter from her cousin Peter, named for his ancestor, was a blessed day. The connection was kept.

In early September 2017, travelling alone, I found my way to the long lane that led to the ancient homestead in Portloe. I had arranged to meet the current owners: a young man called Jamie Trounce and his father, John, who still farmed the land. They had been visited before by both the Canadian and Australian branches of the family.

Stepping onto the property, seeing golden fields stretching under the cloudless blue sky, was overwhelming. I was filled with a connection that resonated deep in my very being. My cousin many times removed had not yet arrived to greet me. For an hour it was all mine. The old stone house, as it stood waiting for the money from Jamie's gran so that it could be renovated, reverberated with permanence. The sea strip at the land's edge and before the rising sky drew me to it and was somehow entirely familiar. I had always been drawn to the land's edge even though I grew up in a landlocked city. Maybe this mystery was finally solved. I was a child born very late in my parents' lives and it was not easy to belong. Just for an hour that day I belonged to a land and a country. The Cornish Celt in me would call this a mystical moment. Dare I say, I was home. It was the way I had felt with my husband.

When my distant cousin Peter had emigrated to Australia in the late 1800s, he got himself a sheep station, called it Walmer II, and my relatives John and Marion Trounce still farm it. My sister, after her divorce in 1982, went adventuring to Australia. She looked up the Trounces and went to meet them in the outback near Wellington, New South Wales. She met John's father Paul, one of her distant cousins, married him and stayed there. Our families were now physically reconnected after generations had passed. John and Marion's children became her Australian grandchildren. Their daughter, Justine, became truly close with her new grandma, my sister.

While visiting and working in Australia with my husband in 2010, I spent precious time with my sister. In a small room in a nursing home close to the sea, where my sister spent her last days, I sat with her one afternoon, and she asked me to promise that I would care for Justine. In that moment I got permanently linked to Australia. Justine as a trendy millennial and she, with the latest in Australian lingo, named me her DNA. Australians, who shorten everything, shorten "relatives" to DNA. We connect on Instagram, which, while it is special, does not have a red kangaroo icon. But it is lively with photos of her life and her adventures.

Thus, Kathy and I have DNA in Cornwall and in Australia. We are rooted together, branches of the family tree going back to 1015. Both of us feel more alive in Cornwall. There is an acknowledged spirituality about the place. In the most southwesterly area of the United Kingdom, there are magical tours given of such sacred places as Tintagel, Rough Tor and Bodmin Moor. There are fairies, mermaids and holy wells there. Kathy and I embrace it all.

We get together at her house or mine when she is in residence in Canada. For fifteen years now, after the sudden and early death of her husband, she has been in partnership with her Dutchman who lives in a village near Amsterdam. They go back and forth, ninety days together, ninety days apart, and so the year goes by. When in Canada, she lives a ferry ride away from me on Vancouver Island. We get together for happy times of golfing and travelling and shopping and sharing our writing. We also indulge our Cornish practice of opening the doors of perception. We do this by reading our Russian Gypsy cards. As children, I read tea leaves with my dad, and she read palms with her college friends. We are at ease with this practice.

The cards are printed in gloriously rich colours. There are many symbols, and as we lay out the cards, sometimes they make a match with the next card put down. Then the two halves of the picture are joined. The completed picture can be in one of four positions: right side up, upside down, facing left or facing right. There is a book that helps you read these joined cards. We do these three or four times a year and never on Sunday, as the gypsies demand. It is as though we have a dream together and we interpret the symbols that turn up as we lay out the cards.

One evening, in the summer of 2018, we were together conducting a reading for each other. We each drew a match for the Number 3 card, which depicted a ship sailing in the left-facing position. Now, in this completed picture, a beautiful ancient red sailing ship was being aided in its travels on the high seas by a round-faced wind figure puffing out a mighty breeze. This ship was on a tear, its mainsail billowing.

"Ann, you got the same reading as I did. We got the ship going the same way. What do you think? Ought we to be making a trip together?" Kathy's voice conveyed her excitement.

Always up for an adventure, I responded, "How about we go to the original Walmer?"

"I want to snorkel on the Great Barrier Reef as you have done," Kathy added.

"I want to see Uluru at dawn. I have never been there, and access is changing. They are protecting it and making it harder for tourists. We just have to go soon."

"I can go to my mother's gravesite in Sydney. You have been."

Our enthusiasm was mounting. Maybe the Celtic fairies were taking over but before long, the trip was becoming a reality. That red sailing ship was moving fast.

HomeLink again came to the rescue and before long we had a house exchange at Palm Grove and a hotel in Sydney, Alice Springs, and Wellington. I would make a side trip to a house exchange on Bribie Island to do some writing while she visited her younger friends. We booked flights and decided not to drive. We both wanted to hike around Uluru and camp under the stars.

Within twenty-four hours we had a trip planned to be there for November 2018, just as spring slips into summer in the southern hemisphere.

We discovered Walmer II, and with it the immensity of an Australia sheep farm. The dusty, ochre land stretched out unimpeded for miles. Sheep were moving mounds, rolling along like tumbleweed in the wind in the distance. It was so dry that my skin cracked and my curly hair clumped and stuck together in dreadlocks. The farmhouse was surrounded by an acre of irrigated land. Marion and my sister had gardened it and made an oasis for every manner of flora and fauna. My sister's part of the house had an acacia bush beside the kitchen window, where it filled with blue wrens. When she was in the nursing home, she told me how those wrens got her through the dry spells when her soul longed for the sea. Tiny hits of neon blue, they dance amid the bottlebrush, protea and kangaroo paw. It was good for Kathy and me to be where she spent more than a third of her life.

Very big farmer John Trounce soon got us into the "ute", his all-terrain vehicle, to see the land. I knew from the time I spent as a young ordinand minister at a congregation on the Canadian prairie that land means everything to a farmer. The ute was open-air and I was hanging on, afraid of being thrown to the elements, so fast were we travelling on no road at all. As we bumped along in an open field, John was telling us about when the hydro went out, or the wind came up or the irrigation wells dried, and the sheep had no water. I caught bits of the story as I tried to keep the dust out of my eyes and ears.

In the shearing shed where we made a stop, I could see his large and weathered hands. His fingernails were dark with oil and grime from shearing sheep the day before.

"I don't want this life for Justine and the boys," he told us. "It is too hard a life."

Kathy and I felt his dilemma. It was the only life he knew. Could

Walmer II ever be sold? Justine has told me that the decision has not yet been made.

Our friendship deepened as we shared our roots, took photos of the blue wrens and feasted on legs of lamb and fresh peas.

Moving on to the exchange house in Palm Grove, we prepared for another highlight adventure. We splurged on an excellent tour boat to take us out onto the Great Barrier Reef.

"I am afraid. How do I do this? Will you hold my hand?"

Kathy was nervously perched on the ramp at the back of the boat that would let her down into the sea. I, having done this before, was already out in the ocean bobbing in my fins and snorkel gear.

"Come on, Kathy, you can do it. Take my hand, I will hold it and I won't let go until you want me to."

Together we moved over the coral and began to be transported into another world. As we relaxed, Kathy grew braver and pointed out angelfish, clown fish, parrotfish and more in a rainbow of colours. Some 1,625 species of fish live on the reef. The yellows and blues and oranges were electric in the sun's rays. Then, braver still, she let my hand go and we swam among the coral formations being immensely careful not to touch them. We went together. We discovered together. We did what friends do. I think we will never stop.

These five women are angels that have a long history with me. One of them is my age and four of them are ten to twenty years younger. None of them live in my city. They do not know each other, though I wish they did. I imagine them meeting at my funeral. I am grateful for the internet and ferries and airplanes. I am grateful that my sorrow was not too much for them. They hover close by, bringing messages of endurance and hope. When I am weak and flailing, they make such a caring fuss, and when I am strong, they rejoice.

Chapter 17

COLLEAGUES
BECOMING FRIENDS

Lots of people want to ride with you in the limo, but what you want is someone who will take the bus with you when the limo breaks down.

— Oprah Winfrey

Have you ever heard of Dunbar's number? Dunbar's number is the number of friends you can have and this limit is 150. It is the number of people you would not hesitate to go over and sit with if you happened to see them at 3 a.m. in the Departure Lounge at Hong Kong airport.

— Stephen Fry, BBC, QI

Perhaps the most surprising finding to emerge from the medical literature over the past two decades has been the evidence that the more friends that we have, the less likely we are to fall prey to diseases and the longer we will live.

— Robin Dunbar

In 1965, freshly ordained, I was sent to the wilderness boonies of northern Ontario to be a pastor: black fly-ridden in summer and freezing in winter. The small church had been closed for several years but was opened to give me a place to start my ministry. It was a one-room frame structure with a giant wood burning stove in the entrance. Wooden pews on either side of a central aisle led to a small stage at the front. There was a central pulpit looking over a communion table. A wheezing pump organ flanked the right side and on the left was a mostly out of tune upright piano. A bare wooden cross hung on the wall behind the pulpit. The windows were gothic in design with plain glass in wooden frames. It was barely a church, compared to the Roman Catholic structure with a steeple on the hill overlooking the town. Protestants were architecturally, and in every other way, an afterthought.

I decided on my very first Sunday to start preaching with the creation story, a text from Genesis. This was before my denomination was assigning a text for each week and I thought I would just start at the beginning of the Bible and carry on through. I was wickedly erudite and wildly out of touch with my congregation. As a fresh-out-of-seminary way of understanding creation, I decided to introduce the congregants to Teilhard de Chardin.

"He is a man most dedicated to the study of organisms," I began by way of introductions. Or at least that's how I meant to introduce the twentieth century's great French Jesuit priest, scientist, paleontologist and theologian.

Instead, I said, "De Chardin is a man most dedicated to the study of orgasms."

Jane and a college student in the back seat were actually listening and understood what I said. They laughed uproariously for what seemed like a long time. It was an auspicious start to my life as a parish minister. I fear my dear congregation was left forever able to only associate creation with orgasms.

Jane ran the local general store in that pastorate. After that gaff in my first sermon, she was drawn to me and I to her. She took me under her wing, filling me in on ways of life in a remote Canadian wilderness village. The village was dominated by a peaceful river with an abundance of fish.

Once during a forest fire, the people had fled onto the river on rafts to escape the mighty fire. The locals hunted in season and their freezers were full of moose and bear. Tourists came for the hunt and for fishing pickerel and bass. The very talented fishers caught speckled trout in the tributaries feeding the great river and cooked them up for shore breakfasts. People had massive vegetable gardens in summer and in winter they had the Legion Hall for curling, drinking and dancing. If you could walk, you curled through the long dark winter days. Most people in the community were French-speaking Roman Catholics. Jane showed up each Sunday at church and before long I realized she had my back. The woman priest, as I came to be known, was a novelty to be tested and assessed.

Gradually we trusted each other. Then the worst thing happened. I got pregnant and now I was not only a woman priest but a pregnant woman priest who had obviously had sex, my denomination's worst fear. During the long winter, with the fire roaring in the stove and the heat uncontrolled, my body overheated and my face flushed, I was quite a sight as I preached God's word.

My second son was born, lived a few months and died in that village. Jane marshalled the compassion of the community and sat with me through terrible nights of grief.

A few months after my loss, she made an appointment to see me in my study.

"Ann, you know Charlie, he is on the bottle again, I don't know what to do. The kids need a dad. I have no right to bother you, especially when you are so full of grief, but I don't know what to do." Her soft lovely face filled with tears. Mine did too.

I didn't know what to do either. I could preach the Word, deliver the sacrament but I was ill-equipped to know how to be with her. I did not understand or have any experience with alcoholism, addiction or codependency. Seminary had not given me these tools. I did know that I wanted to be more helpful. That night before sleep, I promised myself that I would do all it took to be able to help people like Jane. In the morning I applied to a clinical training programme in pastoral counselling.

Nine years later, in 1974, with my training in interdenominational pastoral care and counselling complete, I truly hoped my denomination would be eager to hire me as part of a ministerial team where I could practice my new skills. Alas, that would not be. They would welcome me to parish ministry, to teach at a seminary or to be a hospital or prison chaplain, but in asking for recognition of a specialised ministry in pastoral care and counselling, I was again pushing my denomination into uncharted territory.

I had enjoyed preaching and parish life in that northern community, but I really wanted to focus on a healing ministry. I justified this desire by reminding the decision-makers in my denomination that it was a central part of Jesus' ministry. As I was trying to sort this out, I had a very significant dream.

I had studied theology at the University of St Andrews in Scotland. St Andrews was the home of the largest Roman Catholic mediaeval cathedral in Scotland, built in 1158. In the sixteenth century, in the midst of the Protestant Reformation, John Knox and his followers ransacked the cathedral, and it fell into the most magnificent open-air ruins, which remain to this day. Parts of great stone walls frame lush green grounds outlining a massive 390-foot-long cathedral facing out to the North Sea. As a student there, I walked among the ruins often, touching the altar stone so many times that it is not surprising that this scene appeared in the most significant dream of my career. This was the dream.

I am fully gowned, standing at the back of the ruined cathedral of St Andrews, waiting for the procession to begin. I can barely see the details of the altar 140 metres away. There are several male bishop candidates ahead of me. I am preoccupied with the elegant embroidered robe that is far too long for me. I am particularly concerned with my ceremonial hat, a grand mitre-shaped affair that will not stay on my head. I must also make that long trek to the altar, holding my hat in place with one hand and hoist up the robe with the other hand so as not to trip. It is very intimidating. I am selected to be ordained a bishop along with several other men. The presiding bishop is the Most Reverend Ted Scott of the Canadian Anglican church. He is a man I most admire for his progressive thinking and his empathic pastoral manner.

As the last candidate, I finally arrive at the altar stone. With relief, I kneel on a silk cushion to await being dedicated. Ted Scott's hands come down on my shoulders firmly and with pressure. I hear him saying, "Ann, I dedicate you this day, a bishop of healing and the care of souls from this day forward and forever."

I woke up.

This dream sealed my career. I would need to find a way to make my denomination understand my calling to be a pastoral counsellor. With that as a work in progress, I decided to start my own private practice as a pastoral counsellor. Another church denomination gave me space to use as an office. It was all an experiment. I was not a registered psychologist or a medical doctor but a clergyperson with specialised training in both spiritual and secular counselling. Soon after hanging out my shingle, amazingly people came to see me and paid me from their own pockets for my services. Slowly and surely, clergy and other professionals referred clients to me. It has continued to be so for forty-eight years and counting.

Several years later, my denomination did find a way to recognize my ministry by inviting me to teach the discipline of pastoral counselling at their theological colleges. I did this for years. In that capacity, I tried to prepare ordinands to go out better equipped than I had been, to serve the mental and emotional health of their parish members. In the 1980s, I headed an interdenominational institution as director of training for pastors wanting clinical experience in the practice of psychotherapy. For a year or two my denomination recognized this as a legitimate ministry. I was persistently asking my official church to expand its reach in the provision of care for the mental and emotional well-being of its members. Other denominations sought my direction and service, which I gladly gave. Sadly, over the years the mainline Protestant church found itself in decline and used its resources to focus on survival. By 2000, pastoral counselling as a specialized ministry disappeared in my country.

From the beginning of starting my practice, I knew there was something wrong about it being a solo endeavour. Jesus is all about being accompanied. He called his disciples friends. I needed a group of friends to hold me to account. In the early days of my practice, a group of psychologists with theological backgrounds and a chaplain, all men, invited me to join them for monthly meetings where we discussed cases, gave case conferences and supported each other's work. I was the only woman, and it was awkward for them, but they came to value my perspective. In time I was one of them. When I moved to western Canada in 1997, we disbanded. Most of them had retired by that time and one of them had died. Our work as a group was over.

As I established a new practice in Vancouver, I initiated the birth of a similar group. For a long time, there were four colleagues, including me. Then there were three of us as one retired. At first, we met monthly. Now we meet five or six times a year. We are four again, having taken in a mutual colleague. We have been meeting for twenty-five years. As well as this group, I developed a close collegial relationship with two male therapists, both of whom I had encouraged in their pursuit to be pastoral counsellors.

When my husband left me, I knew I needed to inform these colleagues, Bianca, Yolanda, Linda, Don and Brian. I expected them to be horrified and they were. I did not know that they would transform from colleagues to friends and angels who lifted me with love.

Angel Bianca

All over the world there are people learning to live with celibacy. People choose to do this. I did not. Following my husband's abandonment of me, I hated the space left in my bed by my lover. Our sexual companionship was a combination of kind, tender, funny, imaginative, creative, spiritual, raunchy and sometimes all of these at once. Before he left, on that Valentine's Day after we made love for what became the last time, my husband rather plaintively said, "Ann, I am not leaving because sex was bad. Actually, our lovemaking has been one of the best parts of our union."

My body still yearns to be cherished and touched. My soul longs for physical connection. For years I woke in the night after dreams in which we were together again making love and I hated the waking reality that left me sobbing with grief and remembered pleasure. I know that if he had left me through death, I would be able to treasure these dreams. Then they would be normal. I could speak about them without shame. Do they now indicate that something is wrong with me? Are they a symptom of PTSD? I don't know. I can only report that they happen, and finally, nine years later, they happen less.

I know the words of a thousand songs, the smell of fresh sheets full of the outdoor breezes, the light of the afternoon sun, the taste of egg salad sandwiches, the smell of tea and rose bubble bath and the feeling of being naked together on an isolated beach or in our backyard on the first of May; these things bring memories that will not be forgotten. They leave me crying, "Why?" I am grateful for such lovemaking and damaged by the nature of its loss in the same moment.

Everyone who is dropped into unwanted celibacy needs a "sex angel" and Bianca, a sex therapist, was perfectly qualified. She knew about my body's ache to be touched and treasured. There is this thing about sex angels: they are not afraid to talk about this with their assignment, in this case, me.

Not long after I had told my monthly support group that my husband had abandoned me, Bianca drove me home. Outside my house she stopped the car, turned off the ignition, making it clear she wanted to have a private chat.

"I know sex was good for you and your husband. What is going on now? How are you handling this?" she directly asked.

"Not well. I hate it. If I try to masturbate, I just fall apart. The pleasure is gone, and I can't find it. Maybe it is too soon. Sometimes I end up rocking myself to calm down. Bianca, it's too hard to even try."

"Yes," she said. "Does it happen sometimes in dreams?"

She knew. It was good for me that she could see me and make me talk about it. She knew the raw need in my body would surface, if only in dreams, and she was right.

Bianca persistently fixes things. She is not Canada's leading sex therapist for nothing. She was of the mind that I would be helped by meeting a new man. In the early days, when I was reeling, she had the nerve to assign her husband the task of telling all available men in his circle about me. She was fearless in investigating any such men she knew who might become possible friends (with or without benefits) for me. She encouraged, even pushed, me to be on the lookout for possible partners when I was so far from the idea that it seemed ludicrous to me. Because she persisted and enquired, I began to take note of men in the line at the grocery store, when walking in my neighbourhood and just when I was out and about.

She would text me from time to time: "Have you met anyone? Did you talk to them?"

She stayed with me to pursue my interest. She was a relentless angel appointed to remind me that I was a sexual human being. She made it safe for me to tell her about the ache of celibacy and to confront what I was going to do about it. I certainly needed this angel to stay around.

I had enjoyed Bianca's optimism for twenty years, and after my husband left, she applied that optimism to my situation, believing that even at my age a lover would appear. I became hopeful that in time I would be able to pleasure myself sexually without so much emotional pain. Perhaps this is one of those areas that make grief specialists talk about eight years of recovery time. Perhaps it is just so difficult because I am a woman in my last years of life. There is a powerful ageism afloat that suggests that desire has waned. Fortunately, or unfortunately, I have not found this to be true.

Angel Yolanda

Yolanda was there when the church was abandoning me. She was a Christian from another mainline denomination. It made no sense to her how I was being treated. She attempted to get my church to hire a mediator in order to ease the pain between them and me. She offered to assist them in finding a neutral mediator. They were just not ready at that time to consider her idea.

Also, she had been the one to challenge me to go to Australia and do the workshop there in the very early days of my grief.

"Ann, imagine what it will be like if you don't go. Imagine yourself sitting at home through all the days of the conference. Won't it be worse than being there?" she asked.

And then she added, "Can you imagine the regret you would feel? You would have passed on an opportunity to start to feel better about yourself."

One day in the spring of 2016, while we were walking together, she mentioned that she and her husband would like to go to Bard on the Beach, the Shakespearean festival that happens every summer near my house. Immediately, I went down memory lane.

As a child, I demonstrated very little musical ability. Quite frankly I could not and still cannot carry a tune. Undaunted, my parents enrolled me in private elocution lessons. I have never been able to make sense of this decision they made, as they could ill afford it, but my gratitude is immense.

Our hometown had a reputable theatre, and I spent my Saturdays in the greenroom there and on the stage. In my very first performance at age seven, I had the opening line, and suitably attired in a large orange contraption, I had to say, "I am a squash seed."

The problem was that my mother had become deaf as a teen. This resulted in her having the capacity to speak but with unusual pronunciations for a lot of words. She had a habit of inserting the sound "r" in words where it did not belong. On opening night, I proudly said my line as the curtain went up: "I am a squarsh seed!"

In theatre school I learned to speak properly. I thrived and pursued my thespian hopes in all the drama clubs and performances of high school and university.

In 1952, Tom Patterson founded the Stratford Shakespearean Festival in Stratford, Ontario, a town very close to my hometown. By 1959, as I graduated from university, I had options. I had been accepted to study theology and I had been admitted to the Royal Academy of Dramatic Art (RADA). I had no idea what a coup this was. It enabled me to get a job as an apprentice at the burgeoning Stratford Shakespearean Festival during the summer of 1959.

My world exploded. I was a very naive twenty-year-old. The comedy at the festival that year was *As You Like It*. The tragedy was *Othello*. I did not know what homosexuality was and it was everywhere among the theatre crowd. I was exposed to every aspect of theatre, props, voice projection, understudy lines, fencing and costumes where I had some real talent. I went to all the parties. One of the lead actors, playing Orlando in *As You Like It*, took a fancy to me. The Queen was coming for its opening night. I was to sit on an aisle not far from Her Majesty. The costume department got right on it and designed a dress for me.

It was made of lemon peau de soie. The skirt was panelled and shaped with a stiff lining. The bodice was a skin of silk fitted over my breasts. My black curly hair was shining. I think I looked like a spring tulip just about to burst. The Queen was in her seat, and when the lights dimmed, her tiara and jewels sparkled brilliantly. The actors were in place. I felt Orlando's arm resting on my shoulder as he waited for his cue in the aisle beside my seat. The trumpets sounded and the play began. My heart was pounding with excitement and pleasure.

I was in way over my head. The world of theatre at this level was too exotic for me. I feared that I could not navigate that world safely. I chose to study theology. Perhaps I lost my nerve that summer. To this day, I love theatre and remember a road I did not take. Yolanda's passing comment about our Vancouver Bard on the Beach inspired me. I came home and purchased three tickets for each of the six performances of the bard for that summer. It was a big financial investment. Now I had to find friends to accompany me. Yolanda and her husband were the first. When Covid eased and the theatre began performances again, at their urging I purchased tickets for summer 2022. This simple act got me through many summer nights in anticipation and enjoyment. I was finding myself and maintaining friendships at the same time.

Angel Linda

From 1998 to 2004, I had been the president of the British Columbia Association of Marriage and Family Therapy (BCAMFT). We were a fledgling Canadian branch of the very large American parent group (AAMFT). I needed help with all the work of being president and school psychologist. Linda stepped up as my president-elect.

In 2000, I was in Nashville at the AAMFT national convention with Linda and her husband, a down-to-earth, no-nonsense man's man. It was our first afternoon there and our first local Nashville bar.

"Yes, one beer please," I said to the bartender. "And please, I would like it in a glass."

The bartender, cracking off bottle caps, looked at me as if I had arrived from another planet. Linda's husband found it uproariously funny and never hesitates to tell the story of my refined central Canadian manners.

Linda and I grew close, meeting often as we tried to build a professional body of therapists in Vancouver. We navigated the inevitable tensions with the parent organisation who wanted us to become autonomous. It meant we travelled together to the USA to meetings and negotiation tables. After her run at being president, she retired. She and her husband bought a home on a golf course. Now we often golf together and they graciously welcome my grandson as a fourth when he is in Vancouver.

After one such game on their course in the summer of 2021, we were at a pub following the game. Linda and I were the designated drivers. Her husband and my grandson were drinking. Six beers in, I am getting alarmed no matter how much fun they were having.

"Now what is all this stuff about gender fluidity?" her husband enquires, displaying his half-serious redneck side to my grandson.

My grandson takes this on and explains quite graphically. A delightful conversation ensues as Linda and I watch. My grandson is at his most engaging self. It looks like two men are falling in love with each other: one remembering happy evenings drinking beer after golf and the other being initiated into that world by an old hand. A lively conversation over beer is the quintessential nineteenth hole of golf.

Linda is a much better golfer than I am, but we still get to play at least once a season. I know my grandson is always welcome, alien that he is with his long hair, full beard and, to Linda's husband, sincere ecology commitments that may never earn him a decent livelihood. Linda and her husband bring love and humour into my life.

Angel Don

I met Don a long time ago when, as a professor teaching pastoral care and counselling, he came to see me for a chat. He was studying theology with a strong aptitude for pastoral counselling and English literature. I liked him from that first meeting and just knew he would go far, and he has.

Next thing I knew he was working at my family church as the youth pastor and leading my son, who was in youth group. The kids loved him but were neutral about the church. My son chose not to be confirmed that year, but he had met a fine man he still admires. Teen years were challenging for my son, and I am glad Don was a steady presence for him.

After graduation, Don returned to his original home out west. He trained as a pastoral counsellor in Calgary and became the pastor of one of the largest and wealthiest churches in Vancouver. After I moved west, he called one day and said, "Let's meet."

I learned at that luncheon that, after years of service, he was considering leaving the pastorate. We discussed possibilities for his next career move.

"So, Ann, do you think I can form a private practice as you have done? I have an itch for a new adventure."

"Of course. It makes sense for you to be in practice as a psychotherapist. Most of your training is already done. You will have to do some supervision and BC will be so fortunate to have you in the field."

This meeting was the first of many such discussions we had along the way as he prepared to meet the standards for accreditation in British Columbia to practice psychotherapy. Eventually he joined Bianca's clinic as one of her associates.

I encouraged him to become the president of the British Columbia Association of Marriage and Family Therapy. He accepted the challenge and led our organisation brilliantly as it continued down the path to governmental acceptance.

His love of literature had never died. He had crafted elegant, inspiring sermons. He had studied with our national literary hero, Professor Northrop Frye. Don wanted to write. He already had a manuscript in his drawer where he shared his reflections on walking with Frye through the seasons of the Christian year. I did everything I could to encourage him. I was so proud when his book, *Universal Spirit: The Seasons of the Christian Year in the Company of Northrop Frye* was published in 2019. I gave a book launch party for him at my house and sold all the copies he had with him. I anticipate the arrival of more books from him in the future.

Most months before Covid, Don and I met monthly for dinner. Our friendship grew as we both were practising psychotherapists. For dessert we loved to eat sorbetto di limone, frozen lemons filled with ice cream. He moved to Vancouver Island and practising by Zoom made his trips to Vancouver infrequent. Being in touch is more sporadic but we are unlikely to drift fully away, so enduring is our friendship. I do hope he gets to hold my published memoir in his hands.

Angel Brian

Put simply, Brian and I companioned each other in crisis. He is twenty-five years my junior. I first met him as a young therapist and former evangelical pastor who was assigned me as his supervisor. He did therapy for an evangelical clinic practising pastoral counselling. I had just moved west. I needed to get established and this clinic needed help. The chair of their board had an inexplicably progressive lens through which he convinced the board that I was what their clinic needed. I supervised in that clinic from 1998 to 2000, at which point the therapists took control, fired the more conservative board and reconstituted themselves as a private clinic. I just might have had something to do with this action.

Soon after meeting Brian, he and his wife had their third child. Their marriage was floundering. Brian was distraught. It was touch and go. It is hard to help the marriages of others when one's own is fragile and on the edge of collapsing. I helped him continue to work as a marriage therapist while being in therapy for his own marriage. In time, he and his wife and family all survived as a unit. When, fourteen years later, I found myself devastated, my marriage in ruins and barely able to imagine life at all, Brian walked with me. In time his wife also became part of the team to help Ann thrive again.

They lived in a suburban home bordering on the fifth hole of a stunning golf course set in a forest of redwood trees. Once a month we spent the better part of Friday together. He had an enormous practice; yet he set aside this time to be with me for years. His wife supported him in offering this. We just walked and talked a lot about therapy for men and had lunch. It was an enormous gift to me. Tears well up as I appreciate this. It was a friendship with a consultative benefit to us both.

As a youth Brian had played golf and had been very good. I talked him into taking up the sport again and playing with me. After all, he lived on such a desirable course. I had no idea how good a golfer he would be. I was blown away. Once a golfer, always a golfer. I was so envious and delighted that he was happy to play with me, or so he claimed. It was such a joy for me to watch him drive the ball, pitch the ball and plop it in the hole. If only I had started young!

He and his wife have since sold their house and are moving into the city they were missing so much. As he says, we are now just a little ferry ride away from each other.

Vancouver has a water taxi bus system that just delights tourists and me. These boats look like tiny tugs, hold twelve people and bob around our harbour on specific routes. One docks a ten-minute walk from my house. Each Christmas, for one day, they sell tickets at twenty-five per cent off the regular price. I buy sixty tickets and give them to my friends, taking them on rides across the water to make a change from walking across the bridges.

It means we can walk and walk and, when tired, take a ferry home. It is a little random gift of kindness I am so pleased to give.

Having Brian and his wife just a ferry ride away means easy visits and great food, as Brian is an awesome chef. They seem completely at ease with my being so much their elder.

I had five out-of-town friends and five colleagues that were now definitely friends in addition to Anita. I was 74 when I was left and had somehow managed to accept the care of friends and was beginning to learn to give as well as receive.

Chapter 18

THE ARRIVAL OF
NEW ANGELS
BECOMING FRIENDS

If we understand that neighborly relations are woven into divine love, then we can grasp that God is a near-dwelling God. We know God through our neighbors.

— Diana Butler Bass

It is social aptitude, not intellectual brilliance or parental social class that leads to successful aging. The only thing that really matters in life are your relationships to other people.

— George Vaillant

Lying, thinking
Last night
How to find my soul a home
Where water is not thirsty
And bread loaf is not stone
I came up with one thing
And I don't believe I'm wrong
That nobody,
But nobody
Can make it out here alone.

— Maya Angelou, "Alone"

Angel Moyra

In the months before the sabbatical that was supposed to have been a glorious time for my husband and myself, during Sundays after church, I sat at a book table and sold copies of my husband's books. Moyra, a newcomer at the time, came by the table and purchased a book.

"Can I help you?" she asked.

"Yes, I would be delighted to have help."

Moyra and I became a little marketing team and, in the process, we got to know each other.

She was a Scotswoman, daughter of a Presbyterian clergyman who had emigrated to Canada and found work as a minister in my denomination. Twelve years younger than me, she had just retired as a property and commercial lawyer who focused on environmental issues. Her parents had passed. Her sister lived in Richmond. She was married and her husband was South Asian. There was nothing not to like. She had a slight Scottish lilt in her voice, was a tad exotic, liked my husband's sermons and was committed to saving the environment.

Then my husband abandoned me. I wondered where Moyra's loyalty would be. For a few months she continued her enjoyment of him, signing up for further courses he had offered. We spoke a few times and then we began to walk together. Having just retired, she had the time and the desire to exercise gently. We walked further and further and further.

"Ann, look at your watch. How far have we walked?"

"Oh my, Moyra, we are closing in on twenty kilometres. We have walked pretty far in this direction, and I don't know any shortcuts back."

"We must call a taxi. There is no way I have any more walk left in me." She made her exhaustion clear.

We called a cab and began to chuckle. We had been so engrossed in our conversation we had forgotten all about how far from home we had gone. We agreed to keep better track next time. Within a year of such walking, we had achieved her retirement goal of losing twenty pounds.

On one occasion I took her to a nearby island in the Gulf and introduced her to walking a labyrinth. As a lawyer with an environmental concern, she knew the city and its projects well. She was continually educating me; the architecture, urban planning sites and historical buildings were her favourite topics. I have always thought she and her husband could run a business where they introduced tourists to our city.

From all our conversation and her increasing knowledge of my pain, she realized that I could not handle her staying in my husband's orbit. She also experienced how the church was treating me. Then she chose me. Moyra walked with me on my worst days in those first two years. She was a steady calm presence who often brought her legal expertise to bear on my situation, both with the church and with the legal divorce system in my home province. Moyra was nothing if not thorough.

At one point she decided to take her concern for me and how I was being treated by the church board to the co-pastor. Before she did so, she devoured the manual of my denomination. When studying theology, all students are required to have a working knowledge of the manual and must pass a test to prove competence with its boring and tedious rules. She just thoroughly ingested it. The board must have been overwhelmed with her careful articulation of her thinking in her defence of me. She challenged the church to find a way to support me based on her legal articulation of its mandate found in its own manual. She was summarily dismissed, just as Yolanda had been. All we could do was commiserate in our sorrow about the state of our beloved church.

Moyra is at heart a teacher. In her retirement she teaches Asian students to speak French. My ear is so bad that while she corrects my pronunciation if I try French words, I am not a good pupil. She finds tricks to help me get it right and then I forget the tricks.

In time I got to know her husband, Reg. He is an almost scratch golfer. In the early days after my husband left, I wondered if I would ever be able to play golf again.

"Let's go, Ann. I will take you to the driving range." Once there, he was so patient. "Nice swing. Just repeat that swing. It is really good. The distance will come."

He did this in good weather and in cold wet weather when I hit in a covered driving range. Some days he got very cold, but he never wavered with his encouragement. I felt like he really believed I would be able to play golf again.

Together they gave me a front seat at very elaborate East Indian weddings. Reg has a large family and every summer there are weddings that last for days.

"No, I will not wear a sari. I have to sit on the ground too much. I need slacks and elaborate tops," Moyra was explaining as I tried to shop with her for the right outfits.

"How many outfits do you need?" I enquired.

"There are seven events, so something new for each one. And the top has to show off the jewelry. I must wear all Reg's mother's gold. The top will have to be simply background for the jewels."

One summer, there were three weddings, which devoured the entire season. I had several Punjabi clients and was mesmerized by all this ritual and activity. Moyra willingly shares her world with me.

Reg, on a walk one day, put it this way: "Ann, you know if your husband had not left you, Moyra and I would never have become your friends. It is awkward to say this, but it means so much to us that you are now such a good friend." He was helping me see that sorrow has a power to connect us in ways we could never imagine.

As well as golf, Reg tried to engage me in pickleball, a game combining badminton, tennis and table tennis. It is the fastest growing sport among seniors in North America. Outdoor tennis courts are being turned into pickleball courts. We went to beginner's pickleball. The downside is that it is brutally noisy as the paddle smacks the baseball-sized plastic ball full of holes. It is best not to buy a house near pickleball courts! He got it from day one and soon was excelling in the sport. I tried for a season, saw how much effort it was going to take and decided to stay with swimming and golf. Reg, for his part, tried swimming and was loving it until Covid.

Moyra and I walk weekly and sometimes Reg joins us. Moyra and I talk about politics and books, architecture and travel, gardening and family. If I was sick in the middle of the night, I would call Moyra. Reg would drive her over to my house and they would know what to do.

Angels: The Cruising Pilgrims

It is true. I am overwhelmed with angels. They are a mighty force. They just keep coming and get more and more compelling. If it takes a village to raise a child, it takes a multitude of the heavenly host to raise the dying in spirit. Their abundance is staggering. How is it that they keep coming and coming? Surely this is a witness to a gracious spirit in the universe itself.

In 2016, three years after my husband abandoned me, I decided to go on an educational cruise with Joan to trace the steps of Saint Paul in the Mediterranean. I had always been leery of Paul's teachings. After all, in 1 Corinthians 14:33–35 he writes:

> As in all the congregations of the Lord's people, women should remain silent in the churches, They are not allowed to speak, but must be in submission, as the law says. If they want to inquire about something, they should ask their own husbands at home; for it is disgraceful for a woman to speak in the church.

Yet I was aware that while first century women were tasked with the work of the home, they could open their homes to worshippers and did so. Paul's policy was to offer positions of leadership to the women who founded these house churches. Thus, Phoebe, Chloe and Rufus' mother rise to prominence. More women also gained his friendship and partnership in contrast to Paul's outburst to the Corinthians. I needed to learn more.

I also had a sense that there would have been no Christian church at all had Paul not been its first missionary carrying the story to much of the known world at that time. This became abundantly true on this trip that took us all around the Mediterranean to the places Paul journeyed, not by luxury ship, but mostly by foot and cart and only sometimes by sea. It was indeed time for me to come to a deeper understanding of Paul.

The leadership team of the tour seated us at a table on the ship with Julia and Haydn from Australia, a couple, and Elizabeth and Pat from Philadelphia, friends like Joan and myself. Over time, I christened us "the cruising pilgrims".

We connected in our desire to know Saint Paul, this first and great travelling missionary of the church. Two of us were mainline denominational liberal Christians and four of us were Roman Catholics with a heart for social justice. We were outspoken and we fell into friendship. Haydn was comfortable being the only male among us.

Our days were peppered with lectures and then field excursions to many of the places Paul spent time in: Corinth, Athens, Ephesus, Delos, Mykonos and Malta. We also enjoyed a memorable day on the Amalfi Coast and also a day on Santorini.

On a glorious day, we explored Ephesus. Seeing Joan, a librarian for most of her working life, standing before sunlit two-story high stone columns of the ancient Library of Celsus filled my eyes and heart with pleasure. She belongs in a long, long line of those who maintain the word, I thought.

There is a photograph of me that day, standing in the agora, looking every bit like a tourist guide, my chest strewn with important-looking electronic gadgets. I have a crowd seated before me and I am teaching or preaching in my mind. I am Saint Paul reincarnated telling the gathered group what he preached in this very spot.

"Here in Ephesus, Artemis was worshipped for centuries. She was both a fertility goddess and a huntress. This is a place where women were adored. Paul knew this and while he fought idolatry, he reminded us that we are all one in Christ. He preached unity right here and not division. He understood complexity. He wrote to the Galatians these words from this very place, 'There is neither Jew nor Greek, slave nor free, male nor female, for you are all one in Christ Jesus.'"

I felt chills up my spine then and now in recalling that moment. These new friends were helping me remember that I was a lively capable spirit with wise words to say. I was experiencing healing.

On another fine day in Corinth, Joan and I offered communion to our friends. What is not amazing about two Protestant women pastors offering the Eucharist to a group of Christians of different persuasions in the ruins of ancient Corinth?

At dinner a few days later, emboldened, I expressed my frustration with the tour organisers.

"What do you mean, we're in Rome, and we are not visiting the Basilica of Saint Paul?" I asked all of them at dinner.

"I share your sentiment exactly," Haydn affirmed.

We decided to challenge the leadership of this tour. We assessed that they were tired and cutting corners. We made a fuss, and for those who wished, the Basilica of Saint Paul Outside the Walls was back on the itinerary. We were a feisty table group. We made things happen and we still do.

In the autumn of 2016, we spent fifteen days on that ship. Since then, Julia and Haydn have visited me in Vancouver, their son visited Joan in Toronto and all of us had a week reunion in Philadelphia. There, on a tour of the historical sites, we found ourselves helping distribute sandwiches Pat and Elizabeth had made for the homeless. They think of themselves as Beatitude Christians.

Then we discovered Zoom, and we Zoom. We supported each other as we deplored the actions of Trump. We hold in prayer and concern all the pain of the terrible scandals of abuse by the church in all three of our countries. We had a cruise planned for Newfoundland and had to cancel it due to Covid.

I have since learned that many friendships are born on sea cruises. I think ours is most unique.

Angel Lynda

I went to retreat given by my spiritual companion Peter's wife Sue, to which he suggested that not only I attend but that I make a friend there. The retreat was held at the foot of Mount Seymour in the outskirts of North Vancouver. The snow-capped mountains soared, and the paths among the trees invited us to deep conversation. I had been apprehensive about going.

The retreatants, all women, were members of the church where Peter was serving as an interim minister while the congregation prepared to make a new permanent hire. None of them knew my story and I did not want to tell it. Much of the agenda was interactive. Given an open-ended topic and an assigned partner, we explored the environment and talked with each other. I listened and found ways to say very little about myself. The walking exercises were followed by a group session and much discussion ensued. I listened carefully, looking for a possible person to befriend. At the meal table I also watched and listened. By the end of the retreat and at the final circle, I was so aware that I had not made a choice. My heart was racing with the pressure to fulfil Peter's mandate. After the final prayers following our last lunch together, as women were hugging, making golf dates and arranging for the big upcoming bazaar, I was watching.

One woman stood out for me. I knew I had enjoyed her comments in the larger group though I had never been paired with her. She was pulling on her anorak and gathering her things to leave.

With only my three-year-old confidence in my voice, I walked over and said, "Lynda, will you be my friend? Peter wanted me to come on this retreat to make a friend, so will you be my friend?"

She said "yes" to my request to be my friend, and very soon after asked me to meet her for a walk near her home. Making a new friend is a little like going on a blind date. I was nervous and excited as I parked by her home. I knew from its oceanfront street that I was way out of my financial league.

It was a ten-story high-rise with one apartment per floor, each with its own elevator. I stepped from the elevator and had to settle my nerves. Deep inside me there still beat the heart of the poor kid from the other side of the tracks. My heart was racing as I took in the wraparound view of the harbour of my city, thought to be the most beautiful in my country. The ocean, magnificent bridges and the green of our great park, the snow-capped mountain above it all, cruise ships and tankers all elicited a gasp I had to control. I wanted to be the new "cool" friend.

The entry hallway was home to a series of prints, and I knew the printmaker. I not only knew who he was, but I had met him. In front of me were five David Blackwood original prints telling the stories of fishers at sea off the wild coast of Newfoundland. I had only seen the works in galleries and books but now was just enjoying them with my very new friend. I knew a thing or two about Canadian art and I was finding a point of connection.

"David rented my children's family cottage from us over several summers. My children's uncle is a Canadian printmaker as well. Maybe you know him." And I told her his name.

"Yes, I do, I gave my friends a book containing his works."

Lynda and I were like two kids in our excitement. Friends need connection points and ours was getting off to a great start. It had been a long time since I had met anyone who shared my interest in visual art.

Over time, we visited galleries and craft shows, lunched at places where we tried new food and went to theatre. We discovered that we liked clothes. She was funkier than I was, and I delighted in helping her go for her style. I think the human body is our canvas and every day we get to paint a new version of ourselves as we dress.

In time I told her about what had happened to me and how I was in recovery. She shared that she had breast cancer and had recovered. She was intrigued by the pursuit of things spiritual, and I was only too happy to share my knowledge with her. I discovered that she hailed from an even smaller hometown than I did. She was four years younger, but we had lots of similar experiences growing up in small parochial cities. She was engaged in becoming a holy, mystical and very well-informed Christian. I was delighted to help.

Just as I was, she was raised to be a needle woman. She knits, sews, quilts, cross-stitches and creates beautiful artefacts. Most evenings I wrap myself in the softest raspberry red shawl that she knitted for me. She wears a bracelet I purchased for her. The newest research on friendship shows how it is so akin to falling in love. There is a desire to keep each other close when apart. Before I go to bed, I look across the ocean to where her home lights twinkle on the other side of the bay. I send her prayers for a restful sleep. She does the same for me. I think we are like Anne and her bosom friend Diana in *Anne of Green Gables*. It is a novel that shaped both our childhoods as Canadian girls.

We also golfed. She knew all the rules and while she obeyed them, she did not push me to behave beyond my limits. She taught me with a hands-off approach. One summer we took up golfing at each pitch and putt in our city. It was just fun.

She has a daughter who had returned to university to pursue a degree in fine arts. My son had done this degree years before. One of my grandsons was creating amazing art for a sixteen-year-old. We kept finding ways we were alike.

In the spring of 2022, in my inbox was a note from Lynda: "Here is a link to my daughter's graduation perspective on her work for her MFA."

And on the site, I found beautiful work by her daughter. In one painting, she catches all the joy of our national sport, also played by women.

Keith McClocklin, *Tender Roses or Prickly Thorns*

And I respond, "Here is my grandson's effort at portraiture." And I attach Ben's rendition of rapper Kendrick Lamar.

Our closeness in age and both of us being grandmothers added another dimension to our developing friendship. There is pleasure in homogeneity; the achievements of our highly functioning kids and grandkids were easy to share. It made the friendship flow easily.

She and her husband travelled extensively and extravagantly. I was often envious. I wished I was snorkelling around an atoll near Tahiti or kayaking among the icebergs on the Northwest Passage like them. Her husband was and is an exceptional amateur photographer. I am captivated by visual images. I always anticipate Lynda and her latest email attachment full of firsthand photos and videos from above and beneath the sea. I was an armchair traveller with them. The envy eased.

We are friends, new friends in later life, which we know is a gift for us both. We began to engage in Bible study together and in time invited Joan to join us. The disciple Matthew wisely said that "where two or three are gathered together in my name, there I will be."

Angel Els

I am not unique but one of many abandoned and forsaken women around the world. Two years into my grief, I discovered Canadian Vikki Stark's book *Runaway Husbands: The Abandoned Wife's Guide to Recovery and Renewal*. It articulated so much of what I was experiencing.

Vikki Stark's husband left her suddenly and without warning. She is a colleague of mine and a marriage and family therapist. Being a researcher by nature, she wondered if this shock had been experienced by anyone else. She knew, as did I, in most breakups there are lots of warning signs. In her case, as she shares in her book, she had been on tour promoting an earlier book she had written and came home expecting to be welcomed. Instead, she was told he was leaving immediately. Early in her grief, she put out a request and a questionnaire. Was this happening to anyone else? Four hundred women from across North America responded and the book was born. From the stories these women told her, she identified and colourfully categorized into stages our shared experiences. One of her first stages is named "Amputation without Anesthetic". It has been important for me, through her work, to be seen in these stages she so accurately describes. She has now published a follow-up book with stories of recovery from women around the world, *Planet Heartbreak: Abandoned Wives Tell Their Stories*. Her work helped me feel not crazy but normal in my grief. She created a diagnosis: "wife abandonment syndrome". Thanks to her my condition had a name.

Not long after I read her first book, I thought to go to one of her workshops. It was cancelled. She lived in Montreal, and I was going to be in Ottawa with my daughter. Vikki was just a short train ride away. I asked her to meet with me and she agreed.

It was an autumn day. Montreal is a magical city, marked by fashion, energy, great food and history. It is a French-speaking city, and I was navigating in new territory in my faulty French.

For some reason I was nervous. I guessed she was twenty-five years younger than me. She was ahead of me in her processing of her grief. I met her at her office, and she graciously showed me her space and introduced me to her stable of therapists. She took me to a charming café. It had patio seating with heaters under a striped awning. I felt as though I was in Paris. We ordered and then we talked.

It was so warm and special to speak with a woman whose husband had suddenly abandoned her. This was my first such experience. She was putting her life together. Drawing together and enabling all the women who were coming to her from all over the world was her grief practice. She had found such rewarding purpose. I was inspired.

"Vikki, what should I do? I want to write about my experience. I totally relate to the stages you have described."

For her, being with others and sharing their pain was paramount in the healing process.

"Ann, I have been contacted by another woman in Vancouver. What if I ask her if she would like to get together with you? You could then see what happens."

"Yes, I would like that, and I hope she says yes. And also, I think I want to tell my story in my way. I have had a lot of experience with grief. I think I could share things that have helped me and things I am just discovering. I am so much older than you and for me this is what some folks are calling a 'grey divorce'. I think I could talk about this in, perhaps, a memoir? I want to legitimise the sort of grief we have. I think we have a right to mourn. Loss of a partner through death is one thing, but loss through divorce at my age is quite another. I also bring a spiritual perspective. What do you think?"

"I know what you mean, I hope you do this, Ann. I find, with all the women I am talking with, they benefit from resources that get into the heart of their experience. Maybe you will be a resource that comes from the wisdom of age?"

It was a long lunch and an important one for me. She was encouraging me toward a future I could barely articulate. As she promised, she got in touch with the woman in my province and connected me to her.

Upon returning home, I immediately reached out to the woman she had suggested I meet: Els. We began our relationship over email. We were both nervous. We were admitting to each other that we had been abandoned. It was not a club in which we sought admission. Nevertheless, we agreed to meet in person. I had always strongly believed that healing is encouraged when we meet with others who suffer similar loss. When my children died, I had wished for such a group, long before the Grieving Parents Support Network was created. I was eager to meet Els.

Gradually and slowly, we walked and shared fragments of our loss with each other. She was twenty-five years younger than I was. From my perspective, she had more time to forge a new identity. From her perspective, I had more free time every day since I was not working when we met and she was a very busy entrepreneur. I learned that she was back at school part-time, learning to be an architect. Like Joan, she was opening to a new career. I wondered if I was her age if I would have done that. I might have gone to law school, built a travel company or done an MFA in creative writing.

We discovered that travel was a passion we shared. Els wanted to see the world. She was planning a trip to Holland to visit her family. I, who had travelled extensively, wondered how I could ever travel as a single person. My lawyer and my therapist both encouraged me to try and consequently in 2016, before I met Els, I had committed to my first solo international trip.

"Els, I have a home exchange in Milan," I said. "It is a large apartment within walking distance of the city centre. You can look online and see the photos. It looks very elegant. Would you like to join me?"

"A week in Milan with free accommodation! I can see Museo del Novecento!"

Els was easy to convince.

We barely knew each other as we explored the apartment in Milan, chose rooms and sorted out the basics: food, bedrooms, location and how to share a bathroom. Milan wrapped us up in magic: art galleries, Mediterranean food, the Duomo di Milano and a night at the opera, Teatro alla Scala! We purchased tickets. I was giddy with excitement.

We were women and we needed to dress up. We had a box at the La Scala. We played with our limited wardrobes, created our outfits and took each other's advice.

"I have a stole that would work for you, Ann," proffered Els.

"I have a necklace that would work for you." I did the clasp up around her neck.

Ah, if only we could wear some of the beautiful jewelry our home-owners had left behind. We peeked in the impeccable drawers with sets of matching jewelry but did not touch. Later we learned that we were visitors in the home of the Milan attaché for tourism. They clearly dressed for balls. In fact, they were using my house in Vancouver to attend a gala to encourage Milan as a tourist destination for Canadians.

Crammed into our tiny box at the opera, we allowed ourselves to be transported by Verdi's *Don Carlos*. The king wept out his deep grief and ours as he failed to win the love of his life. I mourned with him and left the theatre knowing I was not alone. Verdi sang for me and for us that night. Susan Cain in her book *Bittersweet* states, "…Sadness of all things!—has the power to create the 'union between souls'". Walking home on those cobbled streets that night, arm in arm, we knew that it was so.

It was a good start for our friendship. Els flew to Amsterdam to visit her family in Groningen, and I flew on alone to Vienna to the next very welcoming home exchange apartment. While there I spent a perfect day at Freud's house and office and another at the museum and office of Viktor Frankl, whose book *Man's Search for Meaning* was on my pride of place bookshelf. My homelink host had arranged for me to attend a magnificent open summer air concert given by the Vienna Philharmonic Orchestra where many of us waltzed in the aisles to Strauss. I continued to Prague and then to northern Scotland. My new friend, Els, helped me make my first major solo trip abroad by helping me get started.

After returning to Vancouver, Els and I continued to build our friendship together. We share theatre tickets, do outings together and despite our age difference have fun together. For me, that we grow and create thriving lives as singles is profoundly encouraging.

Angel Francine

A golf buddy of my husband and myself golfs with me once or twice a season and sometimes more. He pushed me to join women's golf. I resisted. Everything I heard about it made me sure I would hate it. Reg helped me get ready to at least try it. Two years after being abandoned, acutely missing my live-in golf partner and desperate to play golf, I signed up.

We were on the putting green at the first hole. I was fiddling with my ball to get the best line for my putt.

"You have to put your marker on the green if you lift your ball to adjust it before you putt."

And on the number two green, I was adjusting my ball when I heard the reprimand. "Ann, you did not put your marker down before you moved your ball. That is a one stroke penalty," instructed a most rule-bound woman in a foursome.

And on the tenth hole green, I heard again, from the same woman, "Ann, you did it again. You must mark your ball."

I hated rules. *I am not going for the PGA. What is wrong with these women?* was my inner dialogue.

"Ann, you have to hit the ball out of the bunker. You can't just throw your ball onto the green after three tries. You are now disqualified."

I went home and cried. I had always played golf with my husband and two men. They gave little care for such picayune rules, as I called them. I guess they just tolerated me and were happy for me to keep up speed of play. I was good at this aspect of the game. I picked up if I thought I would hold up the game. I tossed my ball out of sand traps. My friend Gail, who regularly played women's golf, told me plainly to suck it up and learn. I did and I still find many of the rules irritating. One should never have to count seventeen points on a hole, no matter what the rules say.

Because I made myself play women's golf, I met Francine at a club breakfast. We were both new members and she had just moved into my neighbourhood. Occasionally I drove the ball further than she did and she did not seem to mind. She always made her fairway shots, and I rarely did. She was super friendly. She knew nothing about my past, she did not ask and it did not matter. This was an exciting new step for me. I did not have to bring it up. She took initiative and before long we were walking together once a week on the weekend. I met her husband and sometimes the three of us golfed. He was a new friend, too. I introduced them to Brian and the four of us played golf and will continue to do so.

Vancouver is not known to be a friendly city. Making friends at any age is a challenge but at my age it is especially so. As a younger woman I had confronted misogyny and in my later years now confronted ageism. Francine did not seem to notice I was an "older", as I called myself. I was very thrilled and pleased when she regularly invited me for walks. Her husband was genuinely pleased that Francine and I were enjoying each other.

Francine was a swimmer. I have swum my whole life. I then learned from Francine that there is a club called SwimTrek. People go on swimming treks all over the world just as one would go on a walking tour. I had to see it for myself by exploring the website. Francine had swum around Greek islands and in Majorca and off the coast of Turkey. She and her son spent a summer swimming around Lake of Bays in Ontario in segments. I was fascinated. Could I do this? Maybe.

I would have to be able to swim in the ocean for two kilometres, rest and repeat this two more times to accomplish six kilometres in a day. As a college student I had trained in long-distance lake swimming. It was in the days that Marilyn Bell had swum Lake Ontario and then the English Channel. She was my childhood hero, and I thought a lot about doing what she was doing. Back then, I decided I could not compete with the likes of Marilyn Bell.

However, throughout my life, I swam a lot but really did not like rough cold water with live creatures in it. I did not fancy being nose to nose with a harbour seal. Still, the warm waters of Majorca had appeal, as did the challenge. I did and still do swim two kilometres in an hour twice a week but in a very clean swimming pool. Maybe I could do this in open water? Francine was keen for me to do an upcoming trip to Croatia with her.

I could go to Majorca with SwimTrek and train. This would be expensive, and I could not help but look out my living room window and see that I lived on the ocean. I thought I could sign up for ocean swimming right where I live and give it a go. Maybe I could join Francine.

Sure enough, there was a club, Fast Lane, that would train me. Why not? I said to myself and signed up! I was to start early in June and have six lessons. In Vancouver we call June "Junuary", a conflation of January and June. That should have been my first indication of the trouble ahead.

I showed up carrying a newly rented wetsuit and a thick towel. Jericho Beach is stunning with snow-capped mountains rising across the inlet. The sun was bathing the beach in the soft golden light of one of the longest days of the year. I felt intrepid. Then I saw my fellow classmates gathered at picnic tables, signing in and putting on their wetsuits.

Vancouver is probably the city in Canada where the fittest specimens of humanity live. Jericho Beach is where the most elite of these hang out, windsurf, paddleboard, sail, run and bike. It is weird how I can forget I am eighty years old. I had not thought about who my fellow swimmers would be. These men, mostly about thirty years of age, were drop-dead gorgeous. I was more than an anomaly. There was a young woman among them, and I could tell she was nervous and not a swimmer. Neither of us could get our wetsuits on. Had she not been there I surely would have fled home.

Our coaches were enthusiastic. First, we introduced ourselves. The guys were all competing in an Ironman in mid-July and were wanting to hone their skills. The young woman had a boyfriend who was into deep-sea diving, and she wanted to be able to manage ocean swimming.

"My name is Ann, and I am trying to assess whether I can swim around the islands off Croatia with SwimTrek." I knew I had impressed them all. Fifty years their senior, they happily did up the zipper on my wetsuit for me as they pumped me with questions about SwimTrek. Maybe this was going to work.

The coaches started their instruction. I was game.

"Tonight, we are going to work on entry and exit from the water. Speed is essential and the water is 150 metres from where we are. The sand is deep so pick up your feet on the way down to the water."

I was beginning to understand that the Ironmen were competing, and speed was going to be part of this course.

"You can run right in but on the way out, you need to do a push-up to lift yourself from the water and then count to sixty before running up to take off your suits and get on your bikes. You must pause or you take the chance of fainting."

Going so fast I would faint was not something I had considered. Maybe I should go home while I was still ahead?

"Today we will just get used to swimming in a pack. You must lift your head to spot every sixth stroke and try not to hit your fellow swimmers. We will video you so you can check if you are spotting well. Let's get started with some push-ups to get us warmed up."

Maybe this really wasn't going to work. Very quickly I progressed to the bottom of the class. Flip turns around a buoy amid the flying arms and legs of my hunky Ironmen classmates in a freezing ocean was terrifying. If I must drown, perhaps this was the way to go.

I had never been this cold in living memory. An hour later, my fingers too numb to unzip my wetsuit, the coach helped and offered me thermal gloves and booties for the following week. Somehow, I got out of my wetsuit, wrapped myself in my wisely brought, very thick towel and tried to run to my car with the heated seat and thank goodness, a heated steering wheel. At home I filled my oversized bathtub and slipped into it like a giant ice cube, teeth chattering and thinking Majorca would have been a lot warmer.

For six weeks I endured this craziness before I admitted I was not going to be an ocean swimmer. Francine, bless her, was willing to be my friend anyway. SwimTrek does look amazing and maybe in warm ocean water it would be easier? In the summer of 2022, she was once again enticing me with a swim in the rivers and lakes and oceans of Montenegro. In my next lifetime?

Francine also liked to travel. I told her about my desire to go to St. Petersburg for the white nights and to go to the Hermitage. She had worked in Helsinki and was wanting to visit friends there. We decided to do it, and off we went to the cruise specialists. We found the perfect cruise on an upscale ship that would take us from Stockholm to Helsinki to St. Petersburg and back. It had been on my bucket list. I would finally see Rembrandt's *The Return of the Prodigal Son*. I wanted to be in Scandinavia for the days of the midnight sun and we were going to do it. We purchased tickets and I bought guidebooks. We were new friends, and it was so full of novelty and adventure. Alas, Covid took this away, and now going to Russia in my lifetime has vanished. It remains an almost-dream-come-true.

Francine and I walk and talk most weekends. She and her husband and I play golf and share meals and good conversation. They are new friends now fast becoming old friends.

I believe there is a benevolence in the universe that is accessible for all. Violence also abounds. For me, the Creator Spirit is an energy that abhors violence and draws us towards compassion. We cannot bear the child fleeing with her body ravaged by napalm. We cannot bear the photo of Alain's body washed on the beaches of the Mediterranean as the refugees fled from Syria. We gasp to see an elderly man dead, dropped from his bicycle with a sack of potatoes spilling out and mixing with his blood on a Ukrainian street in Bucha. Our transgressions go too far. They cannot be dismissed as "messy" bumps on the road towards progress. We are capable of a shudder. Specific shudders ignite the energy of a multitude of beautiful angels.

I did not know that so many angels, with more still coming after them, would show up for me in small ways and in huge ways, all of them so magnanimous that there is no word other than gobsmacked for the gratitude I am feeling.

In Mexico on a visit with Gail during Easter, I found a collection of tin angels at a market. Each is uniquely painted in different colours. Each has a tiny base to hold the light of a tiny candle. They hang in a window during Eastertime in my house and keep me very grateful for the presence of angels in my life.

All the angels, both old and new, who came to me in my trauma continue to stand by me, grounding me. I understand how Jesus came to have an inner circle of at least twelve. You have met my circle as it stands at the end of year nine. Rippling out from that circle are many others who have constantly carried me in their thoughts and sent messages of care and support. Now I am truly confident that there will always be more angels coming. Allowing people to care for me is an astonishing grief practice. Before I knew it, I was caring for them. As I turned the corner on ten years, I had brunch with a new angel, Janice, and she insisted on paying to thank me for all the support I was giving her in her new business as a crochet artist. Mutuality in relationship was returning. I find I am sprouting wings.

Chapter 19

THE LEGAL NIGHTMARE

The number of people who are going to court without lawyers has gone up enormously. We know around half of the people that represent themselves begin with a lawyer. And they run out of money.

According to my research, more than 50 per cent of people going to family court this year, 2016, will not have a lawyer. It's most people, and it's certainly the middle class.

> – Julie Macfarlane,
> University of Windsor law professor

At the very beginning, back in November of 2012 when my husband first told me that he was thinking of leaving our marriage, I knew I should call a lawyer. I did not do this. I did not take what would have been my own advice to any client of mine in similar circumstances. My denial was airtight.

After he left me on Valentine's Day of 2013, he immediately initiated divorce proceedings with me. By mid-March I knew I had to find a lawyer to protect myself.

In the province of British Columbia, Canada, where I live, a change in divorce procedure was introduced at exactly this juncture.

The Family Law Act came fully into force on March 18, 2013 and replaced the Family Relations Act.

Because my husband began divorce proceedings on March 20, 2013, all our negotiations fell under this new law. The press was reporting that lawyers were scrambling to understand the implications and were generally displeased with the new system, which entailed more work for them. A fifty-fifty split of assets was the common practice but this changed with the new law. Assets brought into the marriage by one of the spouses could be protected if proof of the same was provided. I did know that this could possibly give me a legal advantage. I also saw how this complicated both my life and the lives of lawyers.

Finally, I called Theresa, the lawyer to whom I generally referred my clients. I knew her to be direct, feminist and tough in her negotiations. Her office made an appointment for me to chat with her by telephone since she was in Vancouver and I was still in Florida. Mary had returned to Florida for a weekend to help me get through my birthday on March 27 which, for some unfortunate circumstance, was also the birthday of my husband's therapist, now probable lover. The call to the lawyer was arranged for a time when Mary would be with me.

I was in deep denial and did not want to have the conversation. Once Theresa had the facts, namely that there was no chance of repair, she began with true practical legal precision, though not before stating her genuinely startled shock and sympathy. She then moved quickly on to a barrage of reality-based questions for which I was not prepared.

"The condo you just purchased is a big problem. Everything is going to be about assets."

"I don't understand why the condo is a problem," I managed to say.

She went on: "This is a grey divorce. You are seventy-four. The new law has changed everything, and you will need the deed to the house you owned when you first cohabited with your husband and its estimated value at that time. I think we can make the new law work for you. You will not have to split everything fifty-fifty and you will have entitlement to what you brought into the marriage..."

I interrupted her. "I am not eating or sleeping. My daughter is with me. I don't want a divorce."

Then I hung up. I had just blanked out. Mary took charge and got me out walking and talking and recovering from my initial conversation with Theresa. With her encouragement the next day, I called my accountant, Barbara, who knew both my husband and me but had known me for much longer. After she took in what had happened, expressing the same gasp and sympathy, she also moved into high gear.

"Ann, you have to get your own Visa card now and end the joint ones. You must put a stop on your joint line of credit. Empty any joint chequing accounts now. Promise me you will do this immediately."

She was right and I should have done those things, but I did not. I was in massive denial. I still thought things would work out for my husband and myself. I was also ashamed to call the bank.

I returned to Canada a week later. Settling into "our" house was overwhelming for me. Mary helped me by talking with the lawyer on my behalf. She could also see that it was more important to try to help me keep food down and get some sleep than act on the lawyer's advice. She knew I was still more interested in dying than living. Eventually the lawyer also saw that I was not fit for the work of a divorce. I could not focus on the tasks of collecting data and filling in multiple forms concerning my expenses and finding documents. She spoke with my daughter about having me declared "incapacitated emotionally and mentally". The bar was high for this, requiring psychiatric diagnosis and possible hospitalisation. I expect it is a good thing that this idea was rejected as it would be on my medical record forever. Instead, delay tactics were employed to buy me time to stabilise. Appeals from his lawyer drew no response from mine.

Most divorce proceedings are about custody of children. Grey divorce is all about assets and who gets what. The new law made it clear that assets held by a person at the moment of cohabitation could be apportioned to that person. If it is a house, which is often the case, then the fifty-fifty split is only on the amount the house earned during the cohabitation and not on its value when purchased. It was true of all other assets as well. We were going to have to agree on a division of our assets.

My lawyer encouraged me. "Please try to get a hold of yourself. Your husband is likely to be most generous with you in these first months after he has left. It would be good to try to make his guilt work for you."

Even before he left, while he was with me in Florida, he had moved from a generous position to wanting half of everything. When my husband and I married, I had a full-time practice as a psychotherapist, owned a house, a new car and had pension investments. He came with a part-time student job, an old guitar, a beater of a car, several record albums, two feather pillows, some student debt and child support payments. We happily shared what we had with each other for thirty years.

One friend commented when she heard he had abandoned me, "I'll never forget watching him go from Gap tees to Hugo Boss shirts in a week."

Throughout the years of our marriage both of us worked and made about the same amount per year.

I thought, *He is seventeen years younger than me and has years to work. He is going to be with an able-bodied professional woman seventeen years younger than him who has even more years to work than he does.*

I discerned and hoped a judge would agree that, at seventy-four, my financial position was significantly more precarious and that I would be entitled to more than half of our assets.

The fourth month after he left, he insisted that our home and condo be sold and the matter settled immediately. I began to get nasty letters from his lawyer. I was finding it very difficult to work with my own lawyer, who was powerfully representing me, but I was clearly avoiding talking to her, let alone fulfilling her requests.

Gradually my shock was easing, and my denial gave way to reality and anger. Even though I was still crippled by suicidal thoughts, I was forced by the legal system into thinking about what would be next in my life. Selling the house and packing it up and moving somewhere was way beyond anything that I could imagine doing. Had he died, I would have been told to take my time. Wanting to live at all was a daily battle. Where to live was not yet on my radar.

As a child, I hated the oft asked question, "Where do you live?"

In a grade thirteen government-administered composition exam, I read, "Compose a story starting with the view from your bedroom window."

I remember writing something like this in the spring of 1957.

The train tracks run just beyond my back garden gate. My bedroom window overlooks the garden and the rail yards. The railway station is a hub for important steam trains carrying manufactured goods from New York state to Canada and taking Canadian wheat and coal to the USA. The Union Pacific Big Boy, the Pennsylvania K4 and the Canadian Pacific Royal Hudson arrive and leave in full view of my bedroom window. My father knows the schedules and makes stories up for me about their cargo and their destinations. I love the whistles and they don't frighten me. The steam billows about the engine car when they arrive and leave. They are huge behemoths and bigger than the whale in the Bible.

Above the yards and to the east I can see the flashing neon sign of Yello's furniture store just beyond the terminal station, blinking bravely through summer rains and winter snowstorms. The view from my bedroom window is amazing.

I knew I had written a colourful composition and I finished a bit early. I began to reflect, and shame filled me. Who would ever let such a poor kid from the wrong side of the tracks get a mark fit for university? I set the story aside and in the remaining minutes scribbled some inane thing that I deemed would not give my poverty away. It is astonishing that I passed the exam at all. Through all my years growing up I had shrunk year by year from ever having to tell anyone where I lived.

When my husband left me, our home was in Kitsilano. This is a word full of magic and memories for many Canadians, even those who do not live in British Columbia. Kitsilano is the Haight-Ashbury of Canada, capital of the countercultural revolution of the 1960s and 70s.

When people ask me where I live and I answer Kitsilano, it is guaranteed that a faraway look of lost pleasures will cross the face of the enquirer as they tell me, "Ahh, I envy you. That's where I lived when I went to university. That's when I was free. That's when we were all free. I had a bike, a volleyball net and a bathing suit. It was party time, and it was protest time. It was marijuana time. Have you eaten at the Naam? It is still there, you know. You are so lucky to live there. It is out of my budget now but if only…"

I am proud to live in Kitsilano. While gentrified, it is still a happening place. Our house is a block from the sea where I can walk unimpeded for twenty-eight kilometres on a path following the land's edge around our picturesque harbour. I frequently pick up a small ferry boat ride and pop around to various sea stops on the Burrard Inlet. I have taken swimming lessons in the ocean and swim all summer in the longest swimming pool in our country at 137 metres. From my living room chair, I can see the ski runs and the hiking paths in the mountains that are forty-five minutes away by car. I am a ten-minute drive from one of the best public golf courses in my province. The local market, open seven days a week, is a thirty-five-minute walk from where I live. For me it is a paradise.

Hilary Morris, a Vancouver artist, painted what I think of as my pool.

Hilary Morris, *Kits Pool*

The inside of my home is sensational to me. The house is a heritage home that was completely renovated and turned into three strata units. Our unit is the smallest of the three but has most of the original charm. It has a complete wall of stained-glass windows and the flooring is original maple wood from my home province of Ontario. There are twenty-foot pieces of burled maple and other slats of birdseye maple on the floor. They give off a golden glow in the evening sun, echoing the deep amber in the stained glass. The master bath is the pièce de résistance. For me, the large bathtub sitting beneath a gas fireplace mounted on the wall is perfection. I never want to live without it. It also has a two-person shower that my husband and I enjoyed together every morning. People driving by often stop in front to look up and admire the house set above two flights of fifteen stone steps divided by a stone path. All this is set in cedar hedges and lampposts and surrounded by green gardens twelve months a year. It is a house we could barely afford when we purchased it. Together, we worked hard for it and enjoyed it immensely.

Distraught as I was, I did not want to move. I was losing my husband, my church and its community and my lifework project. The house was one thing too many. How could he have the right to take this too?

When I was being pushed to sell the house and filled with uncertainty concerning my next step, I hoped for a dream that might give me clarity on the path forward. Then I had this dream.

A magnificent creature appeared to me. She was radiant with light. On her head was an incredible tiara. It had tulips spinning and bouncing around, moving like a child's mobile. In the dream I loved this creature. She was totally alluring. She took my hand and I had a sense she would never let go. When I woke up, I named her Sophia, a feminine name for God. I thought of her as Holy Oneness and I knew I was hers forever.

She became a beacon calling me to a future self I did not believe existed. While this dream did not tell me whether to try to buy the house or not, this beautiful creature helped me to remember that, maybe, I could find the strength and ingenuity to figure out how to secure the time I needed to mourn. Keeping the house would give me a safe place for that task. Those who loved me wanted me to keep the house for as long as it took for me to be more functional.

I made a collage of her to celebrate her arrival. I keep her image on my cell phone opening screen. She shows me and reminds me that one day I will thrive and be like her, shimmering and flowing with motion and light.

This dream enabled me to engage in the legal process towards this end. I had to find the right lawyer for me. As I researched to find such a lawyer, I was appalled by the cost. I had already spent $30,000 on a lawyer that I only wanted to avoid and finally fired. She had been a good lawyer, but I was not ready. I wanted a new, less aggressive lawyer, one who might be patient with my damaged soul. But could I find one I could afford?

In February 2011, Chief Justice Beverley McLachlin of the Supreme Court of Canada was quoted in our national newspaper, *The Globe and Mail*, saying, "The middle class cannot hope to pay legal fees that average $338 per hour, leaving them little option but to represent themselves in court or go away empty-handed."

Indeed, in ever-increasing numbers, people are doing just this. By 2012, based on limited statistics, sixty-four to seventy-four per cent of family law case litigants were self-representing. By 2016, judges were reporting that it was more like eighty per cent. The law profession knows that this is a genie that is not going back in the bottle. Slowly, help is being provided for self-litigants. A process called "bundling" is taking effect. Here, a person can self-represent on all but the most complex matters, which some lawyers will consent to handle. Knowing all this made me consider representing myself. However, as my new friend and lawyer Moyra helped me see, I had no idea how to acquire the sanity to represent myself within the urgent time frame that was demanded of me.

After a series of interviews, I found a new lawyer, Carla, who saw me through the process. We had both studied theology at different American universities in the late 1960s. It was a serendipitous connection for me. We shared progressive theology and the campus life of the late sixties. She would not give me a price, but she said that her fee was reduced when she did routine work. Her paralegal did this work and charged $250 an hour for it. I could not afford her or her paralegal who earned more an hour than I did. However, she was kind, empathic and shuddered when she heard my story. I felt she would care for me. I felt I had no choice but to opt into this impossible system. I was steadied by the sentiment of our chief justice. It was and is still a flawed system.

I found it painfully difficult to spend so many after-tax dollars to pay for a divorce I did not want and had not initiated. I often thought about the 1970s and the time before the almost universal introduction of no-fault divorce. Then, the person ending a marriage bore the brunt of the financial cost. While I understood that this system was difficult to administer, nevertheless, from my perspective, the old way looked very attractive.

Gradually I became more levelheaded and secure. My new lawyer had assured me that this process would be my full-time work for at least one year. Motivated to possibly make the house mine, I did my best to take on the hardest job of my life. I would prepare for sessions with her and meet in her office, which was downtown. I could take a little ferry across the inlet and walk there in less than an hour and the walking helped me attain some semblance of calmness.

The sessions were long. There were so many facts for me to gather, from past income tax returns to how much I currently spent for toilet paper in a month. My brain was not able to stay on topic. My daughter reminded me regularly that not doing so was costing me money by the minute. In today's world I would have been able to record the session on my cell and not have to rely on my very rattled memory. There were meetings where I just got up and walked out. The lawyer would go to another room to make a copy of something I was giving her and when she returned, I would be gone. I barely knew I had left.

Under stress, I had dissociated. I would not remember where I was or who I was. More than once, it would be an hour or two later that my brain re-engaged, and I would find that I had wandered off into some part of the city strange to me. I would then have to reorient myself and make a plan to get home. Of course, I could not remember much of what had been told to me in the meeting. I was not an easy client and I loathed the monthly bills from my lawyer.

I did understand that Carla wanted documents I did not have. Knowing I needed help to do this, I called my son.

"David, the lawyer says that I need to try to find the deed on the Toronto house that I owned. I need to find the records and there's an office in Toronto where we can go to look. I think it's in the centre of the city. Will you take me?"

As my children were trying to help in all the ways they could, he quickly agreed. I made the arrangements to fly to his house and begin this process. The records office was unimaginable. It was filled with tables where endless red tape had to be entered in outmoded computers with deficient programmes. The office was dark, dusty and full of what I thought to be anxious people like myself. The whole place reminded me of the accounting office of Marley and Scrooge in *A Christmas Carol*: threadbare and cramped with piles of ledgers indicating chaos everywhere. I felt like Scrooge with a candle ferreting about, trying under pressure to surface the right document. Three days later we located the papers that my lawyer needed. I had had to prove what I was worth thirty years ago, which in the end seemed small as markets had since done nothing but increase that value. In retrospect it is hard to judge how worthwhile this research was. It was a piece of the hard work I had to do. Maybe people are supposed to keep records of all this sort of data, but I had not. In fact, two years before he abandoned me, we had shredded many documents, secure in our future together and preparing to live with less of a footprint upon the earth.

As part of this downsizing and preparing for the next project of our lives, we had made a new will. As in any second marriage, it was difficult to do. How would we divide our assets between his one child and my two when we died? Fortunately for me, after much discussion, we had divided our assets in three, a third to each child. This clearly gave evidence to his recent declaration that I had brought the foundation of our current assets into our marriage. In addition, all these papers were in my possession, and I could turn them over to my lawyer easily.

Carla was tiny and effervescent. Her optimism never wavered before my despair. Gradually I think we met in the middle with the understanding that we each had different paths. She became careful with her buoyancy, and I restricted unburdening my deep sadness upon her.

We first had to deal with the condominium that my husband, myself, my daughter and her husband had just purchased in Ottawa some five months before he left me in Florida. It was not yet built and was a year from completion. It had been purchased to allow us to live for two to three months a year in Ottawa to be a part of our grandchildren's lives. I was very happy about this purchase. My daughter and her husband chipped in half of the cost as both an investment and to have us close while their children were growing up. I never wanted to live in Ottawa, but I looked forward to having our own space there while visiting. We never would have made the purchase if my husband had indicated that he was considering leaving the marriage.

Any conversation with my husband regarding this condo became more and more strained. My daughter did not want to negotiate with him when he continually defaulted on his share of the monthly payment. She and her husband and I decided to buy him out of the project, which I am sure was a relief to him. Financially this decision favoured him. When the condo was completed the market in Ottawa real estate had gone down significantly. Consequently, when we sold it, my daughter, her husband and I lost a very sizeable amount of money. The amount was equivalent to half of my gross yearly income before tax. I am particularly angry about this, and I thought about what it would have been like for him if he had done this to his parents or his daughter. He had fully signed

on the dotted line five months before he abandoned me and simultane-
ously this commitment to my daughter's family.

The legal bills were mounting. Gradually I realized that this process
was going to cost tens of thousands of dollars, if not more than a hundred
thousand dollars. These were all after-tax dollars that I had worked well
beyond retirement age to acquire. Our Supreme Court justice was right.
Middle class people cannot afford this and particularly grey middle class
people certainly cannot.

I wanted to do mediation, a process whereby my husband and I and
our lawyers would sit down with a person trained in the art of bringing
about compromise between conflicting parties. I had confidence in this
process, and I knew it would keep costs down. My lawyer wanted this but
his lawyer, known to prefer mediation, was steadily conveying to us that
his client was unwilling. From the beginning, my husband presented a
strong desire to go to court and have a judge decide. The new family law
in BC was definitely against proceeding by trial and wanted all settlements
to be made out of court. The new law clearly preferred decisions to be
made through mediation.

Somehow, his lawyer and mine arranged an attempt at mediation. I put
myself one hundred per cent into giving it my best shot. I prepared in every
way. My lawyer was satisfied with the legal state of the case and the result
of my research. I prepared emotionally by creating a circle of support. I put
a keynote presentation on my computer that I made for myself with letters
and prayers from friends around the world. I planned to read this presentation in the break periods during the day-long mediation. I was determined
to be calm and steady. I was not going to dissociate.

My keynote presentation began with this slide along with a quote from
John O'Donohue. The photo was taken by James and was the one that
saved my life that terrible night in the Florida condo.

And here is a sampling of other colourful slides with photos.

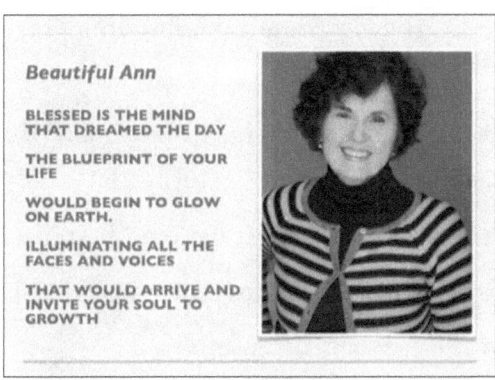

From my son and his family, beside a photo of the three of them at the entrance to one of my son's woodlots, were these words:

Hi Mom, Tried to call but no answer. Just going to bed. I hope Mary arrived safely. I wish you strength and courage for to-morrow. I'm sorry you have to go through this. It's hard that life can be so unfair. I hope on the other side of the mediation you can have some release from the terrible burden you have had to bear. Be firm, resolute and patient as you can. Let the process unfold and take your time. Calculate. I will be thinking of you and I will pray for your well being to-morrow. Call me if you need to talk. All my love, Dave, Cheryl and Ben.

And a prayer from Darlene:

God who holds our past, our present and our future,
We pray to-day for Ann

May this experience of mediation be bearable for Ann
Help her to trust the process, her lawyer and the mediator.
Help her to think and speak with clarity and confidence.

Help her to breathe in your calm presence.

Steer her broken heart away from triggering thoughts
and memories.

Let there be just the right mix of anger in her veins that she stands
up straight but

Not so much that she works against her own best interests.

We pray that justice will be done for Ann through this mediation,

Though none of this is what Ann wants.

God we pray, that you will infuse her with the strength to face it
with grace.

Remind Ann of the loving thoughts and prayers that surround
her.

And we pray for Ann's future,

That she can find release from the devastating orbit of hurtful
memories and rejections

The pain that courses through her will ease

That she will reclaim her beauty and clarity of soul.

And more still, God of the Resurrection, that she will find her way
through this time of darkness and loss to re-enter a gladness to be
alive.

We pray that a new path of connection and pleasure will emerge for
Ann.

And we offer our prayers for Ann's family; David and Cheryl, Mary
and Chris and her grandchildren who have been there for her in
brave and practical ways

Hear our individual prayers and hopes......

We pray in the name of the one who heals.

My niece Kathy, whose husband had died in his forties, wrote these words for me:

I remember going to a silent retreat one June weekend after Paul died and the leader—Elizabeth West, a former Catholic nun, now Buddhist—told me that Life is a river, and we are in the stream. At times we travel a long way with someone and then, suddenly our ways divide, and we find ourselves in a new tributary. This is our new way and the design of it all is out of our hands. She said I must embrace my new river. And learn to swim all over again.

My thought for you on this day is: Grace under fire. May you hold your head up and shine with your inner beauty.

Here are the words from my physician Ellen beside a photo of her rain-soaked at the end of a march.

Dear Ann

Remember that nothing and no one can take away your inner beauty. You are God's child, and you are beautiful.

The photo I am sending of me was taken at the end of the march in the cold and rain for truth and reconciliation with our aboriginal brothers and sisters last October, 2013 and it symbolizes my solidarity against injustice. I am with you in solidarity with your struggle to find inner peace even when justice is elusive.

All of us will surround you with love on Friday. Feel that energy around you.

There were fifty-three slides in total. Every message was deeply meaningful and all of them inspired me to be centred and strong.

His lawyer made the decision on the choice of mediator. My lawyer encouraged me to accept their choice because they were so reluctant to be at the table. Since I was allowed to, I met with this mediator a day or two before so that I knew the office and had met the person. She had a good reputation within the legal community.

When I stepped into her office, I found myself navigating my way through piles of cardboard boxes. The hallways were stacked floor to ceiling with them. Eventually I found her office door and, once admitted, was invited to sit on a box.

"Oh, my goodness, you must have just moved," I commented. I was staring at boxes and books everywhere. *A rabbit warren would have been neater,* I thought.

"No," she said firmly, and moved on to be friendly and to describe the process.

"Ann, you will have a choice about conducting the meeting. We can meet separately from the beginning if you think that best. Or we can meet around a table all together, or a combination of both. What do you want?"

"Let's meet together to start." I felt strong enough to see him and I wanted him to see me.

I left her office dismayed. I thought that she must be a hoarder. Therapist that I was at my core, I wondered how I could help her with this problem. I thought I could refer her to my colleague Don. How could she help me untangle a mess when she herself lived in one? My lawyer was prepared for my call.

"She's not suitable," I said. "How can she have such a good reputation?"

My lawyer assured me, "Ann, we need to go for this. She is good at her job, even if not her tidiness. Mediation is the best solution and they have agreed to try."

I suppressed my intuitive doubt. I was so fully prepared, and my daughter Mary had booked time off and purchased her plane tickets to be with me in Vancouver. Then, the day before the mediation occurred, I learned that my husband had fired his lawyer, the one with whom my lawyer had accomplished successful mediations in the past. I feared the new lawyer might be cheaper and less experienced with both mediation and grey divorce. I used the keynote presentation I had made over and over to calm my anxiety.

The day of the mediation arrived. It was possible to walk to the mediator's office from what was still our home. I invited Anita and Moyra to join my daughter and me. We decided to gather at the foot of the Burrard Street Bridge, the bridge that would take us to the downtown core of the city. It would take us to the courthouse and to the office buildings of the city's lawyers. I asked everyone to wear something red, my favourite colour. The bridge was flying pink cherry blossom banners from all its lampposts. The four of us hugged and began this mediation march. On the way we picked up my lawyer at her downtown office building. She was outside waiting. She is very tiny and there she was with her very big suitcase on wheels filled with my documents. It was a third the size of her. It was a sunny spring day with displays of daffodils and tulips brightening the public spaces in the downtown core. Everything conspired to give me strength.

Our little parade arrived at the mediator's office door and each of my friends hugged me and wished me well as they parted with me. My daughter put her arm around me, holding me just enough so that I stayed strong.

"Bye, Mom. You can do it. Call me when it is over, and I will be here to debrief, and we can walk home."

My lawyer and I quickly entered the office, navigated the clutter of boxes in the entry hall and found our way to the boardroom. The mediator was there to greet us.

I saw his lawyer first before I saw him. She looked to be thirty years of age. Her arms were filled with files and papers, a box of Kleenex and a water bottle. Her eyes and nose were red. She was obviously sick. All I could think of was how my husband was almost a germophobe and hated being around any sickness of the contagious kind.

The mediator spoke, describing how the day would go. She suggested we might desire to break for lunch. She made a pitch for mediation as the best means of reaching a settlement. I hoped my husband was listening.

My lawyer began and it quickly seemed to me that his new lawyer was unprepared. She was scrambling though papers and blowing her nose. I found it unnerving and suggested we retire to separate rooms and that the mediator go back and forth with messages. Their seeming lack of preparation annoyed me. This became more and more evident as the messaging went back and forth. Their side seemed unaware of the details that the new law demanded. Very difficult things were said and transmitted. The mediator asked my lawyer and myself for our patience as we proceeded.

We sent a message to the other side that lunchtime had come, and we suggested a break to eat and think. I began to listen to my keynote presentation and my lawyer made other business calls. Eventually we were told by the mediator that the other side had already left the process, declaring it ineffective. I was devastated yet again. I had put so much into this process and honestly thought it could work. I was so disappointed. My emotional capacity to stay connected fell away and the dissociative state returned with force. I simply let my daughter take my arm and walk me home. She comforted me for a day or two before making her flight back east to her home.

It took me several months to recover and sort out that this process was going to cost more and more money and probably become more and more nasty. Moyra walked with me several times a week, helping me to regain courage and understanding for the process that had been forced upon me. Her legal mind was an indispensable gift for me. She freely gave and I received.

Letters and accusations went back and forth between lawyers. My lawyer strongly favoured mediation most of the time, although occasionally we spoke of what the court trial process would be like. She had to prepare me.

My husband fired his second lawyer and hired a third one who was basically unknown to most family lawyers in the city. I assumed this lawyer was cheaper again. At this point, two years in, I received a subpoena to be present at a date for a trial some months hence that was to be five days in duration. The legal costs threatened to use up all the assets we were fighting over.

My lawyer suggested to me, "There is one more thing we can try. We can force a mediation. If we do, he must attend."

I told my lawyer my concern. "But won't he just scupper it, as he did the last time? I think he wants a trial. I think he wants a judge to decide. I think he wants this so that he does not have to make the decision. Then in his mind it will be the judge's call and not his."

My lawyer persisted. "You must think of the financial cost and the emotional one of a trial. I want to try to force this. Do I have your permission?"

I agreed and their side balked. We received a letter saying he was not in compliance with the request. However, because it was forced, he did not have a choice. My lawyer and I found the city's best mediator. I met with him. The office was clean and full of windows that let in a view of trees and parklands. As before, I met with this man a day or two before the mediation was to take place. I took him the letter from my husband stating his avowal for noncompliance. The mediator agreed with me that this made the situation untenable.

"Please, Ann, leave it in my hands. I will contact his lawyer and see if there is any room for negotiation on this."

This mediator was able to effect a change and the proposal of mediation was accepted. The day was set and the mediation occurred. I put on the table an offer my lawyer and I had agreed was fair. It involved the division of our assets and gave me more of them than it did him. It also gave me an additional three months before I would have to put the house on the market. It was my best offer. He refused it. The process ended with no resolution and the court date remained in place. The trial was to be honoured some months ahead, provided the court did not delay it, which was common practice due to a large backlog of cases to be tried. In my opinion, a trial would have done nothing to speed up the sale of the house.

I remember walking out of that mediation, looking at the man I loved and had given my life to, sitting there in the hallway waiting for his lawyer so that they might leave together. This had been my best friend and the cold rage in his countenance as he looked at me was impossible not to see. The process of divorce is brutal and cruel in many situations. I felt so humiliated that this was happening. I hate that moment now lodged in my memory.

I tried to think positively about preparing for court. I had worked with judges in my practice over the years and I knew them to be good people who struggled with difficult decisions. Maybe a judge would be able to find a way to resolve this. Perhaps it would be good for me to be able to have my story witnessed, knowing that his would be as well. I knew I would be cross-examined and torn to shreds. He would be as well. I thought that perhaps I could endure this experience. I began to get ready by arranging to attend some trials in preparation. Again, Moyra promised to do this with me.

However, the mediator was not finished with us and held out a carrot: he would send my lawyer and his lawyer a letter with his recommendations. He suggested that the final agreement I had offered should be accepted, as this was likely as good as it was going to get in a trial. Weeks went by with no response from his side. We prepared for a trial.

I knew he wanted the house sold. I did not want to tell him that I entertained the possibility of buying him out. I had, as yet, no financial means to do so. The common practice in divorce among younger couples is to sell the house and split the proceeds by agreed-upon percentages.

For a long time after he left, I thought about living in the city where one or the other of my children lived. I didn't want to choose between them. I didn't want to live in either of their cites because both are very cold in winter. The condo in Ottawa would be finished and was an option. But I loved being near the sea. I looked at other neighbourhoods and cheaper houses in Vancouver. As I did this, I knew I loved where I was. I was not able to face any more change. We had prepared this house to see us through retirement. It had new appliances, refinished floors, new carpets, and a new bed. I did not want, as many suggested, to turn the key and get the hell out of it. I did not feel very safe in the world, and I did feel a little safety in this house. Emotionally I knew I was not ready to sort through all the possessions dear to me and move. Perhaps having lost so much, keeping the house took on more meaning for me. In this house was the floor I crept upon when I was trying to put pieces of myself together. I was not finished with this work. I could not imagine relocating to a new city. Here I had a GP who was beyond a blessing. I had my five dentists who helped me save my teeth and I had a hair stylist. I had a few friends. I had walks I loved. The sea was at my door. I thought that if I got well enough, I might be able to work again, and my office was in the house. I liked this too, and I did not want to rent office space elsewhere.

As a retired woman of seventy-six, I began to try to figure out how to raise the money to keep the house. My children, my financial planner and friends all supported me in this desire. I had to think about trying to raise nearly half its value in a line of credit at my age. I did not want a mortgage because it would require me to pay down both the principal and interest costs. Housing prices in my city are the second highest in the world. It was terrifying and humiliating to go hat in hand to banks. I felt stupid and ashamed. How could I have let this happen to me? The bank I had been with since I was ten years old refused my request outright. Each time I was rejected put me back into anxious days and long nights of sleeplessness. The ageism I encountered was cruel and persistent.

As the mediator had predicted, eventually his side accepted the agreement I had put on the table. It was over. For me there was yet another wrinkle, which galls me still. The mediator made a $35,000 error in arithmetic favouring my husband. I had this checked by several accountants. There was a mistake. I wanted this corrected, but my lawyer thought it had to be swallowed. I swallowed. But I do think that, as mediators do not have financial training, there should be accountants in the room when finances are the main issue as they are in grey divorce.

A trial was averted. I now had only a very few weeks to come good on the agreement. I had to raise a lot of cash or sell the house. My husband still did not know I was trying to raise the money and was very annoyed that there was no "For Sale" sign on the house. I had to field realtor calls from a person I thought of as our realtor and I did suspect that he was encouraging those calls.

I repeatedly got close to a bank deal, but I continued to fail. I don't know how I found the grit to try again. Eventually I found a brokerage service willing to work with someone my age. At the very last day and in the eleventh hour, after six weeks of negotiations with my husband's lawyer who threatened daily to cancel our mediated agreement, one bank agreed. Indeed, they agreed just two hours before the whole settlement agreement would have collapsed and the trial order would have been initiated. However, this bank agreed to give a mortgage and not a line of credit. Now I would have to make mortgage payments, consisting of principal plus interest, which made the amount still beyond my capacity.

I frantically called my son, who immediately stepped up. If I could not make the mortgage payments, he would help with the shortfall. He was willing to take a risk on Vancouver real estate. Thankfully interest rates were very low.

Thus, two years and four months after being abandoned, my husband had a separation settlement and the right to divorce me, which he did immediately. It mattered to me, as a point of my integrity, that the court system did not require me to agree to this divorce. It was granted to him two months later. I had kept the house and maybe enough to support my living costs with the help of the National Bank of Canada with headquarters in Quebec and the promise of my son. I had purchased time to continue with my healing process.

In the words of Julian Barnes, when speaking of the death of his wife and quoting himself in an earlier novel: "[P]eople say you will come out of it, and you do come out of it. That's true. But you don't come out of it like a train bursting through the downs into sunshine and that swift rattling descent to the Channel; you come out of it as a gull comes out of an oil slick. You are tarred and feathered for life."

This described me perfectly: "tarred and feathered for life". My life would never be the same and it would never be as lovely as it had been. I was deeply scarred.

Yet, I could hear my grandson Ben's voice. Three months earlier, my grandson recorded his pure boy-soprano voice singing his version of Katy Perry's song "Firework" just for me, for my birthday. He wanted to tell me that for him, I was a firework with colours bursting, shooting across the sky.

I was finally free of the legal humiliation. I was in the process of committing to live as best I could. It was even possible that I might yet lighten the night sky with colour as my grandson wished for me.

Quaking in my confidence, I took ownership of the house in my name on June 30, 2015. I was seventy-six years and three months of age. I had a whopper of a mortgage and a retirement income too small to afford it. On

July 1, Canada's birthday, I gave a small brunch party and raised from my Juliet balcony a new British Columbia flag beside my Canadian one.

My later-in-life encounter with family law had been nothing short of horrendous. I agree with the sentiment of financial planners who instruct people of my age to do everything within their means to avoid separation and divorce. In their words found in a brochure I received at this time, "It will take years to negotiate, and lawyers will take such a huge portion of your nest egg." This has been my exact experience. In every way it interfered with my right to mourn.

Chapter 20

THE RETIREMENT DILEMMA

The progress of medicine and public health has been an incredible boon — people get to live longer, healthier, more productive lives than ever before.

— Atul Gawande

I will probably never retire. I wouldn't know what to do with myself. I also know the consequences for people who retire early: an increased risk of developing dementia.

— Sanjay Gupta

What is the ideal age to retire? Never. Even if you're physically impaired, it's best to keep working, either in a job or as a volunteer.

— Daniel J. Levitin

Imagine starting your life at seventy-two. At just that age, Mary Delaney (1700–1778), a fan of Handel, sometime dinner partner of Jonathan Swift, a wearer of green hooped satin gowns...invented the precursor of what we know as collage.

— Molly Peacock

On a gloriously warm spring day in 2015, just a month or two before I was to take possession of the house, I accompanied my daughter to the campus of Carleton University in Ottawa. She had an appointment to interview the man who would become her thesis advisor for her PhD. Students were studying outside on benches and on blankets strewn about the fresh grassy knolls above the bank of the Rideau River that flowed through the campus grounds. While I waited, I sat by the river as it bounced over rocks, surged, swirled and sparkled in the sunlight. Alas, sadly, suicidal thoughts intruded into my mind.

I have always loved water. I have made it a point to get to the sea, a lake, a river or a lagoon every day. I had often thought that being buried at sea would be appropriate for me. I should have been born under the Pisces sign. Morphing into a mermaid had been a childhood dream.

In the suicidal thoughts that preceded this spring day, I was drawn to overdosing, falling asleep and dying. But I also thought about drowning. In my imagination, I would just walk down to the sea and swim out until I could swim no more. That day by the Rideau River, I wondered how I could drown in a river where I could touch the bottom. I thought, *I will trip and fall in and hit my head.* The water would be cold and sharp in my throat. In a panic, I would swallow too much water. My drowning would not take long. As I sat there, the whole plan began to take shape in my head.

I saw my beautiful, bright young daughter and imagined her coming out from her interview, having just initiated her PhD, the next chapter of her life, and finding her mother dead. Something snapped in me. I found myself with the power to stop the fantasy. I put my hand on the ground of the Carleton campus, tender shoots of first grass slipping through my fingers, and felt grounded. When such dark thoughts arise as they were wont to do, I now had the rushing stream, the Carleton University earth, the jubilant river and my daughter's joy in her new adventure to bring me to the life that now was and that I must live.

Over a year after the Carleton University visit, in October 2016, Roméo Dallaire, a retired lieutenant-general and former Canadian senator, published his piercing memoir *Waiting for First Light,* telling of his battle with PTSD, alcoholism and depression brought on by the genocide he witnessed and could not stop in Rwanda.

He had served as commander of the ill-fated United Nations peace-keeping force in Rwanda in 1993 and 1994 and had tried, unsuccessfully, to stop the genocide perpetrated by the Hutu extremists against the Tutsi people and the moderate Hutus. More than 800,000 people were slaughtered. Seven out of every ten Tutsis were killed. All his attempts to have the world powers stop this carnage were denied. He returned to Canada a broken man and not a single military personnel officer was on hand to greet the returning general.

The resources provided to him by our military were soulfully lacking in any understanding of what he had been through. PTSD was only named in 1980 as a medical condition to be treated. The military was familiar with shell shock and battle fatigue, but they had never researched PTSD or figured out how to treat it. When Dallaire returned, he worked at full tilt for the military during the day and at night he relived the horror of the Rwandan slaughter.

An old friend of his, General Maurice Baril, called Dallaire into his office just before Christmas 1999. He had been getting more depressed daily. Maurice Baril was the one to tell him that he, Dallaire, was going to be relieved of his position, no longer fit to command troops in operations. He was told that he needed to dedicate himself full-time to his healing, although no provision was made for it by the military.

Dallaire wrote in his memoir, "When the uniform came off, the separation felt violent; the system to which I had spent my lifetime being loyal was breaking its loyalty to me."

While I have no right to compare my trauma to his, and I do know his suffering was immeasurably worse, there was something about this sentence that expressed how I felt when my church did not welcome and sustain me.

One night after he was medically discharged from the army in April 2000, former Lieutenant General Roméo Dallaire drank most of a bottle of scotch in his apartment in Hull, Quebec before he opened a metal box containing his father's medals and his fifty-year-old razor. Very slowly, he began to slice himself, first his thighs, then his arms. As the blood oozed from him, a knock came on the door and his sister-in-law found him and saved him.

Dallaire tried killing himself many times with alcohol, pills, cutting and overwork. When his little son or his daughter would ask for a toy or refuse to eat something, he would bark at them, "Do you realize? Do you have any idea what other children…" And he would proceed to describe some horror to them. His family did not know how to help him. He decided to live alone. He became sicker. His suffering from the trauma grew worse with time.

His attempts to kill himself increased and sometimes he lay down weeping for the end to come. In the morning he would wake up in a pile of sick. Eventually he felt a failure and "lousy" at trying to kill himself.

In November 2000, he was picked up by ambulance from a park bench at midnight. A camerawoman from the *Ottawa Citizen* reported it.

> Witnesses say Lt.-Gen. Dallaire was curled in a fetal position and obviously drunk. "When I finally discovered it was him, I was really sad," said Stephane Beaudoin, a night news camerawoman who happened on the scene. "I didn't shoot it because I was depressed to imagine a man like that could be there and didn't have help. He was so important for Canada when he was in good shape."

I was drawn to him in his pain. Like him, I could not sleep. What my church was doing to me was similar in my mind to what the military did to him. Could he survive what he had witnessed? Could he survive how he was treated when he returned? His memoir became a sacred text for me. I read and reread it. When he came to Vancouver to promote his book, I went just to be in his presence and get his autograph if I could. I heard him say that now, twenty-three years later, he had days when suicide did not cross his mind.

As he ended his memoir, he wrote, "As I approach the end of this book, I'm also approaching my seventieth birthday. I am surprised to find that I am angry at that number—angry that I might be running out of time. For the first time since I returned from Rwanda, I am surprised to realize that my wish to end my life has been trumped by the desire to stay alive and continue my mission."

Waiting for First Light draws an unforgettable picture for me. The first light is the seventy-two minutes that precedes the dawn. I still often awake in these precious minutes each day. Dallaire's memoir is my scripture for this time. Permanently scarred both physically and mentally, he now finds life as he commits to the mission of persuading the military to offer healing care for its returning soldiers with PTSD. He also raises his voice to challenge the world to end the practice of child soldiers and in the meantime to offer them special care. He has written books to support his ideas and is a most persuasive and inspiring speaker as he gives lectures around the world. In 2022, he is calling the world to more action in Ukraine.

By securing my home and its peace, I knew that now I was in that first light, inching my way towards dawn.

All the literature on grief suggests that to heal one should engage in volunteer activity. During my lifetime, I had given massive numbers of hours to the work of the church. Usually, I served as a teacher and group leader. I was rarely paid for this work. Once or twice, I received an honorarium. Now I was no longer wanted for service in my own church community, and I was not comfortable or ready to seek another congregation or explore another denomination. I had also given years of hours to my professional association, serving on committees, on the board and as president.

Because I was determined to take the suggestions of the grief experts, I began to think about how I could volunteer now. Since I had always enjoyed film immensely, the first attempt I made was to volunteer for the Vancouver International Film Festival. It would be a contained, two-week experience and a good way, I thought, to start.

The film for my first evening's volunteering was *Beeba Boys* directed by Deepa Mehta. The film explored the life of an Indo-Canadian gang on the streets of my home city, Vancouver. All the volunteers were excited. We would be hosting a private showing for the city's elite. Vancouver's world-famous chef, Vikram Vij, was doing the food and would be in attendance. Hours of preparation yielded banquet tables of lamb popsicles, fenugreek and garlic curried paneer on cumin-spiced flatbread and garam masala portobello mushrooms in porcini cream curry. The buzz was palpable. Women were dressed in gold and red saris with gold bracelets, and many men were dressed in traditional formal brocaded jackets. I was assigned to help Vij's family, making sure their every wish was fulfilled. Finally fed, feted and seated, I was free to find a seat and watch the performance.

For most of the festival, my work was more mundane. I spent a lot of time helping people to be patient in line and to find their seats. In return, I saw many films over the two weeks of volunteering. I discovered that many of my fellow compatriots were professional volunteers going from one cultural event to the next. I could have carried on and continued to volunteer in the many arts events my city hosts. While the experience benefitted me, it was not giving me the purpose in life I was seeking.

Undaunted, I pursued being part of the Writers' Exchange, an excellent programme created to help inner city children improve their reading and creativity skills. In the past, I had happily donated financially to its work. I applied and was accepted as a helper in the programme. Most of the volunteers were university students.

"Hello Jack," I said to a young lad of seven. "I'm Ann and your helper for today."

I expected I was there to help him improve his reading. As we sat side by side at a classroom table, I noticed him eyeing an athletic young man in cool sneakers, playing a noisy and wild game of going under tables and over them. He wanted to be with that guy. Of course he did.

It did not take me long to realize I was out of place. These kids were too old to be intrigued by the grandma factor. Perhaps I had been accepted because I was a donor. I resigned after one term and continued to donate.

I missed the mission project that I had shared with my husband. For a while I tried to sustain it as a volunteer project. I knew I was a very capable teacher. With a friend, I organised study groups in my home in the summer season. We studied the works of some key thinkers in the field of evolutionary Christianity, namely Ilia Delio, Teilhard de Chardin and John Haught. After my friends and acquaintances had participated, I ran out of people to engage in this rigorously academic study.

Each year, our national broadcasting service, the CBC (Canadian Broadcasting Corporation) encourages Canadians to read by having an annual contest, Canada Reads, every March. This contest is commonly called the battle of the books. Five personalities choose one book written by a Canadian author around a theme that the CBC has chosen and defend it in a week-long series of debates. A book is eliminated each day and on the fifth day a winner is announced. This is the book all Canadians are encouraged to read before the next year's contest. This contest first began in 2002 and has both an English and a French version. Every year I read all five of the books. It means I read outside my normal choices. One of my favourites was *Fruit*, a novel by Brian Francis. It told the story of a quirky obese boy preoccupied with his nipples as he went through puberty. Another book that intrigued me was *Fifteen Dogs* by André Alexis. The back cover gives a taster of this meditative, devastating, charming and strange novel:

> "I wonder," said Hermes, "what it would be like if animals had human intelligence."

> "I'll wager a year's servitude," answered Apollo, "that animals—any animal you like—would be even more unhappy than humans are, if they were given human intelligence."

Just over 170 pages and fifteen dogs later we know the outcome of the wager.

I also read a lot of books written by Indigenous writers. *The Break* by Katherina Vermette introduced me to Stella, a young Métis mother who reports a crime she has witnessed to the police. She was made to feel that she did not see what she saw. In the end she triumphs against all the odds of gender and racism. She finds and releases the power of her voice that was there all along. If she could make it, I surely could.

It seemed natural to ask friends to join me in the Canada Reads challenge. I had never belonged to a book group but was excited to form a six-week book club. I found friends to join me, we read and discussed one book a week, listened to the formal debates for one week and met for a wrap-up. We met for two years before interest in continuing collapsed. I continue as a book club of one.

I understand that volunteering is healing for a person in grief and the service offered is enormously meaningful. However, I began to think I might be able to earn an income. This would mean I could stay in my home that I loved without ever needing my son's financial help. In my search for another house when I thought I needed to sell, a realtor, frustrated with my demands to find a similar house, none of which ever lived up to my expectations and exacting standards, commented: "Ann, I think you will only leave this house feet first. You know, at your age it's not a bad idea to stay in your home." He understood me on the housing front. Perhaps, just maybe, I did not have to retire, at least not yet.

During sleepless hours in the middle of the night and long chats with friends and family, I agonised over what to do next. On visits to my children's homes, I looked at properties and assessed whether I could move to where they were. I was obsessed with the question "What next?" I have found that as the years pass, this question has increasing urgency. As elders, we joke about our so-called "terminal projects" as a way of highlighting just how precious the last possibilities are.

What are my contemporaries doing? I wondered. Joan, who had been abandoned when she was fifty-five years old, decided to retire from her librarian teacher position and seek a new career. She studied theology for three years, graduated and became a minister. Els was thirty-eight when she was abandoned. She built a business and went back to school to become an architect. Now, nine years later, she is close to graduation as an architect. Vikki Stark was fifty when she was abandoned. She took her experience, developed a niche in her field of psychotherapy for women like herself, wrote the book *Runaway Husbands* and runs workshops internationally to help abandoned women. What I noticed was that these women were all ten to twenty-five years younger than me. They had something I did not have: time!

Right when my husband abandoned me, I was booked to give a seminar just six weeks later to a group of up-and-coming CEOs in Vancouver. It was a big deal that would expose my work to some of the brightest entrepreneurs in my city. It was to be held in our fanciest seaside hotel in downtown Vancouver. I thought I should cancel it. I told the organiser who had booked me what had happened. I knew him and his wife well. They said they still wanted me if I thought I could do it.

I decided to do the workshop. I knew the material so well that even if I dissociated, with a good keynote presentation, I would be able to proceed. In life I have done things that were not the best choices, like preaching the Sunday after my son died. I have always understood how Rafael Nadal could play Grand Slam finals with feet asleep or a tear in his abdomen. But for me then, the timing was wrong. It was too soon. I was barely coherent. Agreeing to deliver the workshop was probably an act of sheer denial.

The evening of the seminar was a summer solstice night in trendy Coal Harbour in downtown Vancouver. I walked alone along the great wharf stretching out into the sea. Giant cruise ships towered above me. I was calming myself for the presentation. I missed my life partner for whom I had so often been a supportive presence in these exact circumstances.

I knew there would be the expected long periods of wait time between the sound checks and making sure the audiovisual equipment worked. There were the usual panic moments when things didn't work. Finally, thirty minutes late, I was introduced, and after thanking the organisers for the privilege, I began.

"Please find a space for yourself and your partner in this big ballroom. Give yourselves some room from the other couples," I directed.

The noise of dragging chairs ensued and soon there were thirty two-somes looking at me for guidance. Opening the screen of my PowerPoint presentation, I began, "One of you will follow the instructions and answer the questions shown on the screen for five minutes and at the bell the other will do what their partner has just done. Interrupting each other is not allowed.

"It is your birthday. Pick a previous birthday from your childhood and tell your partner how the whole day went. Did you have a party? If you did, what sort of party? Did you get gifts and from whom? Who purchased them? Were they wrapped? Did you like the gifts? Had you made a list of what you wanted? What did you like best about your birthday?"

The energy in the room intensified as the couples spoke and listened to each other. Then I asked them if they could identify anything in their conversations that would help them understand how they gave gifts to each other now as adults. I know from experience the issue of gift giving is often a fraught issue for couples.

The workshop continued with similar questions: Who handled the money in your household? How was anger expressed in the family when you grew up? These questions were designed to help the couples see how patterns of their behaviour reside in patterns learned when they were young. I emphasized that these patterns are just patterns and not cause for personal attacks on the other. Such insight relaxed familiar arguments. It opened avenues for understanding and new choices.

After the workshop was over, I took a cab home alone. I thought about how, after each presentation all around the world, my husband and I had celebrated, often having a bath together and talking about all the details of the evening. This was a night I wept and was quite wild and wet with the grief of missing him.

The next day I was rewarded by this email from the organiser:

The event was well received. I have had people ask for more information about your work and one person ask about a group workshop. I have directed them to your email. The group who sat at my table during dinner discussed your content the entire time.

Nine years later, I am still receiving referrals from that event. Without me realising it, this event certainly kickstarted the new life I was to create for myself.

In those very early days when I was so fragile, at Yolanda's urging,

I had also done the workshops for the Common Dreams Conference in Australia. I had aways liked my work. But could I ever do this work again?

The few hours of therapy I still occasionally did with old clients were always satisfying to me and were appreciated by the clients too. Gradually, it became clearer and clearer to me that I loved my work as a marriage and family therapist and that this was still my calling. My dream in which bishop Ted Scott ordained me as a bishop of healing still held true.

But, but, but. My mind plagued me with all the reasons why I could never practice again. I was a relationship therapist who was divorced not once but twice. Did I have any credibility at all? What couple would want to bring their marriage to such a person as me who had twice failed at marriage? Would I take my sputtering car engine to a mechanic who was failing at fixing the very thing for which I needed service? Never.

During this state of feeling so damaged, I went to our city art gallery with my friend Lynda. I have always found that paintings speak to me and this moment was no exception. I stood mesmerized by Emily Carr's painting, whose title I thought was *Scorned as Timber*. She is my province's premier visual artist. Canada is known in the world of visual art for our very famous Group of Seven, all men. Emily was their contemporary, but as a woman, she was never admitted as a member of this elite club. Of course, she had my allegiance and now is recognized the world over for her brilliance. I stood before the painting a long time. Both it and its creator spoke to me. I knew I was a scorned tree.

I felt this tree in my inner core. I kept a postcard of it on my fridge for a long time and it is in my mind forever. In the image's foreground, I saw the clear cut, and in the emptiness, left by the loggers, I saw a single tree, incredibly still, standing among the stumps of those trees taken for their lumber. It was not beautiful. This tall tree had been left stripped of its branches except for the very top where the semblance of a tree was hanging on. For months, each time I opened the fridge I placed my head against the photo. That scorned tree was truly me.

Emily Carr, *Scorned as Timber beloved as the Sky*

Here is what Emily Carr said about this painting in her journal:

I am painting a sky. A big tree butts up into it on one side, and there is a slope in the corner with pines. These are only to give distance. The subject is the sky, starting lavender beneath the trees and rising into smoother hollow air space, greenish in tone, merging into laced clouds and then into a deep, bottomless blue, not flat and smooth like the centre part of the sky, but loose, coming forward. There is one sweeping movement through the whole air, an ascending movement, high and fathomless.

I then learned the full title of this painting is *Scorned as Timber, Beloved as the Sky* and I also learned that it was rare for Carr to name her paintings at all.

I had never noticed the sky until I read her words. Carr invited me to see this painting as more hopeful and encouraged me to hold two perspectives: the scorned tree and promise of the sky. Slowly I began to contemplate the sky and what meaning it held for me. I must wait for the light and experience Holy Saturday in the expectation of becoming like Carr's sky, loose and sweeping forward.

Not wanting to remain only a victim, a scorned timber, I had to explore all that was keeping me from pursuing the work I loved. My husband's refusal to seek relationship counselling for us continued to undermine my ability to practice psychotherapy ever again. I had thought we were both committed to the efficacy of such therapy. However, he placed no value on the work I had given my life to do. The couple of sessions he attended with me were clearly about making sure that I had a therapist and that the therapist understood that he was abandoning me. It was as if the best he could do was to dump my broken self in a place where, possibly, I could be repaired.

Well-meaning friends trying to understand how he could have done this offered various explanations. "He is having a midlife crisis," said one friend. "He will get over it."

One of our golf buddies put it more crudely: "He's just a guy who can't keep his dick in his pants."

More psychologically sophisticated friends would assure me that I had wound up with a "classic narcissist". Those who had read the latest material in our field wondered if he was a high-functioning psychopath. I did find out that the business of trying to diagnose him was inescapable. Everyone who knew us felt free to offer their armchair opinion. As a therapist myself, I also obsessed over a diagnosis for him, as well as one for myself.

I got an email letter from the leader of the church in Florida where we spent our last six weeks together, telling me that my husband had explained his actions to that church by saying I was not supportive of his career and that I was standing in the way of his commitment to evolutionary Christianity. This was deeply galling and completely false. When I clarified the untruth with clear evidence of my support, the leader later apologized for even having thought such a thing could be true.

When I had pushed my husband as to the why of his behaviour, he wrote in an email, "We have had a beautiful thirty-year relationship, filled with intellectual companionship, great walks and fabulous sex. Now it is time to move on."

I pleaded, "Therapy will help us. I need to understand what you are doing. You need help with the dreams you have had and shared with me. Please, I know it will help me and you. I have helped so many couples who found themselves where we are, and it always issued in better outcomes."

His response became indelible in my mind, repeating over and over. "You have no proof you ever helped any couple stay together or part on better terms. You did not keep evidence. You did not do ten-year checkups. You can't prove you ever helped a single couple."

These words came from a man I had trusted with my life. Whenever I thought about re-establishing a practice, these words stopped me dead in my tracks. My therapist tried to help me with this excruciating, ever-repeating sentence. She said to me often, "If someone is intent on deceiving you, they can."

I have come to understand that it was important for my husband to see me as a person that could be abandoned. My opinions and worth had to be discredited. I now know this is a process called gaslighting. I was encouraged to believe things about myself that were not true. He had wanted me to agree to walk away and to celebrate the decision as God-given. When I did not comply with that idea, in order to leave me, I had to be damaged goods in his eyes. My trust in him was so complete, I believed him.

What was I to do? My confidence in myself as a therapist was incredibly fragile. I would soon be twice divorced. Yet I enjoyed this work. I was encouraged when previous clients and new ones they were referring kept calling me. Bianca, Brian, Don and Yolanda assured me that they would all refer clients to me, were I to start again.

I had been a supervisor for thirty-five years and as such, over the years, hundreds of therapists had brought me their cases for assessment. I would help them figure out what was working and what needed to be changed. I saw videos and listened to tapes and did live supervision where I would be stationed behind two-way glass. Remembering all this, I made a call to an internationally known supervisor and trainer in marriage and family therapy.

"Sylvia," I said, "I'm in a mess. I think I want to work again but..." And I told her my story. "Will you supervise me for as long as it takes for me to make this decision?"

I had met Sylvia fifteen years earlier when I had taken a supervision course with her.

"Yes, I remember our conversation," she said. "You had that very interesting multi-generational case." After talking more about my situation and goals Sylvia said she thought we could work well together to discuss my issue of whether to return to practice.

In October 2014, Sylvia and I began our work together and met monthly for one year. I was still in the thick of the divorce proceedings. I had no sense I would ever do therapy or supervision again, but I was keeping the option open. Meeting with Sylvia was a hint of the future. I was but a scorned tree waiting for first light.

I had not been well enough to work since my husband had left. In order to do supervision with Sylvia I would have to find at least four client cases. When my husband and I left for Florida, my clients understood I was taking a sabbatical of indeterminate length. Many of them asked to be told when I was back working so that they would have the option of returning to work with me. I contacted four of them and they readily came back into my practice. All of them were clients that over a number of years had come to me for intensive periods as they navigated new transitions in their lives.

One of them was a man named Nathan whom I had seen off and on for thirty years. He was the child of holocaust survivors which left him with many issues that tended to surface as he faced new challenges. While I am mainly a couples' therapist, I occasionally make exceptions and he was one of them. I am a therapist who appropriately discloses some of my life story. He knew I was married. I brought this case to Sylvia as I troubled over how to tell him that my marriage was dissolving. It was further complicated as he told me, "Ann, it was great to hear that you are not going to fully retire but you are opening your door again. My wife and I are going to call it quits. We can't make it work. I don't know what to do. I am so relieved that I can talk with you."

"Sylvia, this my worst fear. It just hits me that I have two failed marriages. I just don't think I am good enough. I am trying so hard with

Richard, my EMDR therapist, to quiet this negative noise in my head, but am I able to be Nate's therapist?"

Sylvia helped me centre in what I wanted to say if I did not sink into my low self-esteem. I told her, "I really think that the biggest betrayal that I experienced was that my husband would not come with me to try to repair the marriage or even to help me understand his decision to leave without trying. I had always been sure of this; if there were trouble then we would get help."

Almost immediately my professional self started to awaken. I remembered I had taken a supervisory training course with Dr. William Doherty and been very impressed by his insistence that marriage therapy be marriage friendly. I remember hearing him say, "A good therapist, a brave therapist, will be the last one in the room to give up on our marriage, not the first one." That I could be and would be that kind of therapist again was a thought taking shape in my head.

I wanted to encourage Nate to ask his wife to see a marriage therapist and to work on the issues that were tearing them apart. Yes, I had wanted this for myself and I wanted it for Nate. Could I tell Nate the truth that my marriage had failed and that I thought he would be well advised to seek out help for his before he walked away? With Sylvia's help I did this and Nate responded with sorrow for me and a commitment to make more effort in his own marriage.

I had done it. I had been truthful about my situation and survived. I told each of the other three couples that had returned to my practice that I had been left and was now seeking to decide, under supervision, whether I would fully commit to rebuilding my practice. My worst fears began to subside. The work I had done for thirty years had validity. In each supervisory session, with Sylvia's encouragement and through incorporating her wisdom, my confidence as a therapist was returning. I was shutting the door on false information about myself.

Finally, in the spring of 2015, my healing steadily progressing, I made the decision to prepare to publicly announce a return to practice in Vancouver. My next steps pushed my Luddite computer and social media skills to the maximum. My trauma yoga teacher referred me to Angela. Her very name was perfect, and without hesitation, I contacted her, "Angela, I need to make a video. I need a website and I need to be on Facebook and Twitter. Are you able to help me do all this?"

She readily agreed. She was such a multi-talented person, visual artist, photographer, singer and songwriter, and I got to benefit from all her skills and accomplishments. I talked with Sylvia about the content I wanted to put on my website describing my practice and the sort of therapist I was. I decided that swimming had to be part of the video as it was so much a symbol of the plunge I was taking. We shot many takes at the Kitsilano swimming pool. This shot of me inspired me.

I suppose I was faking it until I made it. Angela had captured me looking like the person I used to be. It had been strenuous, cleansing and right to mourn for her, my old self, in the hope that she might raise her arms with confidence once again.

My website got published. I had made a video that described my skills as a therapist, I had a Facebook and Twitter presence, and slowly I began to navigate all the required technology. My colleagues and former referring bodies came through, and before long I had a ten-hours-a-week practice and I could relieve my son of his standby duties to help me pay for the house. By Christmas 2015, I was out of retirement and into semi-retirement.

I had a house, a debt I could maintain with work I loved, therapists to guide me, family who were proud of me, friends who loved me and I them, deep scars that were still healing, trembling courage and nascent curiosity for the adventures ahead. "Tarred and feathered", I had survived. Now I entered a new phase: the possibility of thriving.

Once again, all the animals of Noah's Ark are lined up, freshly cleaned and bathed, on a glass table in my office. Small pewter figures of Mr. and Mrs. Noah watch over them. In pride of place is the walrus pair, the parting thank-you gift to me from the couple I had thought were my last clients before my husband and I set off together on what I also thought was our next life project.

Walruses are terrestrial marine mammals that can swim in the ocean, walk on the land and traverse the sea ice. Males and females have tusks that are both their distinctive feature and their survival tool. They use their tusks to pull themselves out of the water and onto sea ice or the rocky shoreline in order to breathe. If they are beneath the sea ice, they can make a hole with their tusks big enough to get to safety on the ice. Sometimes they use their tusks to hook onto an ice pack and lie down to sleep. The tusks can be used to forage for food. The mother walrus pulls herself by them onto her own ice floe to give birth. Males use their tusks to show off when they are courting. Throughout their lives, their tusks grow in size and keep them from harm. The sharp ivory tusks of my jade walruses are permanently in place now, reminding me of my enduring strength and capability for the journey I am making.

Little did that couple know I was about to need tusks and angels to help me survive, just as they had needed them. But, slowly and surely, like the walruses using their tusks, I began to be proud and stabilize myself in a safe place with lots of help to breathe and relax. As I do so, I am being lifted into the dawn and the sky of my octogenarian years.

Epilogue

THE NEED FOR
INTIMACY NEVER ENDS

I am long past my own baby season, past even the season of hungry fledglings, but I am not past the nudging thrum of need.
— Margaret Renkl, "The Gift of Menopause"

Oh, those lonely mornings, when you want someone to talk to.
— From the Finnish film *Still Into You*, 2020

This body is mine now. It's mine again. I own it, and I live in it. It's given me this beautiful moment of unbridled, unboundaried pleasure, and I gave that to myself.
— Emma Thompson in the film
Good Luck to You, Leo Grande, 2022

Does a woman who was left by her husband in her seventies think about finding a new partner?

In May 2017, I was with my daughter in a home exchange apartment in the tiny fishing village of Stazzo, Sicily. Perched on the lava rock coast, the apartment's front windows looked south, the cerulean Ionian Sea stretching beneath us. Swirling swallows greeted the morning and came home to rest in the evenings. My bedroom window, which faced north, looked up at the towering, snow-covered and ever-steaming Mount Etna.

Just two months before my arrival, this great mountain had spewed forth her fire and fury in a summit eruption. As I put my head on the pillow at night, I prayed my earliest remembered prayer with new sincerity: "Now I lay me down to sleep, I pray the Lord my soul to keep." As a comforting mantra, I also repeated what the tourist brochure had assured me: "The last time the mountain fully let its full force throw rock and lava down to the sea was in the eleventh century."

It was a working holiday. Mary was finishing revisions to her PhD thesis, and I thought I was doing the final edits of this book. Little did I know that I was really finishing what would become a third draft with more drafts to come. Mary left a week before me, and I stayed to write.

It was now Wednesday. Friday I would pack and clean up the apartment, navigating the rocks to swim in the sea one last time, and Saturday I would fly home, but Thursday...?

I had driven my little teal blue rental Fiat Panda, with its strange combination of automatic and manual gear shift, to and from the airport in Catania, but I had not visited the city proper with its historic landmarks. Could I do it on my last day on the island? I was not sure as my daughter had driven on the tourist outings we had taken in the afternoons after our writing was done. In Taormina, the idyllic town that was just a few days away from hosting the 2017 G7 summit, we had parked in a large building called a parcheggio. If I could get the car parked in a similar parcheggio near the Giardino Bellini, Catania's lovely old gardens named after the Italian composer, then I would be able to pull off a day of sightseeing.

It felt risky but I was ready for an adventure. I organised a walking tour, programmed the GPS on my cell phone and set out. Proud and exhilarated, I hit Catania at rush hour. Yikes! I found myself in the middle of roundabouts with cars weaving in and out. I never sweat but somewhere along the route I noticed I was very hot and breathing hard. The voice on the GPS was calm and reassuring. I was at least on the right road, along with most of Catania, it seemed.

An hour or so later, I could see the stone pine trees rising above the baroque pillared wall and sure enough the GPS voice informed me that I had arrived at the Parcheggio Giardino Bellini. Alas, the large parking building I was expecting was nowhere in sight. I was on a street with at least four lanes of traffic moving very fast and nowhere to pull off. I panicked. I suspected at that moment that I was too old for this adventure. I pulled off into the first laneway that miraculously appeared on my right, my survival energy pumping vigorously. I saw a scruffy man wearing clothes I thought he might have slept in teetering toward me. A little desperately, I opened the window.

"Parcheggio Giardino Bellini, per favore?" He sauntered over, presumably curious to have a look at this lost lady.

"Non parlo inglese. Nessun parcheggio qui."

"Parcheggio" was my big word! It was all I had. He gave me the strong impression that there was no parking at all nearby. Fortunately, I could see the walls of the Bellini Garden, which meant I was in the place I hoped to be. Then I saw another man coming down the street with shopping bags tucked under his arm. He was better dressed than the first. From my position, sitting in my car, his brown leather shoes were what I saw as he drew closer. *They must be bespoke,* I thought. I understood finely cobbled shoes and I relaxed. I called to him, and he came to the car.

"Parlo inglese? I asked.

"Yes," he said, in welcome English. I told him that I was looking for *parcheggio*. Like the first man I spoke to, he assured me that there was none where I was and launched into directions that would take me to it. He lost me at the second left turn. He could see my distress.

"Signora, could I get into your car and direct you as you drive, per favore?"

I remember thinking, *I am in Sicily, home to the Mafia. I am on a some-what unsavory street. How would I ever explain that I let a godfather into my car?* But I did.

"Please," I said.

He got in and immediately introduced himself, "Giovanni or Gianni is my name." He told me to drive up this street and make this turn and that turn. I began to panic again. He clearly did not know where the *parcheggio* was.

As he directed my turns he said slowly in perfect English, "I arrived in Catania two nights ago. My mother lives here and I come from Roma to take care of her once a month. I am on my way to market to get food for the evening meal."

After a few more turns and directions, he went on, I think to reassure me, "I grew up in Catania. I am seventy years old and have just retired. I am married and have two children who are grown and have their own families."

There was no *parcheggio* in sight, but the gardens were always visible. Gradually I realized we were looking for a single parking spot and not the large parking facility I had used with my daughter in Taormina.

"I see one," I exclaimed. He agreed and small as it was, I thought I could get this Fiat Panda into the spot. I tried and failed. I tried and failed again. He looked slightly pleased.

"Could I have a try, signora, per favore?" he politely, if smugly, asked.

Again, I said, "Si, yes," wondering what I would tell my children and the police were he to go speeding off in my teal hire car. I stood on the curb, and he failed to park the car. This seemed very embarrassing to him and rather pleasing to me. I presumed that Italian men prided themselves on knowing how to park a car. I offered to try one more time and he refused.

Eventually he succeeded and explained himself. "I drive a manual car and this one is very strange." He was not wrong. It was.

"I drive a much bigger car, a BMW," he said quietly, by way of further explanation. Okay, I knew he had great shoes and a BMW and, so far, had been very polite.

Then I had to navigate the parking machine. He kindly offered to do this and refused to let me pay for the meter.

"How long are you staying?" he asked.

I noted it was now 9 a.m. "I will leave at 3:30 this afternoon," I said. He had lots of euros and began putting several of them into the machine. We secured the parking pass and placed it in the car.

I then introduced myself. "My name is Ann," I said.

"Annnna," he replied, drawing out my name so beautifully I was quite smitten. I asked him if he would point me toward the starting point of the tour I had organised on my walking map.

"Better," he said, "I can walk with you through the gardens and show you the way."

Nodding vigorously, I gratefully accepted.

As we walked, he told me that he had not spoken English for twelve years. He had been the marketing director for a large US company before he had retired. He had lived in California for many years where he had perfected his English. He seemed to be so excited to be speaking English again and was doing a great job. He asked when I was leaving Sicily and I said on Saturday.

"Oh Anna, that is too soon. I would like to show you my home city. You must see my Sicily. Will you spend the day with me?" He was already telling me about all the statues in the park.

I was very pleased, quickly accepted his offer and thought to remind him to let his mother know. He told me that he had given up using a cell phone to help him relax into retirement. He borrowed mine and called his mother. I texted the host of my Sicily home exchange who I had planned to meet for pastries at later that day and said that something else had come up.

I told him I would figure out another way to return keys and discuss the closing of his coastal apartment.

Then I just let go, so weary was I of being on guard ever since I had been abandoned. It seemed forever since I felt myself trusting a man!

Gianni was a tour guide waiting to happen. I was the lucky recipient. He showed me his city and his loves. He shared how as a boy he had walked to school through the Bellini Gardens. As we walked, he asked, "Do you know the 'Casta Diva'?"

I was not sure what he was asking. I feigned a slight knowledge. He kept saying *"Norma."* My head was scrambling it with normale. I did not know that Bellini's most famous opera was called *Norma. What an odd name for an Italian opera,* I thought. I did not know that "Casta Diva" was the central aria and also featured in the *Godfather* films. I was caught out being uninformed. I was embarrassed as I thought myself very cultured.

"You must know the 'Casta Diva'," he insisted, clearly unable to understand my ignorance. He was visibly upset that I did not know the music. Almost as an explanation of his urgency, he continued, "My brother plays in the Italian Symphony. As a young man I chose theatre and Sicilians are famous for their comedy."

"I was in theatre, too, when I was a student at university," I said, suddenly on more secure ground.

He took me to the Roman theatre in the Piazza Stesicoro. Unearthed earlier in the twentieth century, the theatre was found to have been built of lava rock over the ruins of an even earlier Greek theatre. He was proud to tell me that originally the Sicilians had been more cultured than the Romans. In our exploring, we crossed back and forth on many busy streets. As we did, he held out his hand to me. "Come, Anna, bella Anna, come."

Oh my, I thought. All this attention was making me quite giddy. He was calling me "beautiful". He touched my arm or my shoulder often, guiding me, being careful of me. At one point the wind blew my hair in my face and mouth. When I was trying to get a strand out of my mouth, he cradled my face with one hand and gently removed the hair with the fingers of his other hand. It had been a while, if ever, since anyone had done this. His confidence with me kept increasing my trust. It was very good that I knew he was married. It was becoming too easy to forget.

Not yet noon, in the bakery, he insisted I eat a granita siciliana, which he assured me was breakfast. It was an icy liquid of sweetened lemon juice topped with cream and a brioche bun. He purchased a bomboloni, an Italian version of a doughnut, and two cannelloni, a cylindrical type of lasagna for me to try back in Stazzo, which he tucked in one of his bags. He guided me to the Piazza del Duomo, the central square in Catania, dominated by the central statue of the *elefanti* and the great Cathedral of Sant'Agata.

"The elephant is a dwarf Sicilian elephant, and this statue is now thought to have magical powers to keep all of us Sicilians safe from eruptions of Mount Etna." His arm rested on my shoulders as he confided the great talisman story. To my mind, the elephant was enormous and, based on his instruction, comforting. I learned that sleeping under an active volcano was challenging for more than me.

Taking me into the cathedral, he proudly announced, "We, the people of Catania, have the body of Saint Agatha, which makes this a very holy place and better than other cities in Sicily which have lost the bodies of their saints." He took me to her resting place in her chapel where a Mass was being said. He kept me close, and he spoke in whispers so as not to disturb the service. I could feel his breath in my ear. Involuntarily I shivered with pleasure. I felt like a mischievous child being told the story of Catania's prized possession.

We left the cathedral and I caught sight of the sea in the distance. Wanting him to know me, I said, "I love to swim. I have been swimming off the rocks in Stazzo. It is amazing, crystal clear and so secluded still. The tourists have not yet arrived."

He responded almost casually. "I played water polo as a young man. My brothers and I have a yacht and sail the Mediterranean in the summer. Now I am retired I will be able to do it more often. I love to be in the water." He did not seem to brag but rather wanted me to know what he enjoyed.

Ah, this was the origin of his gorgeous fit body. He loved the water. *He has a good and fortunate life,* I thought. We also talked empathetically about the young Sicilians that are struggling today and the sorry state of the Italian government. His chagrin was heartfelt. My home exchange host, a young law student managing the property for his father, had persistently asked me if I could help him emigrate.

Continuing our exploration, we walked up a long hill on a very narrow street lined with shops. He led the way and I followed. I was struck by the poignancy of just being able to follow. As I remembered what this was like, tears welled up in me and caught me off guard.

After the climb, we were tired and paused to have a rest, sitting side by side on a bench.

"We must tell each other our emails," he said as he got out a notebook and pen to write in. He wrote them twice, once for him and once for me. He tore the page out and gave me a copy. He took meticulous care to get the letters exactly right.

"Maybe we will be pen pals," I dared to say, following his hint at a possible future for us.

"I am not good at keeping up correspondence," he said. For a brief moment, he seemed to have changed the direction of the mood.

At last, we arrived at his original destination, Catania's market. The cobblestones were glistening wet with seawater sloshed from the fish stalls. Everything was vibrant with life. Red, yellow, aubergine and every shade of green imaginable assaulted the eyes. Vendors shouted and greeted each buyer with joyful energy. Food called out to be celebrated. Visions of alfresco dinners danced in my head.

"Anna, be careful. Bella mia bella, it is easy to slip." Taking my shoulders firmly in his hands, he instructed, "Look at me, bella Anna, remember me as I will be speaking with the vendors who know me. Don't lose me." He was clearly at home and full of himself. He was a chef about to launch a creation: his mother's dinner.

"I won't." Not likely, as I was fascinated just watching him. I was not going to lose him, not just yet. He carefully surveyed the olives on sale.

"Open up, apri le tui labbra mia, Anna," as he popped various olives in my mouth for my approval.

"Try these!" And next I found my mouth full of deep burgundy cherries, my very favourite fruit. He told me all about the dinner he would cook for his mother that evening. He showed me how to buy zucchini by the centimetre. He named the fish and told me how to cook and serve them.

Attempting to calm my jumping hormones I said, "You are not behaving like the Sicilian Mafia. You are being so courteous and so proud to show me your culture." I could see he was pleased with my comment.

He spoke intimately again into my ear so that I could hear above the market din. "I am having such a good time speaking English and being hospitable."

For my part, I trusted him even more, and felt safe with him. Should he have invited me to meet his mother, at that moment, I would have moved the universe to do so.

Once again, the "Casta Diva" came up in our time together. He was genuinely sorry and incredulous that I did not know the aria. As the late afternoon hour loomed and we knew we would be parting when he would board a bus to his mother's house, he took me to Bellini's statue in Piazza Stesicoro. Bellini sits atop the massive stonework with a music score on his lap. Lower, down, four statues surround him, each representing one of his operas: *Il Pirata (The Pirate)*, *I Capuleti e i Montecchi (The Capulets and Montagues)*, *La Sonnambula (The Sleepwalker)* and *Norma*.

"Please sit exactly here on this bench which will allow you to directly gaze upon the statue for *Norma*, bella Anna. Norma is a priestess from Gaul who is secretively in love with a Roman proconsul. She sings the aria 'Casta Diva' in the opera. It is a prayer to the moon to bring peace. It is one of the most difficult arias that Bellini ever composed."

I happily complied, not knowing what would happen but expectant nonetheless. He stood feet firmly planted directly under the statue of Bellini himself. Then he just opened his mouth and sang the aria for me, all seven minutes of it. This is the honest truth. Passersby just kept on with their business as though this was a totally regular experience for them. I was blown away. It was the perfect end to a very special day.

No sooner had he left me than I began to question this encounter. The distrust came quickly as I drove back to Stazzo. I did not know if this is just how kind and cultured Italian men behave or if there was a small air of flirtation? I discovered that Italians do not have an equivalent for the English word "flirt" in their language. They use the word for seduction, *seducente*. Had I been seduced? My heart was pounding, causing me to catch my breath, and I could feel the sexually stimulating response in my body. In the following weeks, we exchanged a few emails that were kind and generous. He sent me a YouTube video of Maria Callas singing the "Casta Diva." Wisdom and reality prevailed, and then, after five or six emails, the exchange stopped.

Gianni affirmed that I am a beautiful woman and a pleasure to accompany on an adventure. In that brief outing he reminded me that a man could cherish me, if only for a day. He lived up to that exquisite capacity for attentiveness to women that we attribute to Italian men. It was the right moment for me to be reminded of erotic delights and my body's capacity to respond.

For a few months, after returning to Canada, I mooned about with a crush on a married Italian man from Sicily. Gianni gave me permission to think I might meet a suitable person who would be my friend and companion in these late years of my life. I began to think I might find a way to date someone.

When I turned my mind to this thought, but for Gianni, I would have been embarrassed. It was easy to think I was too old for such thoughts. There was something unseemly about it. I judged the idea harshly. My mother had been too embarrassed at forty to admit she had had sex, staying in the house for most of her pregnancy when she carried me at such an advanced age. Maybe she was right?

The holiday season after Sicily, I was invited to a New Year's Day party by a couple who had been friends of my husband and me. They were glamorous and had such an erudite social circle. It would be a gathering of my hometown's literati. Could I go alone where I had always gone as part of a couple? I checked and my husband had not been invited. Sweet friends to me were these hosts. I went, stayed, met and conversed with lots of informed and witty people. I actually enjoyed myself at a party without a partner.

As I told Bianca about it, proud of my achievement, she pushed. "Did you meet anyone you felt some connection to? Someone who, like you, was there solo?"

And there was, I confessed. He was Scottish.

"You must think of a reason to connect and meet him," Bianca encouraged.

I had been planning a trip to Scotland, my first entirely solo trip, and I was nervous. This Scot lived nearby, and I managed to find him through our mutual friend, the party host.

I could legitimately connect and accordingly emailed him, "I met you at the New Year's Day party. I was the gal going to Scotland. I am going to Loch Lomond where you said you had a condo. I am looking for travel ideas. Would you be willing to give me some local scoops?"

He invited me to his house for drinks before dinner to give me his ideas. I had a conflicting engagement. (I do regret not treating this with the utmost urgency.) His helpful advice all came by email. He was friendly, and I learned that he had been recently left by his wife.

Two months after I had completed my journey to Scotland and thanked him for his help, I was sitting in a very basic Vietnamese shop in our neighbourhood, having a manicure and pedicure. He stepped through the door a little awkwardly and asked for a manicure and pedicure for himself. Quite unexpectedly and from my perspective, serendipitously, we were seated side by side for nearly two hours while gracious non-English-speaking women attended to our feet and hands. We talked easily and freely.

After chatter about Scotland and the Vancouver housing market he asked, "Are you interested in meeting a new person? I am and it is a very interesting process. I have met a lovely woman in my work environment. I quite like her, and we are seeing each other."

Sadly, he was taken, and I put on my therapist hat as he chitchatted about his new delight and how his kids were taking it. I had come close, I thought, to such a nice man.

I called Bianca, wanting her to know that I was trying and how close I had come to such an eligible bachelor. She was not deterred but even more determined to help. While having her hair cut and styled a few weeks later, she overheard another stylist confiding to his client that he was having trouble dating in Vancouver. Bianca's ears perked right up and before she left the salon she spoke to this stylist and asked if he would like to meet her friend. He agreed, and when she told me and described this man, I agreed. I was thinking I needed to say yes or Bianca would give up on me.

This man was a grieving widower in need of care. As a hair stylist, he was a superb listener. I told my daughter about him.

"He has asked me to go the Sylvia Hotel for lunch."

Her response was quick and protective: "Mom, you cannot meet a strange man for lunch in a hotel!"

After I explained that the Sylvia Hotel was a coveted lunch spot among the senior set, she relented. We agreed to meet at the water ferry terminal and walk to the hotel. I quickly discovered, due to too much soccer, his walking days were mostly over. We met several times after that but had little in common.

In talking with my friend Lynda about him, she cautioned, "My mother would have said beware of those who need a 'nurse and purse'."

I had never heard the expression and was startled by it. Yet in a brutal way, it named my dilemma. It was something I needed to consider. I was financially managing, and I had great caregiving skills. Nevertheless, I did appreciate this dating experience. He was such an attentive listener, but we both knew we were ill-matched. On the plus side, the few dates we did have encouraged me in the crazy pursuit of dating at my age.

I was learning. I had several clients who were online dating. Els and I talked about it from time to time. I had heard there were sites for older people. As I was giving this thought, Janene, with whom I had done a house exchange in Australia, asked to visit for a couple of overnights at my house. I encouraged her to come stay with me and she did.

She arrived six weeks later and after a glass or two of wine one evening, we began to talk about what it is like to be single. She had been recently widowed in her early sixties and, while bereft, she did wonder about dating again. As with my clients, I encouraged her to think about online dating, but she was most hesitant.

"Janene, did you have a young love that you still wonder about?" I asked. "You know, sometimes such people find each other online and it's a good thing."

Her eyes got a bit dewy as she told me about her most important love that did not work out. Before long we were on our computers tracking him down. He had a common name, which made it difficult, but we found him. Unfortunately, he was married with several kids and beginning to have grandkids.

It was an enjoyable evening all the same, and in the morning, as we parted, she said to me, "Thank you, Ann. Great fun we had last night, and thanks to you, I think I am ready to go home and give online dating a whirl."

She did and after a few tries she emailed to say thank you and that she had met someone. Her news made me glad that I had helped her, and I was proud she had taken the leap to online dating.

Not long after her visit, I noticed I had a persistent Facebook message alert. I usually ignore them but this time I checked. "Are you the Ann Evans who went to Governor Simcoe Public School and knew my father-in-law, Jerry?"

I was. I had been looked up online by someone who had no idea what was going on in my life. I responded, that yes, I was that Ann Evans and enquired as to how Jerry was doing.

"I think my dad would like to reconnect with you. He has spoken of you often over the years. He and my mother-in-law were divorced a long time ago. I haven't told him I have reached out to you."

Wow, his daughter-in-law was trying to set her father-in-law up. Maybe that is what our children will increasingly do for us. I could tell from her website that she was an avid Facebook user and promoted her love of dogs on it.

I wrote back in a private email, "I would enjoy speaking with Jerry if he is interested. It has been a whole lifetime since we have spoken." It turned out that Jerry did not use the internet all that much and was happy to speak with me by telephone.

Both Jerry and I started school together. However, in that kindergarten class, Billie was my first love and not Jerry. For some reason, as we left the school to go home for lunch, Billie would wait for me and never failed to plant a big kiss on my face wherever it happened to land. The senior students often cheered on Billie in his ardent expression of affection.

By grade eight, Jerry was the desire of my life. His family had the very first TV set in our neighbourhood. As a gang of kids, we hung over his fence and peered through his front window at a circle of snowy, blurred, black-and-white images on the "box", as black-and-white TVs were called at the time. We were waiting to see an image we could decipher, unable to imagine that one day television would bring sharply defined, brilliant Technicolor images into our living rooms. We screamed when we saw Elvis on Ed Sullivan wiggle his hips! When we tired of the blurry images on the "box", we played basketball in the school grounds until dark. Then we played spin the bottle behind the school on summer evenings. I never got to kiss or be kissed by Jerry. Nevertheless, in grade eight we were linked by being elected the top students in the class. By virtue of living on the north side of my street, my school catchment area put me in the high school for rich kids. Living south of me, he would have gone to another high school. Every bit as smart as me, he chose instead to go to a technical school to learn a trade, as most of the poor kids like us did.

I was turning sixteen in 1955 and had never been kissed by anyone, unless you count Billie's daily smackers and the hit-and-miss spin the bottle episodes. Typically, and pragmatically, I saw this lack of being properly kissed as a problem to be solved. I thought Jerry was my best bet. He was such a handsome sixteen-year-old, six foot two and drop-dead gorgeous. I invited him to my birthday party and indeed before the party was over, Jerry opened his mouth and kissed me just like in the movies. The deed was done. As I searched my memory, I could not remember why we parted but I have always remembered that first real kiss by the big oaken chair in our living room. It bounced off the wow factor scale.

The moment finally came, and Jerry and I were on the phone talking.

It was remarkably easy. Jerry had never left the city where we were born and grew up. His memory was meticulous down to the finest detail. Apparently, I jilted him, or more likely my father did. Jerry remembers my dad telling him to stop hanging around me. I recall falling for the new, most handsome guy in my grade nine class at my high school now that I was confident in my kissing prowess. My dad and brothers were blessed with awesome looks and I clearly had always thought I deserved only the best-looking guy. Jerry held his own in this league, but I had found a new version in my new school. I was young and a tad callous.

"Ann, do you remember your red polka dot bathing suit?" he asked.

I remembered dirndl skirts and cincher belts maximising the glory of my eighteen-inch waist. That was clearly another lifetime, as was anything approaching a bikini.

"I remember you standing drinking Orange Crush at Mackie's in Port Stanley. Remember the straws were coloured twists of orange and vanilla? You had on red lipstick, and it stained the straw."

Jerry had a lot of memories of me like this that I had long forgotten. Like Gianni, he made me feel special with all the details. I realized that he had held me in his heart and mind in ways that I had not held him. We began to talk weekly. One Christmas when I was in Ontario at my son's house, he met me there and we had lunch. Ah, but he, like me, had grown old. He was still tall and straight and proud of it. Somehow, I was not prepared for the toll life takes. Once he had ignited my heart. Now there was kindness and tenderness. Our lives have gone such separate ways. I was worldly and he was parochial. We continued to talk on the telephone and be friendly. We lived 4,300 kilometres apart. He did not travel very far from his home any more. I think we loved each other, or at the very least enjoyed remembering loving each other with the passion of first love. He sent me exquisite gifts. I reciprocated. I suspect his daughter-in-law helped.

One day the call came: "Ann, I have bad news. I have cancer and it is invasive. I don't think I will see the year out. I will not be able to talk so often. I don't want to burden you with my condition. My children are caring for me and I am loved."

I spoke with him monthly until just before he died, six months after that shocking phone call. His daughter-in-law wanted me to visit him, but his son did not. I knew and honoured his son's wisdom that their dad liked remembering me the way we were. We rejoiced in those last calls and in the fact that we had been each other's first adult loves. Our names are forever preserved side by side on a brass plaque in our public school.

Not long after I heard from Janene that she and the man she met through online dating were planning to marry. Once again, it made me wonder if online dating could work for me.

To be more helpful to my clients who were online dating I decided to take a course called *The Love Codes*, given by Feminine Power, a California organisation I respected. Knowing how effectively it helped women embrace their power, I had often referred clients to its workshops. The Love Codes course was designed to help people find a serious, lasting and thriving relationship. Taking the course was also a discrete way for me to check out the scene.

The course was full of practical actions to take, as well as encouraging a deep loving of one's body and one's soul. It was a preparation course for relationship. I made several changes in my behaviour inspired by what I was learning. To this day, I keep the area under my bed absolutely empty, although I've never understood why this is so important. These days it just makes me chuckle as I imagine a would-be lover needing to make sure there were no dust mites under my bed! I make sure that the décor in my house is representative of me. I purchase new underwear regularly and I wear night clothes that at least invite me to have sexual thoughts. I think my body is my canvas that I decorate each and every day. But I always have thought that. In the recent film *Good Luck to You, Leo Grande,* sixty-five-year-old Emma Thompson's character, retired schoolteacher Nancy Stokes, stands naked before a mirror and celebrates her body. I know how she feels as I too was encouraged by this course to be proud of who I am in my body.

Like Nancy in the film, I also had moles removed from my skin that I had never liked. I whitened my teeth. I had professional photos taken. I let my hair, which I usually kept coloured chestnut brown, become its natural colour. This was a monumental step. I was quite literally terrified. I was not at all sure what colour it would be. I imagined mousy grey, as my mother's had been.

When my daughter-in-law had breast cancer and chemo, we went to a wig shop to choose a wig for her. While there, I asked if they had any white-haired wigs. As they did, I began to try them on. However, they were all made with straight hair and given I had always been curly headed, it was a double whammy. The mirror showed me as a sophisticated straight-white-haired woman! Undeterred by my shock, my daughter-in-law took photos of me. I looked rather stunning. She was appalled by the wigs for herself, however, and decided to endure her chemo experience with hats. But I was intrigued and took the photos to my hair stylist, who was quite enthusiastic.

"Let's do it," she encouraged. "I can bleach it out and then put in some straw colour to ease the dead white."

A few weeks later I was in the chair, and just like that, all it took was one day to bleach and one day to soften the bleached-out effect.

When I first looked in the mirror I squealed! "OH MY GOD, I look like Trump!"

And I did, for about six months. Now people often stop me on the street and comment on my glorious hair. Even I can't believe it. All those years of dyeing it were now gone, and my natural hair was turning heads.

A woman stopped me on the golf course recently and asked, "Is that your real hair colour and curl? It is gorgeous!"

It was one of the most gratifying life decisions I have made. I wash, fluff, scrunch and go out in public with a halo of soft white curls framing my face. I simply love my hair after decades of wishing it was straight so that I could have a ponytail. Lately I have taken to having sparkles like foil icicles attached to the roots. Maybe feathers for the summer will be next.

During the course I also learned that online dating works very well for people between the ages of thirty-five and fifty. Even for this age group it takes a lot of work. It is a full-time second job. Mentors exist to help you get the right photos, write the best profile and manage your responses. There are excellent books written to help you. There is YouTube footage to help you manage your fears. It is encouraged that you join at least two dating sites and meet five to ten people in person each week. Apparently, it is important not to waste time thinking you can make something work if you have doubts. There are lots of fish in the sea. "Such an important decision requires diligent effort or you will not find what you deserve" was the message of the course.

For my part, I had new skills to offer my clients as they searched online for the love of their life. While I have confidence that it works very well for the right-aged women and men, I am not convinced it is a workable option for octogenarian women. I think there is not yet a service truly developed for the older set. No doubt when the baby boomers get old enough, they will develop a dating service to meet their needs.

I think it may be very different for older men, my brother at ninety-four being my best anecdotal example. His wife died in November and by early spring he was being courted by six women in his neighbourhood! Mind you, he is very charming. It did give me a lot of concern though. Worried for his safety, my son and I decided to pay a visit. We met all six women and came away convinced that he was managing all the attention from decent women who were not gold-diggers. With at least one of these women, he might have been viewed as the gold-digger himself, given that we travelled about in her smashing Porsche. The dating certainly helped him get out and about—he played golf almost daily with one or the other of them. I had concern, I confess, with the lady admirer who was teaching him the Jerusalem salsa and was inclined to fill him with views from the Christian Right. Still, he was ninety-four and dancing daily in his living room with YouTube videos blaring.

Not long after the completion of the twelve-week online course, I was returning on the big ferry from Vancouver Island following a golfing visit with my oldest friend Gail. A call came on my cell phone, and I answered.

"Hello, I'm Michael, a friend of Bianca's." There was a hint of shyness in his voice, but he rather blustered on, "She gave me your name more than a year ago and it has been in my pocket ever since. I have been away Down Under and am just back. I am lucky to have got out. Covid is just stopping so much travel."

"I am outside on the ferry so please excuse the noise," I said, wishing I had my work diary handy. I stepped inside. "Michael, what is it that has prompted your call?"

I was quite sure that he was calling for an appointment to see me as a psychotherapist. Bianca made a lot of referrals to me. People often tuck my name away for years before making the call they should have made when they first got my details.

His tone became more familiar now that he knew I was on the ferry. He told me how he could see the ships going by from his window. Finally, he got to the point and asked if he could see me, as on a date.

While thinking that I must find out from Bianca who this Michael was, I told him I would be delighted to meet with him. Since I now had his number in my cell, I told him I would call him when I was home, and we could set up a time and place. He agreed and I had bought time to get the scoop from Bianca.

Thus began my Covid dating episode. We met in person, decided to be a bubble for Covid so that we could actually be with each other in person and met weekly for all two years of the shutdown. Very early he claimed to be completely entranced by me. He was often speechless and breathless in my presence. He could walk miles, play golf, swim, had no need of my money, was kind, well educated, a widower, had good kids and grandkids that he deeply loved and whose love was reciprocated. Bianca had scored big time. What was not to like?

For me there was a "but". I never felt for him as he claimed to feel for me. I was honest with him and told him this from the beginning. I did genuinely hope that, in time, my feelings would match his and that as we got to know each other I would gradually feel more as he did. I often thought my desire for what was missing was age-inappropriate. I was not a person in need of flashing hormones to ensure that I had babies and did my part for the population. Maybe how I felt with Gianni was not to be trusted as a gauge for relationship. But my desire for a shared level of self-awareness just would not go away. I wanted him to be interested in his behaviour and why he thought as he did. I wanted him to be curious about why I thought and felt as I did. I wanted him to be a meaning-maker. He was plenty curious about how things worked. One day in a rainstorm we decided to go for a walk on the golf course. For me it was an opportunity to talk about how we were feeling about one another. For him it was an opportunity to check out the drainage system on the course and discover why the seventeenth hole had been redesigned. Alas, this outward-directed curiosity left me wet and cold. I was missing faerie dust. My kids met him and found him decent and kind.

However, my daughter said, "You are chalk and cheese. I feel it as you do." She knew. At last, two years after we first met, I could hold out hope no longer and told him that I just could not find within me that love for him that he claimed to have for me.

"I am happy to be friendly and play golf or go for a walk. I will leave it with you and if you would like that, then let me know."

He pulled away and I have not heard from him since. I often think about this with sadness. I wish for us both that we might have shared the chemistry connection. Most days I am good with myself that I would rather be alone than live with the effort of hoping a spark would ignite in me.

Bianca, my dear sex angel, does not quit, and from time to time she introduces me to another person she has met and thinks might like to meet me. Just recently she introduced me to George, her mentor. We have met a few times and he inspired her to make sexual therapy her area of specialisation. In fact, he is well known in our country and sports an Order of Canada medal for having created the first department of sexual medicine in our country. He jokes about his fame and tells me to ask him, "What have you done lately?" We have the most delightful and unusual conversations. He, too, is a widower, ten years older than me and lives in my city, but bridges and deep ocean inlets sprinkled with traffic jams divide us. Navigating distance is a problem in octogenarian relationships. A few blocks of distance are just right. I imagine sauntering down to the sea after dinner and sitting side by side on a bench watching the sun go down, bodies close, sharing our innermost thoughts.

At our first lunch together, as we wait for the main course, he confides, "I think that intimacy is far more important than sex for people our age. Do you?"

I know what he means. He is talking about caressing and tenderness, not penetration and orgasm.

"People our age need this sort of intimacy," he goes on, "and we need to help the youngers in the world know and respect this."

I tell him that I have just read an article in *The New York Times* that directed me to the words of Roger Angell, American essayist and for many years the chief fiction editor of *The New Yorker*. He was in his nineties when he penned the following words, which I find on my cell phone:

Getting old is the second biggest surprise of my life, but the first is our unceasing need for deep attachment and intimate love! ...I believe that everyone in the world wants to be with someone else tonight, together in the dark, with the sweet warmth of a hip or a foot or a bare expanse of shoulder within reach.

"I agree with Roger," I tell my new friend. "I have always thought that if I were God, I would create a world where two people who cared for each other would sleep safely close to one another."

As we talk in the Cactus Club restaurant patio on the waterfront in west Vancouver, we are two very old people just meeting each other for the first time and yet we are engrossed in a deep conversation about the meaning of sex and intimacy. Casting an eye around at the other tables and the people dining, I smile inside as I surmise that no one at the other tables would ever guess the nature of our conversation.

At this time in my life, I am not blessed with a loving person in my bed at night, but I do know that the desire for this is healthy and normal at every age. It is good to thrum with that need, rejoice when it is present and anticipate its arrival, and it is right to mourn its absence.

Annette Nieukerk, *the long road home 3*

ABOUT THE AUTHOR

Ann Evans is a couple and family therapist (CACFT), supervisor, and educator. She is also a retired ordained minister. Her current hobbies are nurturing her friendships, aging well, travel, golf, swimming, gardening, walking, theatre, visual arts, and blog writing. Her two adult children, along with their spouses and four young adult grandchildren, are an unending source of challenge and delight.

www.ingramcontent.com/pod-product-compliance
Lightning Source LLC
Chambersburg PA
CBHW030909120626
46554CB00001B/78